Cassien.... and Beyond

by Steve Briggs

Freebird
Publishing

Cassien.... and Beyond is a limited edition book.
Published in 2009 by Freebird Publishing
☎ 01293 405781 or 07941 637336
© Steve Briggs 2009

Edited by Keith Jenkins
Proofed by Lynn Chillcott
Illustrations by Tracey Lewis-Wilson
Layout and Design by Cathy Card
Print Management by Linda Jenkins
All photography supplied by the Author unless marked.

Printed in Great Britain by
Butler Tanner & Dennis
Caxton Road, Frome, Somerset BA11 1NF

ISBN Number 978-0-9562497-1-5

CONTENTS

Dedication

This book is dedicated to Joan, who always believed in me
and made me believe in myself.

Acknowledgements

I know it's impossible to list everyone here, as I've shared good times with so many people down the years and I've been helped and inspired by most of them along the way. So, if you are not mentioned here it's not because I've forgotten you, as you all have a place somewhere in my memory – so thanks to all of you. But some people do deserve a special mention.

My old mate Paul 'Glum' Sanders, who was a great friend in so many ways but was sadly taken from us far too early.

Gary 'the legend' Hillson – a man who knows about carp, but even more about wine!

Tim Paisley for being an inspiration, not only in fishing but for life in general and, of course, for inviting me along to fish the World Carp Cup at Fishabil.

Pete Noonan for the great times in the 1980's and for the Mini van!

Pete Jones for all the happy memories and the great laughs we've had.

Rod Hutchinson, Martin Locke, Dave Coakley who have helped me a great deal as sponsors and as friends.

Rob Maylin for those years when fishing was really fun – and we still caught a few!

Rob Hughes for sharing many good times on the bank and for always being a mate.

Simon Crow for always having plenty of bait and biscuits, and for putting up with my snoring - (not!)

Charles Thompson and everyone at Boyer Leisure for letting me fish their lovely waters.

Paul Hunt for introducing me to Rainbow Lake and sharing swims on a few occasions.

Bob, Sheila, James and Cris Davis for the good times at Serreire.

Pierre, Anne Marie, Philippe and Veronique Picot for making Cassien even better than it already was.

Pascal, Nadine, Paul and Max Jousseaume for making us so welcome at Rainbow Lake.

Simon Crow and Carp Talk for the extra photographic material.

Keith and Linda Jenkins and Chilly and Lynn Chillcott for somehow putting all of the following together when I didn't have a clue what to do with it all.

All of the people who I've shared some time with on the banks over the years, there have been a great many of you and you have all made a difference.

Foreword

The name Steve Briggs is known to carp anglers all over the world, and I am in the very fortunate position of knowing not just the name but also the man himself. Having read about his captures and seeing his picture in the magazines in the 80s and 90s I first really got to know Steve in 1998 when we were invited, along with another of our long time pals, Simon Crow, to form the Dream Team, a group of sponsored anglers put together by Rod Hutchinson to promote his brand. Briggsy was a quiet but likeable character and we immediately hit it off as mates.

We fished together a few times as part of that team and my first experience of sharing the banks with Steve was for the making of a video at Lac de Madine in France. I'm proud to say that I managed to catch a bigger one than him on that trip but it's a feat that hasn't been repeated very often since as Briggsy is definitely no slouch when it comes to knocking out the bigger ones.

Of course, we've fished together a lot more since then, as well as become business partners in our own tackle company, Venture, and some of my favourite ever sessions have been with Steve at far flung destinations around the world, such as Africa, Romania, America, and France or back home on some of the Colne Valley pits where we concentrated our joint efforts for a season or two.

Now, Steve is probably best known for his continental captures, of which he has had a few, but he has an incredible record back home as well. He has been around carp fishing from the very early years, having experienced success at places like Johnsons Railway lake, Longfield, and more recently Wraysbury where he bagged Cluster on one of his first trips. He is definitely no slouch at "big fish" hunting and his laid back attitude sometimes disguises the fact that he is absolutely dedicated and channelled to the capture of large carp. He has this knack of knowing where in the swim the lumps will be loitering and I could regale you with numerous stories of his ability to tease out a big fish against seemingly impossible odds. One time in particular jumps out, when we were fishing a "friendly" match for England against Romania. The lake was full of small fish, doubles and twenties, with a few thirties and the odd rare forty. I flew off and started knocking out the doubles, getting numbers on the board, but Steve's side of the swim was remarkably quiet. My tally kept impressing the spectators as more and more small fish came to the bank when suddenly, eventually even, Briggsy's in. An upper 30 wowed the crowds, followed shortly afterwards by a low 40 and another 30 very soon after that. I must have had 10 fish with possibly 1 over 20. Briggsy had 3 that day all of which were biggies.

But it's when you look at his big fish captures overseas that you realise just how successful an angler this man is. He has "Been there, done that!" with Cassien, probably the highest profile and most credible water in the world. His success at Rainbow in more recent years is enviable to say the least and he has also landed carp from a whole host of other waters around the world, including 50lb plus fish from waters in Africa, Austria and France. Add to that the fact he has not one but TWO titles of World Champion to his name in his illustrious carp fishing match career, and the facts speak for themselves .

In closing, probably the best thing about Steve, taking out the natural angling ability that makes him stand out amongst mere mortals, is that he really is an all round nice bloke who is sensible, modest, grounded and just loves his carp fishing. True, he wants to catch more than the next man, but you tell me a successful angler that doesn't. It's fair to say that virtually everyone likes Briggsy. He is one of those characters that you just have to get on with, and we've often commented that if you don't get on with Steve Briggs then you must have an underlying problem yourself.

This book has been long awaited. It's finally arrived, and like everything that Briggsy does, I'm sure it will be massive.

It's been a pleasure serving with you "Me old Twist and Bend".

Long may it continue.

Rob Hughes

Introduction

Well I've finally done it – I've written a book! That will come as a shock to a few people, but I got there in the end. I don't know how long I've been meaning to do it, or how many people have said that I should write a book, but I do feel that it's probably a few years overdue now. On countless occasions I did indeed make a start but invariably, after getting halfway through the first chapter, something would get in the way – normally fishing! You see, most of my fishing involves fairly long sessions and once I was away for a week or two it was difficult to pick up where I had left off, and there were always other things to take care of, so it was invariably put on the back burner. But then I finally got the bit between my teeth and got going and, all of a sudden, it started to flow.

The biggest problem was what to actually base the book on – what should I include and what should I leave out? There was no shortage of advice, in fact everyone who I spoke to had a different opinion. Quite a few people thought that I should write a book just on Cassien alone and, at one stage, it nearly came to that, but that would have left out too many other important times, such as the many sessions at Lake Raduta and of course my fishing in England – and what about the World Cup wins? They were such important events in my life but there certainly wasn't room to cover both of them. My original thoughts were to cover the more recent American competition as it was fresher in my mind, and perhaps my favourite of the two wins I've been lucky enough to share with Tim Paisley. But the reaction from everyone I spoke to was that I shouldn't leave out the Fishabil competition as it was such a fantastic occasion and it would be difficult to go back to it later. So, I took the advice on board and included the Fishabil chapter for that reason and now I'm sure it was the right thing to do. Other than that I just had to do what I felt was right. A lot had to be left out, which would be enough to fill another book right now – I suppose it just shows how much fishing I've done over the years!

Cassien has dominated my life for over twenty years and I love the place, which is why much of the book revolves around my trips there. I've covered some of my most memorable trips to Cassien, but it isn't all about big fish. The chapter 'Dinner with Roger and Kerry', for instance, is about a time when I was discovering new sides to my favourite lake but also witnessing how easily it could all change in a short time.

'Cassien.... and beyond' is very much a story of my fishing since 1985. It seemed an obvious time to start from. I had been carp fishing long before then but I just couldn't see the point in going back to the beginning, my photography wasn't up to much in those earlier days and although the memories of those years are special to me, it was hard to see how I could put them down on paper and make them interesting. 1985 was when it really all started to happen and my life changed in many ways, as you will see. One notable omission you will find in the following pages are any guest chapters, I had my own reasons for that. Most books seem to include guest chapters these days but although many of them are very good, personally I like to get in to the mind of the book writer and when it comes to a guest chapter, the atmosphere changes straight away with the different style of writing, and I've normally skipped past those chapters until I've finished the rest of the book. Plus I just had too much to fit in anyway, so it was the way it had to be. If I ever do all this again I probably would include a few guest chapters, as some of my good friends have had some great results which deserve to be written about, but that's for another time. I've written this book very much in the style of what I like to read. I don't like to get bogged down too much in technical details although having said that I have still included the chapter 'Tips, Tackle and Tactics' as I felt it covers some of that stuff which is missing from other chapters.

So, after all of that, I really hope that you enjoy reading what follows. It was every bit as tough and as time consuming as I thought it would be. I literally wrote each chapter and then went back over it several times, changing bits or adding parts until it got to the point where I couldn't do any more and just had to settle for what I had in front of me, but I'm as pleased as I can be with the end result. So, with that I will leave you to start my journey through carp fishing from 1985 onwards, a time when carp fishing was going through big changes – changes which meant my life would never be the same again – read on................

Cassien – The Early Years

Cassien – The Early Years

A New Dawn

Every story has to begin somewhere and this one starts off around the time of 1985. Sure, I had been carp fishing for several years before that, in fact my first carp was caught way back in 1974 from the famous Brooklands Lake down in Kent. But looking back, those earlier years were almost like my apprenticeship into carp fishing and 1985 was the time when I turned a corner in my carp fishing life and a lot of things started to change for me.

I fished the winter on the Tip Lake with Pete Noonan and caught my first thirty.

I was looking for a new challenge and had joined Darenth Lakes, which are in the same area of the Darenth Valley as Brooklands, but just a couple of miles further down the road. There were four lakes on the Darenth complex, all of which held carp, but it was the Tip Lake that interested me most. It had the reputation of being the most difficult of all the lakes on the complex – and for that matter in the whole valley, but it also held the biggest of the fish, at least three known thirties and several more big twenties. I was ready for a tougher challenge and ready to try for some larger fish as, up to that point, I'd yet to catch a 30lb carp, or even see one for that matter. I lived in Dartford at the time and so I didn't have to travel too far, virtually all of my fishing had to be done on local waters back then as I had no real form of transport, apart from a little moped, although I was learning to drive at the time.

Big 'H' was one of the most sought-after fish and another thirty just before Christmas.

That year I met a young guy called Pete Noonan whilst fishing on the Big Lake at Darenth. I remember very well our first meeting as we had set up in adjacent swims. For what seemed like hours he was casting this tiny little bait dropper out filled with tiger nuts. At first I didn't take much notice but in the end it was starting to get quite annoying and I was pleased when he'd finally emptied his bucket of bait. At last I thought I was going to get some peace, but soon after his alarm started screaming and then rarely seemed to stop all weekend! I know I caught one fish by casting a little nearer to Pete but he caught several, including a brace of twenties which I'd never seen before. I couldn't help but be impressed and, over the following weekends, I got to know Pete a little better and we ended up becoming good friends. I always found him amusing and good company to fish with. One thing we both had in common was that we liked to do our own thing and, if anything, go against the grain rather than following the trends which other people were setting. It was a period when the Darenth Valley anglers were very much into making their own baits and all the talk was of milk proteins and high protein levels, PH of flavours etc. But it was also around that time that the first readymade baits were starting to be produced and they certainly weren't flavour of the month in the Valley, in fact you daren't mention the name Richworth for fear of being a total outcast and labelled as a 'noddy'. But Pete and I had tried the Richworth freezer baits and not only were they more convenient and a lot less bother – we also caught a few fish on them, which put them right at the top of our list! Pete liked the Tutti-Frutti's while I preferred the Honey Yucatan's, although in truth there really wasn't much between them. The first night that I used them on the Tip Lake I caught a 21lb mirror and lost another and really it just carried on from there. This was after a period

One lump or two? We saw plenty of ice that winter.

One week after Big 'H'
I was back in the Rats Nest for the capture of the Pilgrim.

of trying all sorts of other baits in an attempt to catch these 'difficult' carp and in the end it was the bait, which on paper was probably the worst of the lot, which the fish decided that they liked more than all the others. Pete and I not only started to catch, but started to catch more than anyone else and it's quite funny, looking back, because all of the other anglers thought that we'd come up with this incredible bait that was taking the lake apart and many of them, all of a sudden, took a very keen interest in us and wanted to know a little bit more about what we were using. Of course, it was a long time before we finally let the cat out of the bag. It was such an easy secret to keep as, even when we eventually did tell people, many of them just didn't believe us.

The winter of 1985 was one of my favourite spells of fishing, even up to this day. After getting off to a good start with a few twenties from the Tip Lake, on one Friday evening in November I managed to land my first thirty. It was an unknown fish to us and certainly not one of the regular thirties, which we'd seen several pictures of by now, but it became known later as 'The Parrot'. In all probability it was more than likely a fish that had been moved at some point from the Big Lake next door and had not been captured for a while, but on that cold November evening I was more than happy to be looking down at such a lovely big mirror.

In those days we used to get proper winters, and snow and ice were never really that far away, it was often a matter of luck as to whether the lake would be fishable or frozen when I arrived. Several times it did indeed freeze over and fishing after that had to take place in between the regular freeze-ups and of course still only at weekends, but we kept on catching right through and I was lucky enough to catch most of the other known thirties in the following weeks. In December I caught both the lovely 'Big H' and the 'Pilgrim' from the tiny little Rats Nest swim, which by then had become my favourite swim on the lake. Then in January, when the lake had once again thawed after being frozen for over a week, I fished for a weekend in The Gap swim and landed the fish that I wanted more than any of the others, the old warrior known as Scar Bar at 30lb 12oz, to complete the set. They were probably the four biggest carp anywhere in the Darenth Valley at that time and it was also the first time that anyone had caught four thirties in a season from there, so the apprenticeship had been served and, besides having a really good time through what were

It was the one I wanted most, Scar Bar at 30lb 12oz my fourth thirty of an incredible winter.

quite testing conditions, I had also gained a fair bit of experience and the confidence in my angling which hadn't always been there in the past. From then on I wouldn't be worried about fishing any water for carp, in fact I was looking for new challenges.

It was during this time that I started to hear about another lake, which was rumoured to hold carp which were far bigger than I'd ever dreamed about before, only this time the lake wasn't a local one, but

was over in France of all places. This wasn't like any lake I'd ever known before, if the stories were to be believed, as I have to admit it all sounded almost too good to be true at the time. But gradually it dawned on me that it really could all be true!

The story went that Kevin Maddocks and Paul Regent had ventured down to the south of France to fish a lake that they'd heard contained some very good carp. I can clearly remember staring at the cover of The Carp Catcher magazine, which was the magazine of the Carp Anglers Association, and on the front was a picture of Paul Regent holding a good thirty that he'd caught during just a few hours fishing with sweetcorn. I was intrigued and wanted to know more, although I have to say that it was nothing more than a passing interest at the time, as I was so wrapped up in what I had been doing at Darenth. The other thing, of course, was that I had never been out of the country at that time so I couldn't even comprehend travelling all that way to fish for carp.

The lake they had been fishing was called Lac de St. Cassien and it was situated right in the middle of the 'millionaires playground', between St. Tropez and Monaco, and very close to Cannes. It sounded lovely and perhaps even more so when it was claimed that the lake was known to hold several fish over 50lb! I remember reading that statement at the time and thinking that it was probably an exaggeration, I just couldn't believe that a lake could hold so many big fish. What you have to remember – and in fact this is the most difficult thing for people to understand - that until that time, carp fishing didn't really exist outside of England for any of us, at least not in the way we know of it today. Of course, there were carp anglers in other countries across Europe but we had little contact with each other. I only knew of one carp to be caught over 50lb and that was the fantastic mirror

For me it was one of the all-time great captures – Kevin Ellis with his magnificent mirror.

caught by Chris Yates from Redmire, so to be told that one water, albeit a very large water, could hold several over that weight was a bit difficult to take in. It was just like carp fishing from another world - and that was the way I viewed it at first.

Gradually reports started to filter through from Cassien and it really did appear that this was some kind of carp fishing super-lake. Max Cottis landed an amazing fish of 68lb 8oz which made him the first English angler ever to catch a carp weighing over 60lb. But for me that was eclipsed when Kevin Ellis landed the same fish some time later at a mind-blowing 76lb! Now, that really did make me sit up and take notice! I know that Kevin isn't the biggest of lads anyway, but that fish just looked unbelievably huge – and probably because it was! To me that was, and still is, one of the all-time great captures. It affected people in different ways; I spoke to some people who said that it was too big for a normal carp and it was more of a freak than anything else, and I sort of know what they were saying as it was so much bigger than anything else that we'd seen before, but I remember looking open-mouthed at those pictures of Kevin struggling to hold it, and I wanted to hold something like that too!

Kevin's was the biggest capture from Cassien at the time, but it was just the tip of the iceberg as more people decided to take up the challenge and head away from British shores in search of the Cassien monsters. Some of the best-known names were quick to make their mark, perhaps the most famous of those being Rod Hutchinson. His early writings on Cassien were a real inspiration and he had a way of putting it across in words like no one else could. His article: Cassien Revisited '85, where he fished with Roger Smith, remains to this day one of my favourite pieces of writing. That one feature not only described perfectly how it was back then for people travelling down to Cassien, it managed to capture the whole atmosphere of the adventure. The article appeared as a chapter in Rod's book, Carp Now and Then and I would advise anyone, if they get a chance, to read that chapter just to get a feel for what it was like for the early pioneers. Rod managed to break his personal best several times during those first few trips with, amongst other fish, three mirrors over 50lb.

It wasn't just the famous anglers that were making their mark, though, as many remarkable stories were being told in the papers and magazines – as well as first-hand from some of the people I knew who had also been out there. One of the most vivid memories came from a guy called Blair, who had also been a Darenth angler, but had been to Cassien twice already. His second trip could have been so memorable but had a rather sorry end. He had travelled down with his girlfriend and things hadn't gone too well having had not one, but two punctures on the way, but as ever, after a stop in one of the local French garages, they found themselves some time later pulling up at the now-famous Chez Pierre's restaurant. After making up some fresh bait in the car park they set off in search of a few fish and, having fished in the West Arm of the lake before, Blair was keen to have another go in that area. Things didn't go too well at the start and just one run resulted in a lost fish, but after chatting with a couple of the other English guys who were fishing there at the time, it seemed that there were a lot of fish congregating right at the bottom end of the West Arm so they decided to join forces and all move to that area. At the time there was a spawning area which was closed to anglers, right at the end of the arm, but in reality this posed few problems with the 'modern day' equipment that they had at their disposal. Two other English guys, Joe Taylor and Phil Smith, were already fishing at the boundary to the spawning bay on one side of the arm, but the other side was free and the only question was how to fish it? Obviously, they all wanted to have a go there but with effectively four of them fishing with three rods each it wouldn't be easy. In the end they decided that they would fish all of their rods in a line right next to the boundary sign and fish as much as they dare into the bay – which effectively meant all of the bay being covered!

It was an unfortunate sequence of events – especially for Blair on the left.

Blair and his girlfriend had six rods between them and were each taking care of their own rods. The other two guys were sharing runs between them, as many people do. Things started off okay with Blair landing a new PB of 34lb and his girlfriend catching a mid double. However, when it got dark Blair's girlfriend went into a deep sleep which she couldn't be woken from, which was quite convenient for Blair when one of her rods went off. Not wishing to wake her from her sleep, Blair 'kindly' took care of the rod and whilst playing the fish, which incidentally proved to be another PB of 34lb 8oz, he vaguely heard another alarm sounding. Whoever it was from the other two picked up the rod and began playing the fish. By the time Blair had finished dealing with his fish, the other one had now been landed and it turned out to be a massive mirror weighing 64lb! As you can imagine, there was joy and congratulations all around until one of the guys said:

"It's just a shame it was on your rod, Blair!"

Then everything fell silent before the atmosphere changed. It had been an honest mistake as the angler in question had thought that it was his mates rod that he'd picked up, but Blair thought that the fish should rightfully be his as it was on his rod and it was his rig and bait that had fooled the fish, and I can certainly see that side of the argument, but of course the other guy also wanted to claim it as he had played the fish thinking that it was on his mates rod and really, if he was going to take a turn on someone else's rod then what did it matter who's rod it was? In the end, they did the only thing that they could do

Joe Taylor was among the successful early visitors.

and they both photographed it together. It was so unfortunate that the misunderstanding had to happen with such a big fish and, of course, what you have to realise is that back then, a fish of that size was probably amongst the top ten biggest carp ever caught. I had to feel a little sorry for Blair as I know how few chances you get to catch a fish of that size in your life, but at least he got to hold it for the cameras.

Whilst all this was going on, something happened to me which would have a huge influence on my life – I passed my driving test! It was like having a whole new lease of life and, for the first time, I had the independence to travel further afield. Soon after, I managed to save up a few pounds and I bought myself a yellow Mark 3 Cortina. I felt like the dogs do da's in that. The heater didn't work and the gear stick used to come away in my hand and you could literally unlock it with a wooden lolly stick! But that didn't matter, it was mine and it went like the clappers. Whilst rummaging and pulling bits and pieces about, I also found that I could remove the back seat, meaning I could fit a lot more fishing tackle in. I'm sure it wasn't meant to come out that easy but hey, that was the least of my worries. Looking back now, it was no wonder that I used to get pulled up by the police everywhere I went, I couldn't work out what all the fuss was about at the time.

With my newfound independence, all sorts of ideas were starting to go through my mind as to what I could do and where I could go, but topping the list was definitely the prospect of a trip to Cassien. Around that time I'd just got myself a new girlfriend, who, unlike the previous one, had some sort of interest in fishing – especially if it meant fishing in the south of France, and so for the first time I started to seriously think about my first foreign adventure. It was coming up to September 1986 and I had still only been driving for six months but all of a sudden Cassien wasn't just somewhere other people went to, it was somewhere I could go to myself! Two weeks holiday were already booked from work and the mammoth task of preparing for the trip got underway. Back then my assortment of fishing tackle didn't amount to much. I had no boat or echo sounder and I only owned two carbon rods which were 11ft 1¾ lb test curve. They had served me fine up until that point so I figured that they would do okay, along with a couple of my old fibre glass rods which had been collecting dust in the shed for some time. Really, I could do no more than go with my normal gear and just hope that it was up to the job. Bait-wise, I knew that the carp liked peanuts so I bought a 20kg sack of those and I already had half a sack of tigers. On top of that I bought ten bags of the old faithful Honey Yucatan's. I didn't doubt that they would work. The carp were, of course, still very naïve at Cassien and I already knew from the various articles and stories that they loved the boilies which the English anglers were giving to them. Before then, all they ever really got from the French anglers was a half-cooked potato on a treble hook and if they were silly enough to pick that up it normally meant a smack on the head with a lump of wood and a car ride to the local village. So, being able to eat nice tasting boilies and get put back in the lake afterwards to tell all their friends about it must have made a nice change!

The Friday afternoon of our departure finally arrived and I remember cheering out loudly as I skipped out of the door of the factory where I 'worked', much to the annoyance of everyone else who had to stay behind. A mad dash home for a quick wash and brush up and one final check of everything and before we knew it we were on our way! We caught the 10pm ferry, which meant landing in France at around midnight and of course with the hour time difference it was actually 1am, so by the time I'd done a couple of hours driving the other side I was stopping for my first sleep. Considering that this was already my longest-ever journey, I thought I'd done quite well!

I turned the corner and there it was – a sight I'll never forget.

I awoke some hours later to my first real view of France, albeit a service station car park. A quick cup of coffee and a croissant later and we were on our way again. Driving on the wrong side of the road was easier than I expected and I just knew that I needed to head for Lyon at some stage when getting near to Paris, so I was a little concerned when I passed a sign saying that name but figured that there would be more turnings – wrong! The next thing I knew, we were in the middle of Paris having a proper nightmare. The Eiffel Tower, Arc de Triomphe, we saw all the sights but I was just trying to get out of the place, and it was only when I jumped a red light (which I didn't even see) that I was pulled over by a rather stern-looking Gendarme. I'm sure he was ready to impose some sort of penalty on me but, with one glance into the car, he must have realised how flustered I was getting by the whole experience and did no more than direct me to where I should have been going in the first place, which I was more than grateful for.

Before long we were back on the correct Autoroute and heading south, much to my relief. This time I looked more carefully at the signs and managed to get down below Lyon before having to stop again for the night. The next morning I remember well, firstly for the intense heat that woke me up and then for the size of the ants that I saw when I got out – they were huge. But at last I was in the south of France and not far from my destination. I'd only seen signs for St. Tropez and Marseille on the TV before and yet here I was, seeing them in real-life, and it was all a bit surreal. I somehow went past the right turning again and ended up in Cannes, but after looking at the boats in the harbour for a while, I slowly but surely made my way along the roads which were getting smaller and more winding all the time. I knew I was getting close and around every bend I was stretching to see if I could see water – and then all of a sudden there it was – Cassien! I just stopped the car and looked. It was just the most beautiful sight I'd ever seen, blue water and green hill sides just like I'd seen in all the pictures, but somehow it looked even better than I'd imagined it ever could. I figured that I was at the top end of the North Arm and somehow needed to drive around the mountain road to get to where we were heading in the central area of the lake, which I have to say was fun and I would say that it is the best way to see Cassien for the first time. After a few more glimpses of the lake along the winding roads we soon arrived at the now famous Chez Pierre's.

I pulled up outside Chez Pierres for the very first time.

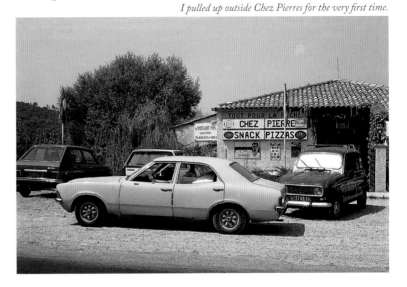

Pierre, with his smiling face welcomed us in and we could do no more than have a couple of ice cold "dare bears", as Roger Smith would have put it, before heading down to the waters edge to blow up my little inflatable boat. It was a lovely sunny day with a warm westerly breeze blowing in. All around were scantily-clad people (mainly girls thankfully) enjoying the sun and I was already enjoying being there, I never thought in my wildest dreams that carp fishing would bring me to a place like this. The first place to look at was the West Arm, after knowing that some good fish had been caught there earlier in the year, and after what seemed like an eternity I was up near the spawning bay, looking around. It was a hell of a row up to there in a small dinghy and I suppose that I just wasn't ready for the scale of the place. But I have to say that, although it looked very nice, I didn't find it particularly inspiring. It was all a bit small and narrow. For some strange reason I had it in my head that I wanted to fish in the North Arm and, after a quick swim to cool off, I headed off in that direction. It's hard to believe now but, before leaving England, people were telling me that it would be a waste of time fishing the North Arm as it was too deep and the carp would never go there, let alone feed there. I had listened to their advice but to me it looked like the nicest part of the lake – and also the quietest it has to be said, which came into the equation as I knew that no night fishing was allowed, but if I could get away with it then I would.

It was easily the most stunning water I'd ever seen.

I had taken a marker rod with me to test the depths and I stopped about halfway up on the right hand side of the arm to have a chuck about. I cast out as far as I could and then waited.....and waited.....and waited! And then after I don't know how long, when the line was almost hanging vertically from the rod tip, the lead finally went 'donk' on the bottom! I didn't know how deep it was but I knew that it was too deep to consider fishing - I also knew that the marker rod wasn't going to be a lot of use to me after that. What I did instead was to look at the surrounding landscape and although the bank shelved off very quickly where I was standing I could see that on the far side it looked a little flatter and maybe that would be a better prospect. As I rowed across I could see a couple of umbrellas further up on the left, although I had no idea who they were, or even if they were carp anglers.

This side of the lake looked a lot better, it was still deep out in front but by counting down the lead to the bottom I figured that it was around 25 or 30 feet deep, much deeper than I'd ever fished before but I was sure that it would do for a start. I rowed back to Pierre's and got all the necessary gear and permits etc. which probably took me a couple of hours or so, and the sun was already making its descent by the time I got back. I vaguely remember a fish jumping somewhere out in front as I was getting the rods set up, but I was so tired from the journey down and the rowing about that I didn't really take much notice, I was just ready to collapse on the bed chair. The set up was pretty basic with 15lb nylon (Sylcast I think) straight through, including the hook length, that was connected to a size 4 Kamasan hook with a 2oz running lead. A couple of Honey Yucatan's were attached to the hair and three rods were cast out around 50 yards with a few freebies scattered around them. I thought I'd better turn the alarms up a bit just in case anything happened and I slept through it. It was all a bit rushed but I had some baits in the water, that was all that mattered for that moment. I lay down on my bed chair and must have been asleep within seconds.

It was an eventful first evening – but I'd caught my first Cassien carp!

The next thing I knew my ears were hurting from the sound coming from one of the alarms. It was my first experience of how silent everything went after dark up the North Arm – except for my alarm that is! It was an absolute belter but the weird thing was that as soon as I picked up the rod there was no fish on the other end at all. It was a strange occurrence but it woke me up a bit, that's for sure. Everything was still intact so I just recast the rod to roughly where it was and climbed back in the bag. A short time later I heard someone approaching and feared the worst but it was the anglers from further up the bank who'd heard the alarm, actually it transpired that even Johnny Allen, who was fishing at the start of the West Arm, had heard my alarm, so needless to say they were turned down a little after that. The guys further up turned out to be Joe Taylor and Phil Smith, who explained that they had caught nothing so far but their friend Andy had caught a good fifty a couple of days before my arrival. We chatted for a while but they soon left, saying they would come back in the morning and we were left in silence once more.

A short time later the same rod belted off again and this time there was a fish on the other end. The moon was big and bright in the sky and even at that time of night I could see the line cutting through the water. It felt really powerful and I thought that it must be at least a mid thirty the way it was going, several times it ripped line from the reel in a bid to gain freedom, the raw power of the fish took me by surprise. Thankfully, it came up high in the deep water as there was a lot of weed in front of me and I thought that it could cause me a few problems, but after a while I was able to steer it through the weed and into the waiting net. It was nowhere near as big as I was expecting, I weighed it straight away at 22lb, but I wasn't bothered about that, it was my first Cassien carp and I'd only been fishing for a couple of hours or so. I did hook another fish a short time later but I soon experienced the dreaded snags for the first time. The line grated around something and although the fish was still on for a while, I just couldn't budge it and eventually it just slipped the hook. I was a bit disappointed to have three runs and only land one fish but my first ambition had been to catch at least one Cassien carp, so I'd achieved that straight away.

Morning arrived along with Phil and Joe from up the bank. We took a few pics of the fish and then they decided that they were going to move in either side of me, which didn't exactly fill me with happiness, although it did make me feel a little more comfortable with other people around. I thought there might still be a few fish about so decided to reel in and put fresh baits on, the only trouble with that was all the rods were snagged solid. I couldn't work out how that had happened and I ended up pulling for a break on all of them. I had heard that Cassien was full of snags, they were made up of all of the stumps

The water was so clear it was like looking into an aquarium.

which were left when they had chopped the trees down prior to flooding the valley. I'd never fished anywhere with snags like those and it seemed as if they were all over the lake bed and they had already claimed my first three rigs. If that was going to happen every time then I would soon be running out of leads and hooks if I wasn't careful.

The day passed quietly but it was my first 'proper' day in the sunny south of France and it was lovely. I loved everything about this place; it was just wonderful to be there. The weather was great, the scenery was great, the warm, crystal-clear water was great and there were great big carp out there somewhere – what more could I want? Well, a few more fish would be nice, I suppose. The evening arrived and I was expecting action, much like the evening before but for me it didn't happen and the indicators remained motionless. I think it was that evening when Joe had a rod dragged in. We were all together, having a chat, when we heard a couple of bleeps, no more than that, but as we all went around to see what had happened, one rod had completely disappeared. In the morning we could see the rod butt sticking out of the water some 70 yards out and Joe retrieved it minus the fish,

Tucked away out of sight in the trees.

but otherwise it was all a bit quieter. I thought that once the fish had found some easy food that they would keep coming back for more, but it was my first experience of fishing a lake of this size and it was becoming obvious that the fish were very nomadic and because they were there one day, it didn't mean that they would be there the next. I only hoped that if the fish could move away that quickly, then they could also return before long.

Two or three quiet days followed and we went back to Chez Pierre's for a decent meal. This was where I met Johnny Allen and Albert Romp for the first time. They were in Pierre's, enjoying a social with some of the German guys Geert Abelo and Dieter Tillenberg. They invited us to join in but they were already several bottles in front and to be honest it all looked a bit too expensive for me – although looking back I wish we had stopped now. I got to know most of those guys better in the years that followed and I still see Geert from time to time down there, and we are probably the only two anglers who still go to Cassien regularly from those early years. But anyway, I remember Albert leaning over to me and saying,

"Have you seen the shoal of bigguns yet?"

To be honest, I didn't take too much notice of what he was saying, he looked like he'd already had a few – if you know what I mean - and it all sounded like the stuff of make believe, but he was sure that there were a shoal of big fish that moved around the lake and if you could find them then anything was possible. I listened to what he was saying, but I didn't take it too seriously. They were all coming towards the end of their time on the lake. Johnny and Albert only had a couple of days left but they had caught some decent fish from the West and South Arms and had moved swims on several occasions to try and keep in contact with the fish. I was happy enough with where I was fishing and decided to stick it out with the same swim and just hoped that fish would pass through at some stage.

With only a day or two left of their stay, Joe, Phil and their friend Andy decided to move off to the South Arm as Phil and Joe had still yet to catch. Although the company was quite nice, I preferred the idea of having the area to myself again. From memory I think they both blanked that trip which showed that it certainly wasn't easy and nothing was guaranteed in those early days. Walking around on the beach after they had gone I noticed that where Phil had been fishing there were several large peanuts dotted around, so I gathered them all up. By now I had come to realise just what a problem the crayfish could be. I'd never fished a water with them in before so it was a totally new experience for me, but I soon found that as much as the carp liked the boilies, the crayfish liked them even more and the fairly soft freezer baits that I had weren't lasting very long once they had been found. It was knocking my confidence as, an hour after casting out, I really couldn't be sure if the baits were still on or not. If the fish were going to return in numbers then I had to be sure that I was fishing effectively. Peanuts were the obvious answer but the ones I had were quite small in comparison to the ones the other guys were using, but now at least I had enough of the larger ones to use as hook baits over the top! Three or four of those on the hair was a reasonably large hook bait and one that I could leave out with confidence.

After a quiet spell the fish returned.

That evening was one I will never forget as long as I live. I must have dozed off early as I just remember a loud noise coming from out on the lake somewhere, bringing me to my senses. We've all heard it said many times now, but it really did sound like a cow falling in. I remember muttering to myself that it couldn't have been a fish as it was too big! But from out of the darkness huge, oily ripples began to roll into the bank as another huge crash erupted from the water, just further up to the left. My heart was now pounding like a drum and I got up straight away and crept down the beach to where my rods were situated. Another huge crash was followed by another….and another. There were massive fish all around me like nothing I'd ever heard before and I thought back to what Albert had said to me in the restaurant, a day or two earlier about the shoal of bigguns. I'd more or less disregarded what he said but here I was, witnessing it all at first hand. I took the gamble of reeling all the rods in and recasting them, hoping that I wouldn't spook the fish, but they

I had tigers and peanuts with me but it was the peanuts which came out on top.

carried on crashing out and I kept glancing at the rods, thinking that one of them had to go off sooner or later. I don't know how long I sat there, but amazingly, as the hours passed by, the horizon started to get a little lighter and the fish gradually moved further and further away. I was left wondering how I hadn't caught the fish of my dreams – because they had been in front of me, of that there was certainly no doubt. Instead, I flopped back on to my bedchair and was soon dreaming of what might have been.

By now it was becoming fairly clear that fishing in the daytime was more or less a waste of time, not only was it very quiet fish-wise but the rods would inevitably be snagged when I went to re-bait so it seemed easier just to leave them in the rests until later in the afternoon. That week there were also a group of guys on one of the Regent trips. They used to arrive early each morning and then get picked up again in the evening to go back to their hotel. I spoke to a couple of the lads and, with nothing to show for their efforts, they wanted to stop later into the evening when they knew that the fish became more active. I was a bit more sociable in those days and made the offer that they could fish next to me as they wouldn't be there long. Well, all I remember is a huge bucket of peanuts being dumped over where I was fishing as they arrived. It was probably their weeks worth of bait and I cringed at first but, looking back, I'm sure that it was about to do me a big favour.

That evening I had my first run for a few days and landed another nice mirror of low twenties. The other two guys also hooked fish but, unfortunately, lost them both which was a shame, although I remember them being happy that they'd at least had a chance of a fish before going home, which they had to do the next day. With most of the people heading for home, and no new arrivals, the lake seemed even quieter than before – and really much nicer. I had the whole of the North Arm to myself and I felt a bit like Robinson Crusoe marooned away from civilisation. Again, I cannot emphasise enough what it was like in those days, where I had gone from fighting through the traffic to get a swim amongst the crowds on Darenth, to lying on a sandy beach with hundreds of acres of blue water out in front of me in the sunny south of France. It really couldn't have been any further away from what I had been used to.

It was like nowhere I'd fished before and I fell in love with Cassien straight away.

After the previous evening, where I had lots of fish jumping in front of me but could not buy a bite, the next evening couldn't have been more different as very little showed but I had four runs! It wasn't the most memorable of results, though, as I lost two fish in the dreaded snags and landed two double figure commons. Up to that point I had been playing all the fish from the bank, which was all I'd ever known, but I decided that I needed to do something different in order to have the chance of landing more fish and figured that I would be much better off hiring one of Pierre's large boats, which would make life a lot easier for baiting up, de-snagging some of the rigs and of course going out to play any other fish that I might hook. I was learning all the time. I was literally making it up as I was going along, but I was gradually getting the hang of it and gaining more confidence in what I was doing.

As the sun began to set over the hills behind me, the excitement began to build once more and it wasn't long before the first run occurred, but it only lasted a few seconds before the fish slipped the hook. It was at least a couple of hours later when another screamer had me running across the sand. This time the fish stayed on and everything went to plan as I followed the fish out in the boat. It was a very still, warm evening with the bright moon

Returning the first of my personal bests, the 39lb mirror.

again shining down, and the eerie silence around me only made the whole experience more intense. As I got around 70 or 80 metres from the bank, I looked up to the north and saw the lights from the distant town twinkling like Christmas tree lights. It was the first time I'd played a fish from the boat and I was a little unsure of quite what to do. As the fish was heading for deeper water it seemed best to just let it go that way and follow behind, I had little choice however, as, with both hands controlling the rod, I couldn't really do much with the boat anyway, but I was really enjoying it and it felt safer to be above the fish. Every now and then I could see the light flank of the fish as it twisted and turned down in the depths - it was a magical experience. On my light gear the fish fought really well but, finally, I managed to edge it nearer and nearer to the surface until it was ready for netting. I had no idea how big it was, only that it was bigger than what I'd caught before and I knew that my 32lb Avon scales wouldn't be any good, so I sacked it up until the morning when I could hopefully borrow a decent set. Thankfully, I did manage to borrow a set the next morning and the needle went round to 39lb, easily my personal best and I couldn't ask for much more at the time. In the sack were more than two handfuls of crushed up crayfish shells and peanuts, so I'm sure it would've weighed a bit more if I could have done it sooner, but I'd caught it and that's all that mattered.

This was by far my longest session but as always the time goes quickly and after another bite-less evening the last day of the trip was upon us. The rods were baited and recast in readiness and I sat out to watch the sun go down for one last time. I wanted to make the most of what time I had left but, as ever, tiredness took over and I soon retreated to the comfort of my sleeping bag. The next thing I remember is the sound of the clutch on the reel screaming as something very angry powered off into the depths. After playing and landing the '39' I knew just what to do and was soon in the boat and, although the line was grating around something at the start, it soon became free and the normal battle commenced. It followed a similar pattern to the previous fight, but it felt even stronger and no matter how many times I gained line the fish would just take it back and power off even further. I'd never known a fish with such strength and I knew that I couldn't rush things, but I did wonder how long it would take the fish to tire – if it was going to tire at all. It must have been over half an hour later when it surfaced for the first time and at least another ten minutes before I finally had it beaten in the net. I looked down and, even in the darkness, I could see the shape of a lovely big mirror, certainly bigger than the other fish but again I had no scales to find out for sure. It would be light in a couple of hours so the fish was sacked up in the margins until I could again go on the search for other anglers who I could hopefully borrow a set of scales from.

One last fish and it was the best of the lot. My first forty at 43lb 8oz.

At first light I was off. The lake was more or less devoid of anglers now, but I had heard that Geert and his friends were in the West Arm, so I rowed down there and just as I came around the corner of the old Blue Boat swim, sure enough there was Geert and he was out in the boat playing a fish. He'd already had it on for 30 minutes and it was pulling hard but he soon had it in the net and it turned out to be my first sighting of the famous Floppy Tail, which weighed 47lb I think. He also pointed to a sack that held a 45lb mirror that his friend had caught earlier and explained that Dieter had caught an upper fifty a little further along. Some people may remember that those three fish featured in one of the old Tri-Cast adverts from the 1980's. Once they had done everything with their fish, Geert kindly loaned me his scales and I set off back to the North Arm to find out what my fish weighed.

My first trip away had gone better than I could have imagined.

After seeing Geert's fish I knew that mine wasn't quite as big but it still pulled the needle around to 43lb 8oz – another personal best and my first 40lb carp! If I was happy with the 39 then I was over the moon with this fish. As far as I know, myself and the German guys were the only ones left fishing at that time and all of us had caught fish over 40lb, at the time that was something remarkable. I suppose memories fade over time and that was over 22 years ago as I write this, but catching that fish is still one of my favourite carp fishing memories. Looking back, it was amazing that I ever got there at all really, but I'd not only got there, but had caught some great fish including two personal bests. The thought of two weeks fishing in advance of the trip had seemed like an eternity, but it had gone by in a flash and it was with real sadness that I packed everything away to head off home – it was far better than I ever dared hope that it would be and for me, carp fishing would never be the same again.

Cassien – The Early Years

The Return – May 1987

My initial thoughts were that my first Cassien trip would be my only one. That seems almost daft now, looking back, but I thought it would be nice to say that I'd been there and done it before getting back to the 'serious' fishing back home. That was, of course before I'd experienced Cassien at first hand and I had no idea just how much of an effect it would have on me. I returned home and got the pictures developed and all the memories came flooding back. It started to dawn on me just what a special place Cassien was. The first thing I remember doing after that was driving straight off down to Darenth where I knew Pete Noonan was fishing. Pete didn't really have much of an interest in going away at that time and, like many of us back then, carp fishing only revolved around England. Well, the poor blokes ears must have been ringing by the time I'd finished telling him about that first trip.....huge lake.....huge fish.....blue skies.......warm water....... naked women!!!!!! Well, forget the first part of all that, I think it was the naked women that really got Pete's interest!

"Yes you can fish for 50lb carp while watching nude women running around."

Pete's eyes widened all the time and I could see that he was really getting quite interested in his first trip abroad.

There was another reason for getting someone else interested in going as I'd been a very silly boy and had got stopped driving home after having one drink too many. It was a tough lesson for sure, but a good one and I would never do it again, but now I was looking at a year without my licence, which I'd not had that long anyway. Pete was keen to go and the best option seemed to be if we went in my car with Pete doing the driving, but after checking with his insurance we found that he wouldn't be covered. Pete had a car that he was very proud of but unfortunately it was a Mini van – okay it had wide wheels and a 1200cc engine but it was a Mini van and I couldn't see how that would be of any use to us. Gradually it became obvious, though, that if we were going to go, then the Mini van was our only option.

"This is more like England than France!" Pete remarked.

In the back of the van I would say that about a third of the space was taken up with a huge homemade wooden box that housed the speakers for the 'sounds'. Pete came from a part of London where you were judged by how good your 'sounds' were in your car and the fact that the car literally shook from the bass as it went down the road gave him a bit of 'street cred' in his neck of the woods, and he wasn't about to give that up for anyone or anything. There was something else about Pete's car that needs mentioning and that was in order to start the van, someone had to stand at the front and poke a screwdriver through the grill to hold the front of the starter motor on until the van was running! It all sounded a bit risky and I'd heard about this Five Star cover that you could get from the AA, which covered you for just about everything, and I suggested that it wouldn't be a bad idea to have some of that just in case things went wrong. Pete wasn't too keen on that but went along with the idea anyway.

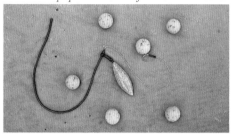
We were well prepared on the bait-front this time around.

Having one trip already behind me, I had a few ideas on how things could be improved a little, next time around. The main problems seemed to lie with the crayfish and the snags. Going out in the boat to play the fish seemed to help a great deal and I'd only really sussed that out towards the end of the first trip. The Kamasan hooks did the job but weren't really strong enough to cope with what we hoped to catch so I switched over to the Drennan Super Specialist size 2's, a much stronger model of hook altogether, but the biggest change came with the baits. The soft freezer baits were simply no match for the numerous crayfish that always seemed hungry, so a plan was hatched to make our own, extra-large, much tougher hook baits which we hoped would be the answer to all our problems. We purchased a few bags of 50/50 mix and some flavours, I used Rod Hutchinson's Cream, while Pete went for Maplecream, and a few evenings were spent rolling some big baits, which were probably 35mm to 40mm. They were well over-flavoured really but that was to make up for the extra long boiling time which was to be our method for making them harder. They looked brilliant and I couldn't see how we could fail.

"We'll catch a few on these I reckon," I said.

"Yeah, they look good," said Pete. "Now tell me about those naked women again!"

Peanuts had worked really well first time around but, strangely, I didn't receive any action on the tiger nuts, although I hadn't persevered too long with them it has to be said, but it does seem that peanuts are a more instant bait to start with and so we got a couple more sacks to use between us and of course a few more bags of Honey Yucatan's and Tutti-Frutti's to use as freebies. One more thing I did make sure I bought before the trip were a decent set of scales which went up to 120lb, maybe a little bit over the top but there was no way I was going to get caught out again!

The day of the 'off' arrived and I poked the screwdriver through the front grill while Pete started the 'mean machine'. Don't ask me how but somehow we managed to get two lots of gear and all our bait in and we were soon on our way to Dover. That part went okay but before we even reached Paris the Mini spluttered to a halt. The fan belt had broken and plumes of steam were rising from the bonnet.

"No probs, Pete, that's why we got the 5 Star cover!"

A phone call later and we were towed off to a little garage where we exchanged a new fan belt for a few tokens out of our 5 Star booklet and we were on our way again. This time I remembered where all the correct road signs were and we negotiated our way down through France quite well, although we did overheat a few times and I distinctly remember something that almost resembled the engine nearly seizing a couple of times when we were almost there, but although I know we both felt it, we both stared straight ahead in the hope that it would just go away. But it got us there and we arrived just into darkness. My girlfriend and one of Pete's mates – 'Spock' - had wanted to come so they had flown down and were already waiting for us at Pierre's. It was a very warm evening and too dark to see anything. The first thing I had to do was just go down to the edge and feel the water. It felt warm and it felt good to be back. The excitement of arriving was soon overtaken by tiredness and we were soon crashed out on the bedchairs in front of the restaurant.

I awoke to the now familiar sight of Pierre's smiling face.

"Bonjour mes amis," he greeted us with.

"Bonjour Pierre," I replied and looked out to a sight I didn't expect to see – rain! I had promised Pete wall to wall sunshine and naked women and there were neither.

"This is just like good old England" said Pete.

I didn't know what to say other than it was bound to clear up soon and one of Pierre's omelettes and chips would set us up for the day. A couple of cups of good, strong coffee helped to bring us around a bit and we gazed around at the pictures of the huge fish up on the wall. There were a few new pictures added since I'd been there a few months earlier and knowing that those fish were swimming around out there somewhere made us feel a lot more enthusiastic.

Meals were paid for, permits were bought and we were soon loaded up in one of Pierre's boats and ready to make a start. As this was my second trip and only Pete's first, it was left to me to choose where to start. Although I'd done okay in the North Arm last time out I quite fancied a go in the West Arm, especially around the Blue Boat area, where I'd seen Geert Abelo in action towards the end of the last trip. I knew that May was a good time to be in the West Arm and I also knew that the Blue Boat swim was a good interception point. Thankfully, after the long row up the lake we found that the area was free. Actually, we hadn't seen any other anglers at that point, although we knew that some were about somewhere on the lake. I explained to Pete that it was a good place to start and if nothing happened we could always go and fish up the North Arm where I had been previously. With the rain still falling quite heavily, though, it was just a relief to get an umbrella up.

Pete held the rods while I rowed the hook baits out.

Considering how narrow the West Arm is, I was quite surprised to find it still quite deep. It seemed at least as deep as the water I was fishing previously up the North Arm, which I hadn't expected, but I knew that the fish would feed comfortably in that depth of water so we set about putting a couple of markers out and baiting up. We basically just spread the best part of a bucket of prepared peanuts and one hundred or so boilies across an area where we could cast three hook baits to. Although I had 'mastered' the art of playing fish from the boat, I had still yet to use one for dropping the hook baits.

The first evening and the next morning passed by very quietly, the sky was a mass of grey with the rain still falling steadily. At that early stage it didn't look too promising and I could see in Pete's face that it wasn't quite up to his expectations so far, but it was still very early days. The one thing that did really please me was that when I reeled into check the baits I found that, apart from a few scratches from crayfish, they were still more or less fully intact. It was a big plus that the baits appeared to be 'nuisance proof' but we just needed a few carp to find them.

The swim in the Spawning Bay was free and we wasted no time.

Another quiet evening followed and it was approaching the third evening, with the rain still falling, when a guy rowed up the lake obviously just on his way home. We hadn't seen him arrive and it must have been really early but as he called across we realised he was English. He asked how we were doing and then explained that this year the spawning bay had been opened up to anglers and he had been down there for the day and although a couple of other people were also fishing down there, he had managed to catch himself a couple of low-twenty commons! We chatted for a while and the guy went on his way. As soon as he was out of sight Pete and I looked at each other – both with the same thoughts! They might have only been small fish, but they were carp and the area needed to be checked out. I took the boat and rowed down towards the end of the West Arm. With all of the rain the water was as high as it could possibly be and the spawning bay looked a whole lot different to the previous October when the level had been around ten feet down and the bay was literally half empty. Over towards the left hand side of the bay I could see that someone was fishing, but on the right there was no-one. It looked really good; the bay was more or less split into two sections by a point of reeds that extended from the far bank. To the right of this point could only really be fished from where I was standing and, looking around, there was definitely enough room for us both to fish.

Looking back, I'm amazed that we didn't move straight away, but with the rain still falling and the night closing in, we decided to leave it until the following morning. Needless to say by the next morning nothing had occurred – but we did wake up to the incredible sight of blue skies! It had to be an omen and we hastily scrambled around and got all our gear together in the boat and headed off towards the spawning bay. With relief we found that the area I had looked at was still free and we pulled into our new swim with renewed hope. I could, however, see a pedalo moored on the other side of the bay with two guys fishing from it. I found it hard to believe that we hadn't caught any fish on their way into the bay but perhaps they had already been there before our arrival and anyway if the other guy had caught from the bay, then there was every chance that we would too.

With the sun shining it was nice to get out at last and have a good look around. Most of the area in front us was much shallower than where we had just come from. The reed beds looked the obvious spot to fish to but I did have my doubts as to whether fish of any decent size would go there as it was only around three feet deep.

Pete Jones and Travolta were fishing from a pedalo each day.

The spot we were fishing was only about one metre deep next to the reeds.

The other thing that I found a bit strange was that there was no movement anywhere and I felt that if there were a few fish about then, surely, we would have seen some signs of them either in the shallow water or in the reed beds. While we were looking about we decided to go over and see the two anglers on the pedalo, who turned out to be Pete Jones, who we'd met previously at Darenth, and his friend 'Travolta'. They told us that they were just looking after the area really for their friends Terry and Karen who'd been there for a while but wanted a break. Pete and Travolta found that it was easier to fish from the pedalo rather than tow the baits across to the reeds from the bank and although they had lost a couple of fish, they had also landed a couple of double figure commons. So there were definitely fish about, although it did rather seem that we'd found where all the smaller commons lived. Either way, by now we just wanted to put a fish on the bank so we would settle for whatever was out there.

Fishing from the pedalo looked quite restricted. Pete and Travolta were only using one rod each, but we both preferred the idea of towing out the baits from our swim with the boat and dropping them fairly close to the reeds and then playing any fish from the bank that we might hook. It was the first time either of us had fished this way and we worked out that the best way to do it was if we rowed out with our own baits while the other person held the rods on the bank. That way, we could still bait up around our own hook baits, which we both felt was important. I know a lot of people like to share runs between the rods but that's never really been for me as I could never be excited about catching a fish on a rod and bait that someone else has put out – but each to their own.

Travolta looking well pleased with his 'surprise' thirty.

With everything in place there was an air of expectancy that was missing before and, even if the fish didn't seem to be that big, at least there were some around, although as the light faded it still seemed very quiet out there. It was very late evening when one of my alarms finally sounded. I was on it in a flash and Pete was soon beside me. Although we were fishing about a rod length from the reeds, with the 15lbs mono and light rods that I was using I could already feel the grating, which told me that the fish had already gained too much ground. I could feel it pulling away on the other end so we quickly took to the boat and made our way out towards the reeds. As we got closer I could feel that although the fish was in the reeds, it wasn't snagged and I was playing the fish effectively through the channels in between. Gradually the fish and the boat came closer together and Pete was able to scoop the fish up in the net.

YES! – A fish – we were off the mark!

The surprise was that it was a mirror and not the common that we were sure we would end up with. I don't know why, but after all the grief before with weighing the fish I just couldn't find the scales! It was my first fish and for all I knew it might be the only one so I wanted to weigh and photograph it properly, so decided to sack it up until daylight. We estimated it at around 28lb.

As is normal when I've got a fish sacked, I didn't sleep very well. Every now and then I could hear the fish struggling but by dawn it was all quiet and when I went to check I could see why – the fish was gone! Somehow it had found the opening and gradually pushed its way out. I was gutted, after all of the effort involved in getting to the lake and finally getting on the fish, when I did catch one it had got away with no pictures and no weight. At least I knew that I'd caught one I suppose. Pete Jones and Travolta arrived soon after, Pete was quite sympathetic after what had happened but Travolta just gave one of those disbelieving looks as if to say "Oh yes I've met people like you before!"

The daytime was all quiet for us but I seem to remember Pete Jones catching one that day from the pedalo, again it was a common of high doubles if I remember rightly. We had already been out with fresh baits by the time evening was once again upon us. Baiting up was quite easy from the boat, we could easily know just where we had dropped the hook bait just by looking at the reeds and once marked we spread peanuts and boilies over about a ten yard area around each bait, which we did by throwing several small handfuls around the area rather than just dumping the whole lot in one spot. We both felt this would keep the fish searching around a little longer as we were beginning to think that the fish weren't stopping long to feed in the shallows.

With darkness upon us it was Pete's turn for a run and he soon had it under control in open water. We took to the boat anyway just to avoid tangling with the other lines, but it wasn't long before he had his first Cassien fish on the bank. It was another mirror, a little smaller than the first one at 24lb but the first one is always special and I know it made Pete feel a lot better. There obviously weren't loads of fish in the area but we'd both caught and so anything else would be a bonus. It was a couple of hours later when one of my alarms sounded again. This time the fish came away from the reeds a little easier than before and we took to the boat as before to continue the fight. It was hard to make out what was on the end but I remember the fish thrashing its tail on the surface and Pete catching his breath and saying "That sounded good!" Then the fish headed straight for us and actually

Pete Noonan about to return his first Cassien carp.

bumped into the boat, which felt quite forceful. Even with just my little 1¾ lb test curve rod I was able to keep it under some sort of control and in the shallow water the fish seemed unable to really gain any line. A few minutes later I was able to guide it into the net. It did look like a good 'un in the moonlight and we both guessed at around 40lb or a bit more. However, back at the bank I was about to get the shock of my life as we went to lift it out – this was certainly no forty!! In fact I'd never seen anything like it! We just looked in amazement.

"How big do you reckon that is Steve?"

"I don't know mate but it's got to be over 50lb" I said.

This time I had the scales and the sling ready and the needle whacked around to 61lb 8oz – Bloody hell !! I was expecting a mid double common from the shallows and ended up with a mirror that looked more like a hippo! We were all in a state of shock – I certainly was! I couldn't believe what I'd just landed. I'd seen the pictures of big carp but somehow had never expected to actually catch one myself. I was shaking like a leaf as I sacked the

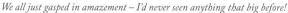

We all just gasped in amazement – I'd never seen anything that big before!

fish up and I wasn't going to take any chances this time after what had happened previously. I don't know how many knots I tied in the cord, but it was quite a few. I was understandably well over the moon and was no doubt beaming from ear to ear but when all the excitement had died down a little I remember Pete sitting there shaking his head and saying "God, I want one of those!"

Morning arrived and as I opened my eyes I could see Pete Jones and Travolta were once again already fishing across the bay. We had to tell them about the fish so made our way over to them in the boat.

"Morning" said Pete, while Travolta came out with

"Oh good morning, now don't tell me, you've had a 50 – and that's got out of the sack!"

Well I had the perfect reply,

Struggling for one last shot of my 61lb 8oz mirror.

"Well actually it's bigger than that – and it's still in the sack!" (you've no idea how much pleasure that still gives me).

They both had open mouths but quickly reeled in to come over and see the fish. As it turned out Travolta had already caught a 30lb mirror that morning and was keeping it quiet ready to 'surprise' us with it – bless him.

Until that time I'd only caught the one forty and seen another, so to see this fish in daylight was like nothing I'd experienced before.

Pete Jones said "It looks like a hippo with no legs" so that was it, the fish had to be named 'The Hippo' after that. We photographed all the fish and then sat around chatting and just re-living events. I just felt like all my birthdays had come at once.

If it had been quiet for the first week, then it was all about to change as there were quite a few other people starting to take an interest in the spawning bay. It looked like we had been really lucky moving into the swim when we did as there were a lot more people arriving now. Geoff Shaw was a name I knew of and he

The alarm screamed and Pete bent into a good fish.

arrived in the swim to see what was going on, in fact he came down every day to see what we'd caught. Two Dutch guys, John and Rob, were further up the bank and we would get to know them a lot better in time to come. We were trying to keep things quiet for obvious reasons but it was very difficult. Some of the other English guys were coming every day and were getting a little annoyed that we weren't telling them the full story, but we were only trying to protect what we had while we could.

Pete still wanted one of the big ones so I made the only offer that I thought I could and said that if he wanted I would take his bait out and drop it exactly where I had the sixty from. He had nothing to lose so that's what I did that evening and although it was quiet through the night, the following morning that rod went flying off in the early morning. I was already up and watched Pete scramble out of his bed to bend into the fish. It was unusual to get a run at this time but it was good to be able to see what we were doing for a change. The fish had kited left away from the reeds and we were soon in the boat in hot pursuit. It was a decent enough fight and we were sure that it was going to be another good one. Sure enough, as it went in the net it was clearly another massive mirror. I shook Pete's hand and we went back to the bank. At 54lb it was the monster that Pete had wanted, a big-framed fish with a huge mouth and even the big hook bait just looked dwarfed in there.

At 54lb it was the one he wanted.

Later that afternoon we heard cars and people moving behind us and went to investigate. I couldn't believe what we saw. It was a group of Germans, not just anglers but friends, wives, children – the lot. There must have been about twenty of them in all and they proceeded to set up tents and beds and they even had gas bottles for cooking that were nearly as big as me. Until now we had been discreetly tucked away under the trees out of sight, but this was bound to cause some sort of trouble. We went off to the shops and by the time we returned the rangers had already paid a visit. A couple of the new arrivals had been carted off and the gas bottles had been confiscated. That was the good news but as we looked out there was another guy moored out in the lake in a boat with four rods fishing to our spots. It was all getting a bit silly but we weren't going to give up our swim that easily and a few choice words here and there seemed to sort the situation out and in the end it was all quite amicable really. People knew we were catching and they just couldn't help themselves. I suppose when you've travelled all that way and you're struggling, while the guys up the bank are having a result, then it's tempting to try it on a bit.

Thankfully, all the commotion didn't really affect things too much for us, otherwise. We only had a

A 37lb mirror about to go back.

Pete just missed the 40lb mark by ounces with this cracker.

few days left of the trip by now, anyway. I don't really know where the fish went to during the day but I can only think that they went back to the deeper channel of the river bed to lie up. There was very little sign of them during the day but they still kept coming back in the evening to feed. We both caught a few more before the end - Pete's best was 39lb while I had another of 37lb. Amazingly all of our fish turned out to be mirrors, as previously only smaller commons were being caught, but I have a feeling that we just happened to move into the spawning bay at precisely the right time. It was just a matter of who we would hand the swim over to as there were plenty of contenders. In the end it was 'Big Bob' the Hells Angel and his mate as we'd got on quite well with them and he was bigger than all the rest! The other side of the bay was taken over by Dave Moore and a young Rob Hales who had only recently arrived.

Another pit stop for the infamous Mini van!

It was actually a bit of a relief when it was all over, to start with it had been rather quiet and pleasant but in the end it was becoming a little bit of a circus. We rowed back to Pierre's, said our goodbyes and loaded the Mini van up – Ah Yes, the Mini van! During all the excitement we'd forgotten all about the small problems that we'd had on the way down. Now, the journey home could be a chapter on its own but I'll shorten it down a bit. We left the lake and the stalling in the engine didn't go away, in fact it got a lot worse! The car was bucking like a kangaroo and we tried to keep going but the exhaust broke away from its mountings and made a hole in the petrol tank, which we blocked up with a rod sleeve. We were overheating every ten miles or so and were stopping anyone we thought could help us. Then the cap snapped off the top of the radiator and we were soon in another little garage being patched up. But the problems weren't solved and we bucked and rattled our way, somehow, up to Calais where the van just stopped and we were there for two days. By now the AA Five Star token booklet was completely empty and we were down to our last bit of cash – "It's just as well we caught those fish" Pete kept saying, and he was right! That was all that kept us going. Eventually we hobbled on to the ferry and by thrashing the van in second gear and with a cab full of smoke, we came to the end of my road, where the exhaust pipe fell off altogether and the Mini van just cut out – and believe it or not, never went again.

Mick Daly with a fish that Rod Hutchinson had caught previously.

Back in the safety of my own home I could laugh about it, but it had taken us five days to get home in all and looking back I was amazed that we made it at all. Our catches had already hit the carp fishing grapevine and of course there were no mobile phones or internet back then but Mick Daley and John Buckley were waiting on my doorstep as we arrived back. They had been booked up to go to Holland and fish the Twente Canal but on hearing of our results they immediately switched plans in favour of Cassien and spent the next five hours grilling us for info. I told them to try the West Arm and if that was no good to go up the North Arm to where I had fished the previous year. Well they did that and the next thing I was hearing was that John Buckley had landed a massive 70lb mirror from up the North Arm. Apparently they'd gone to the spot where I'd fished in the North Arm and one evening John had heard a very big fish crashing in the margins around to his right. He took his rods around to the spot and fished virtually stalking-style in the margins and the rest, as they say, is history.

Soon after that the floodgates opened and Cassien became virtually a household name to anglers. The lure of those big fish proved to be attractive and despite the distances involved

John Buckley with his 70lb monster from the North Arm.

Another of the big fish from the earlier years, Julian Morgan with a Cassien 70.

and the restrictions with the way you could fish, more and more people started to fish Cassien. I couldn't blame them as I'd already fallen in love with the place. The big fish were of course fantastic and I'd doubled the weight of anything I'd caught in England by that time. But it went deeper than that. Cassien is a special place set in one of the most beautiful parts of France. I liked everything about it and I could only thank my lucky stars that I'd made the decision to go there in the first place as it would have been quite easy to have stayed fishing on my local home waters. I feel lucky because it was a special time and one that can never be repeated. I meet many people who say that they regret the fact that they didn't go and fish Cassien in those early years when it was just becoming known to us and I know what they mean, it was a once in a lifetime opportunity and I'm just glad that I was there to experience it.

Cassien – The Early Years

The Secret Beach

The early years of my carp fishing abroad were, of course, dominated by Cassien. There were two reasons for that, one, because it was such a fantastic place, and two, because there were very few other waters known about at the time. The other waters which did become known to me on the grapevine didn't have such an appeal, such as the River Lot – a beautiful place for sure but the difference was that it was known for producing plenty of action but with fish mainly in the mid-double bracket and I just didn't want to travel those sort of distances for the size of fish that I could be catching just down the road.

However, one day another lake did come to light which really got me interested. I was living up at Farlows Lake at the time and a group of the regulars had been out to France to fish with a friend out there that they'd got to know, who had taken the group to a fairly small water by French standards, but one which obviously held a good head of big fish. They were very guarded about the lake and didn't want to tell me or anyone else the location of the venue, but at the same time they'd had a good result and couldn't help showing me the photos of what they'd caught – which included several fish over 40lb! The story went that this lake had been stocked with carp some years before but they had been left well alone as the locals were only really interested in the pike and zander. The lake, although being man-made and not containing all that many features, did hold a fair amount of crayfish and with plenty of food and little pressure the carp had grown on very well and by all accounts the lake held several better fish than what they had caught, going to at least upper 50's and possibly over 60lb!

We hadn't long returned from Cassien.

On the surface I was very calm about the whole thing and said that I totally understood them wanting to keep it secret, but of course underneath I was absolutely gagging to find out where the lake was! There was just no way they were going to tell me so I sort of put it to the back of my mind until, one day, I was just chatting to someone else about fishing in general, as you do, and he just came out with the statement that he knew about the lake where they'd been fishing and knew the name of the town nearby. Now, I'll be honest and say that I cannot even remember who I had the conversation with but I stood there almost open-mouthed as, out of the blue, I'd just got the information that I needed. I went straight back home and got the map out and, sure enough, there were two or three small lakes in the vicinity of the town in question and undoubtedly it was one of those. Now, I hadn't done anything underhand, but I knew the other guys wouldn't be too happy if I just went off and fished there without them knowing so I guessed it would be good manners, more than anything, if I told them I was intending to go there. I spoke to one of the guys and said that I knew where the lake was and was going there fairly soon. He looked surprised, of course, and not particularly happy at the chance of this lake becoming more widely known and I could understand that and I replied that even if I wrote about it, I would keep the location and the name a secret. The problem was going to be that if I could find out this easily then other people would too and I could see this lake becoming very popular, very quickly and I wanted to fish there before it became general knowledge and a lot busier. So I did no more than book the ferry straight away.

It was now the start of October and a good time to be fishing, of course, but I didn't want to leave it any later that year, and next year it might be too late, so time was very much of the essence. Bearing in mind that I still had a full-time job and I'd only just been to Cassien in September, it wasn't so easy to wangle another week off, but I managed it somehow and for that matter so did Joan. She was manager of the bar and restaurant at Farlows back then and she had very little holiday time owing, but when you've gotta go, you've gotta go as they say!

I glanced across at the water and I knew that I'd found it.

We drove through the night down to the south-west of France until in the early hours of the morning we spotted a bit of blue water from the road and knew that we had found the elusive venue. I was tired from the journey and just wanted a few hours kip, but actually getting to the waters edge wasn't that easy. Eventually, I found a way in next to some chalets and before long I was pushing out a few Z's. The next thing I knew someone was banging on the car window. For some reason I expected that it wasn't going to be good news and let the window down waiting to be told to leave or something, but instead a French guy peered into the car and said,

"Have you got any scales? My English friend has a nice fish but his scales aren't big enough!"

How he knew we were anglers I don't know, but I peered across to where I could see a small green umbrella with a couple of figures huddled underneath, so I said that I would come around. Christ, we'd only been there a couple of hours and already I was going to see a good fish on the bank.

"Use big beds of bait in the middle of the lake" I was told.

The fish was an absolutely cracking mirror of just over 52lb. In those days I still hadn't seen too many fish of that size on the bank and it looked massive as the guy held it up for the cameras. If there were more of those in the lake then I was pleased that I'd made the effort to get down there. It wasn't all good news, though, as I found out soon afterwards that the fish had in fact been taken away to another lake, although the English guy was innocently fishing there believing that all the fish were to be removed – which they definitely were not! However, if fish like that had already been removed, I didn't know how many others had already gone. The French guy seemed to be hanging around for much of the time but wasn't fishing. He seemed to be helpful enough, but I took an instant dislike to him although I wasn't going to rock the boat too much as I'd only just arrived at the place, so I had to bite my tongue a bit every time he came around. He obviously knew the lake well and told us that most fish were normally caught by fishing at range, over large beds of bait. I listened to what he said but made up my mind that I wouldn't tell him of any fish that I might catch in the coming days as I didn't want to play any part in whatever he was doing. The English guy had already packed up and left after feeling very uneasy about what had gone on, so that left the whole lake empty of anglers and just hopefully not empty of fish.

I had already seen a couple of fish show out in the middle area of the lake, so I knew there were at least some to fish for. The centre of the lake could be reached by boat from any bank so we decided to set up close to where the car was parked by the chalets. The lake was roughly rectangular in shape and I suppose about 60 acres in size, it was set in a nice enough area although the lake itself was quite barren with a gravel path encircling its entirety. It was obviously a busy lake in the summer with holiday makers and swimmers, there was a small man-made beach at one end with a water slide, but with the autumn weather now closing in, the holiday makers had long gone back to their everyday lives, leaving the whole place almost deserted.

The plan was to place some markers out in the middle part of the lake and bait up heavily with particles, I had a couple of buckets of hemp and tigers already cooked and soaked. To go with those I also had some White Seed Richworth boilies which I had been doing fairly well with, but the hook baits were all home-made jobs and were generally around 30mm in size and well air-dried to make them very hard, in actual fact it was all the bait that had been left from the Cassien trip as I'd had little time to organise anything else, but I figured that if it worked at Cassien it should do the job here too. The skies were looking grey and it seemed as if we were in for a few days of rain but the Frenchman insisted that the carp liked "The dirty weather" so hopefully I'd be in with a shout of a fish or two. I hastily assembled three rods and took to the boat. There wasn't really much to find out there, by the look of it the margins seemed to slope off fairly quickly and after that the bottom just levelled off and it stayed much the same right the way across. Obviously, when it came to building lakes, the French didn't build them with carp anglers in mind and so didn't include much in the way of interesting features. If anything it was the margins which were most interesting as there were several areas of large stones, which I presume were there to stop the banks eroding, but it was the only obvious place where the crayfish could hide away and so really it should be where the carp would look for food. The only reason that I could see for them going to the middle was just that it was a safer area for them, but if that was where they were then it made sense to fish there.

Conditions did look good, with wind picking up and rain starting to fall intermittently, but the night passed quietly. Being close to the road it was a little noisy so, after breakfast, we made the decision to move down to the end of the lake to our left where there was not so much a point, but a section of bank that jutted out into the lake, but it gave a much better angle to fish from and was a little quieter and I could still fish to the same areas as before easily enough.

The rain was falling more heavily by now and the river at the back of the lake, which is normally not much more than a trickle, was now becoming a raging brown torrent. We were confined to our little bivvy for the most part. Of course, in those days we didn't have many of the comforts that we now take for granted, just a tiny little pop up tent that could just accommodate two lilos with the rest of the gear just squeezed in around us. It was all a bit confined but there wasn't much we could do until the weather changed, at least it was comfortable and quiet enough for the three of us – yes there were three of us now as, at some stage unbeknownst to us, a mouse had decided to move in with us! As anglers we get used to all sorts of critters wriggling and crawling around us, but one thing I cannot handle is a mouse in the bivvy! The first we knew of him was when I went to get my trusty pack of chocolate digestives out to have with a cup of tea, only to find that one end of the pack had been well and truly nobbled – well nibbled is probably nearer the mark. No one interferes with me and my biscuits! So everything had to be pulled out of the bivvy with bags being shaken and rattled, but there was no sign of our unwanted intruder. That was until later that night when something walking across my hand startled me and I jumped and threw the thing off, which then landed straight on Joan's head! She screamed and we both jumped up and out of the bivvy, which now left us out in the rain with the mouse in our nice warm bivvy - with my biscuits. Well I wasn't having that, so out came everything again, bags shaken and things rattled but again no sign of the furry fiend. The rest of the night passed by without much sleep and with me listening out for any little scratching noises, and of course keeping a close eye on the biscuits!

Anyway, before I knew it three nights had passed with no action of any sort. It still looked good but sightings of fish had been few and far between and the big baited areas hadn't worked so far. It did get me wondering about the Frenchman's advice. I'm sure he believed in what he was saying but I wondered if it really was the best way to fish. It's often the case that if someone's had a good result fishing a certain way

Most of the natural food was amongst the marginal rocks.

in the past, word gets around and people just presume that it's the best way to fish without really trying anything else. On a lake of that size I didn't think that it would take much for the fish to become wary of being fished for the same way after a while.

During the afternoon I just happened to glance up in time to see a fish head and shoulder at the far end of the lake in front of the beach. I kept watching and sure enough another couple of fish showed in the same area. That was good enough for me and although the weather was grim I just had to move down there. I knew it wouldn't take long to move everything down to that end and at least it would get us away from the mouse!

They gave themselves away and I knew that I had to move to the beach.

We moved in no time and set up right on the beach itself. It was quite nice to be on the sand as the surrounding grass was just becoming more soggy and wet all the time. With a new swim always comes that renewed confidence and I was looking forward to getting the rods out. It wasn't long before we had a visitor to the swim, though, in the shape of the local gendarme. I knew he wasn't there just to see how the fishing was going but he spoke no English, so that was a bit of a problem as I spoke only a little French. He had this finger that was all bandaged up and he kept pointing with it and saying "Voiture labar".

Now I knew that 'voiture' was 'car' but had never heard 'labar' before. He kept saying it and finally the penny dropped and I realised that I'd parked the car in the wrong place and there was a car park over the back where it should've been. 'Labar', as we later found out, means 'over there'. I agreed to move the car, but then he turned to the bivvy and started pointing at that. I guessed that we either shouldn't have a tent or shouldn't be set up on the beach?

"Pluie" I explained, pointing at the rain coming down and he seemed to accept that one as we could hardly just sit out in the rain. He checked the fishing permits and, satisfied that they were in order, he then went on his way. That was a big relief for sure as I feared the worst, but all I had to do was move the car to the car park and then concentrate on the fishing once again.

There were a few things out there that I had to be careful of.

I knew that the fish I'd seen from the other side were quite close in to the beach so for the first time I decided just to cast out the rods from the bank and do away with the small inflatable that I'd been using. There were a few obstacles to be careful of in the shape of a couple of buoys anchored about 40 metres out and a platform which was used for diving off in the summer. All of those were fixed to the bottom by chains. They looked a bit dodgy but hopefully I could miss them if anything should happen. The first rod was flicked around twenty or thirty yards out and landed with a nice 'thump' on the bottom, the second rod was placed at about the same range but twenty or so yards to the right of the first. The third rod I put more down to the right towards the corner of the lake and although the bottom seemed a bit softer there, it still felt okay. I catapulted around twenty boilies over each bait and that was all. I figured that I would try a slightly different approach and see where that got me. I was confident that I was right on the fish now anyway. I felt that there weren't as many fish in the lake as I'd hoped, but then with the stamp of fish that I knew the lake held, I guessed that it could only hold so many.

Some time later in the hours of darkness the right-hand indicator dropped back a few inches and then rose slightly again. I took my time as I was sure that a bream was to blame and sure enough there was little resistance on the end as I wound it towards me. Whatever was on the end was coming towards me quite easily and I wasn't getting too hopeful, however, as it came closer I could see the shape of something larger than a bream and scooped it into the net a bit sharpish. Then all hell broke loose as the fish, which was definitely now a carp, woke up and went ballistic! It obviously didn't realise it was hooked and I'd just been able to lead it in without a problem, so the whole fight took place in the landing net. I could put up with that even though it soaked me. The fish was in fact a common of 30lb 8oz, a long fish, different to the others I'd seen but one that I was certainly pleased to catch after the efforts of moving earlier. Off the mark!

A short time later one of the rods in front was away and I was in action again. This one certainly did know it was hooked and it took several yards of line on the first run before kiting left. I just knew from the angle it was heading it would come into contact with something and soon I felt the horrible grating sensation as the line went around one of the chains. I eased off a bit not wanting to get cut off and then just inched everything slowly towards me. It felt horrible and I was waiting for something to go wrong, but with a sudden jolt I felt the fish come free of the chain and that lovely feeling of just the fish nodding on the end made me breathe a sigh of relief. After plodding up and down in front for a while, Joan was able to bundle the fish into the net. This was more like the other fish I'd seen, a deep-bodied mirror which looked much bigger than the common and indeed was at 43lb 8oz. A cracker of a fish and now it was all happening! Before daybreak the one remaining rod was also away and with another nice mirror of 32lb duly landed, it completed a hat-trick of carp with two 30's and a 40 plus – now that's what I had travelled all that way for!

I took the indulgence of doing a 'Billingsgate' shot with the three fish. It's perhaps more frowned upon these days with fish care taking such importance and I can see why and wouldn't do the same nowadays and wouldn't recommend that anyone else tries to photograph more than one fish at a time, but the fish all went back none the worse for their ordeal and I just hoped that there were a few more of them out there still willing to feed for the remainder of the trip.

The next night was eagerly awaited and as soon as it got dark I was waiting for the first run, but it wasn't quite the same and nothing happened through the hours of darkness. It was actually getting light the following morning when the bait around to the right in the corner once again rattled off with a hard-fighting fish on the end. The water to the right was clear of any obstacles so

I did things my own way and what a difference it made!

Another good fish followed the next morning.

I walked down that way with the rod to keep everything clear of the buoys and stuff to my left and I could then play the fish in relative safety. It was another strong fish and several times it made powerful runs but I knew that as long as I took my time everything would be okay and I soon had another good mirror of 35lb 4oz on the mat.

Small world isn't it?

Until then we'd had the lake more or less to ourselves but, later that day, a few people started to arrive. First was a French guy named Joel, with one of his friends. He was a nice enough guy and we had a chat before he went off to set up around on the 'mouse corner' that we'd vacated a couple of days earlier, while his friend went off to the bank across to our right. Then I saw another three guys approaching which at first I didn't like the look of, but then we realised who two of them were. I couldn't believe it when we saw Roger Smith and Kerry Barringer walking towards us.

"It's a small world," I said and Roger replied, "Nice here, innit?"

They didn't know anything about the lake but they had made friends with the young French lad with them called Jerome and he had brought them down knowing that there were good fish to be had, indeed Jerome had already caught fish to over 50lb from the lake and seemed to know what he was doing.

Jerome set up to our left further down the beach, whilst Roger and Kerry fancied a quieter time and went to the far end of the lake which was the farthest point from civilisation and from anyone else who was now fishing. One more angler turned up that evening and he went in not far from Joel on mouse corner and in the space of a few short hours the lake had taken on a totally different feel. It was obvious that the lake was becoming quite well known and fairly heavily fished already but, on the plus side, everyone was more than friendly and the atmosphere was at least a good one. Jerome was really good company and definitely one of the many great characters that I've met on the bank. He spoke pretty good English too, which always helps. We spoke about all things carpy and we got onto the subject of baits, he too had some very large hook baits, similar to mine which he had air-dried, but Jerome's were coloured red, white and blue of the French flag! He went on to say that he'd been using the same baits on a recent Cassien trip which was where he had met Roger and Kerry and everything started to fit into place knowing how much time they both also liked to spend at the great lake. Then Jerome got out a large 10kg bag of chopped baits which looked very familiar and he explained that when he was at Cassien, he went into Pierre's restaurant and had noticed the bag of boilies in the shop and had bought them before leaving. Well this had obviously all happened soon after we had left Cassien the previous month. I say that because the bag of boilies was one that I had left with Pierre at the end of our trip as a way of a little 'thank you' for all his help and now, around 500 miles away at another lake, here was the same bag of boilies just a few yards away in someone else's bivvy. I'd already said to Roger earlier that it was a small world and this just made that statement even more poignant.

It was nice to have the extra company but it was inevitable that the fishing would slow down with so many other lines now in the water. I think it was the following night that Jerome caught a grass carp of about 22lb, but other than that it was all quiet for everyone – well not quite for everyone. Joel came around for a chat in the morning and of course the first thing was to find out what had been happening for him.

The small stream at the back had become a raging torrent!

"Any fish in the night, Joel?" I enquired.

"No fish for me" was the answer, "But I was lying there in the night and a mouse bit me on the finger!" A plaster indeed showed where Joel had been bitten. I couldn't help but have a little snigger to myself.

"Ahh, you haven't got any chocolate biscuits then, have you?" Joel just gave me a strange look before moving on to talk to Jerome who obviously made more sense than me. That mouse obviously had the hump with us moving swims and taking our biscuits with us, so poor Joel had to bear the brunt of its anger!

Time was fast running out now and although I'd caught some nice fish, it didn't mean I didn't want to catch at least one more before leaving. With the rain still falling I peered out across the lake. There were markers all over the place but it seemed as if the fish had now moved from the beach, or if they were still there then they were lying low. However, as I scanned the water I noticed there was one area in the middle where, for some reason, no one was fishing. It wasn't a big area but I thought to myself that if I were a fish then that's where I would go. I looked at the area and figured that I could get a bait out there without interfering with anyone else. I had already packed my boat away by then but Jerome kindly said that I could borrow his if I wanted and as he had a proper Zodiac with electric outboard it seemed the obvious thing to do. There was little in the way of features anywhere out in the middle so I picked the spot that was furthest away from everyone's

I peered out in the gloom as the bait runner began to tick.

It felt like a biggun and at 50lb 8oz it was!

markers and just dropped the bait with around ten or so freebies around it. I was only trying to get one bite at a time and as most of the others were baiting heavily (as I guessed they would) but had nothing to show for their efforts, I thought it would give me at least a chance of a bite.

The night again passed by quietly and the rain was still falling steadily the next morning when I heard an alarm sound. I unzipped the door of the bivvy and peered out. The indicator on the long range rod was pinned up against the rod as the line steadily began to tick from the spool. As I picked up the rod nothing seemed to happen, it felt solid but I knew there were no snags out there and then everything began to move slowly towards me. It was then that I realised it was just the heavy, solid weight of a big fish on the other end! I can only describe it as like trying to pull a parachute through the water as the resistance was really heavy with just the occasional 'nod' on the rod tip to let me know that it was a carp on the other end. There was no way that I could rush things and to be honest there was no need to as there was a clear path through to the bank, unless the fish kited left which it showed no signs of doing. Inch by inch and yard by yard I eased the fish towards me until, after what seemed like ages, the fish was just out in front of me, although I still hadn't seen it yet as it circled around in the deeper water. I was desperate to get the fish in but somehow managed to remain calm enough to just let things take their course and finally the fish came up to the surface and seemed to resign itself to being netted. My arms were aching so badly by then, I just dropped the rod to my side and breathed a huge sigh of relief. It was still early in the morning and no one else had been awake to see all this going on. In the net was a lovely big mirror, I wasn't sure just how big but certainly bigger than any of the others that I'd landed that week. There was one more arm aching job to do and that was to weigh the fish. I held on to the scales as the needle swung around….47…48…49 …….50! The needle settled on 50lb 8oz. YEEEESSS!! What a fish – what a lake!! After seeing the big fish at the start of the trip I hadn't dared to hope for one like that myself and especially when the other anglers arrived I really thought that any real chance of another fish had gone. But, just taking the chance to put a bait somewhere different had paid off big time and I'd got one of the bigguns. A slight break in the rain meant that everyone was able to gather to take the pictures. It was only then that I was able to have a good look at the fish and see how nice it really was with its chestnut brown flanks and starburst scales – a special fish indeed!

With only one night of our trip left it was too much to expect another fish and there were to be no more runs for me before packing up. I had been so keen to find this lake as I was sure that it was going to be something special – and it was. I also thought that it would be a place which could soon change as it was so accessible and becoming known to more

I returned the following May and had another good fish of 46lb.

people all the time. I did go back again to the Secret Beach the following spring and already I could see that the best days were over. I arrived just as a carp match was finishing. Fifty anglers had fished for five days and had only caught a few tench between them. Again everyone was friendly enough and the Mayor, who was there to present the prizes, even said that we could night fish without worrying – before then it was tolerated to some extent although it was actually not allowed. I went on to catch one good fish, a mirror of 46lb, but things had changed and it was attracting a lot of attention from anglers and also from the authorities who, later, started to clamp down on what carp anglers were allowed to do, and so I felt the time was over for me at the Secret Beach. Soon after, I heard that it was restocked with small commons and then legal night fishing areas were brought in. It was always going to happen and really it's the way it had to be. But I was glad that I took the chance to fish there when I did, I doubted that I would ever return to the Secret Beach but for the short time that I fished there it was a very special place.

Cassien – The Early Years

Dinner with Roger and Kerry

A ll Cassien sessions are memorable for one reason or another, it's easy to pick out the ones that have brought the biggest fish, as they are the stories which most people instantly pick up on. But there are plenty of other times when the trip has been memorable, but for different reasons. One such session took place during September in the early 1990's.

September was always seen as the prime time to go away. After the long hot summer in France, it was when the temperature just dropped slightly, making the fishing far more pleasant, and the seasonal change normally triggered the fish into feeding a little heavier too! I suppose that I always had a soft spot for that time of year, as my first-ever trip to Cassien had started in late September and I'd caught my first ever 40lb carp on that trip too, so I'd continued to head down to Cassien around that time. The swim that I'd fished that first time down was also quite special to me and it was normally somewhere that I would return to, at least for a few days. It was now known as the Third Point in the North Arm, rather a shame I thought that a place of such beauty, that holds so many memories for so many people, should just be referred to as 'the Third Point', but that is how it has become known to everyone, so who am I to disagree?

Predictably, that was where Joan and I started off this time too. Really the swim covers quite a large area in the middle section of the North Arm. Around to the right, the swim faces back down towards the bridge and the Second and First Points. It's certainly a good area and has many nice features to fish to, but I've always preferred the left

Cassien in September is a great sight.

side of the swim more. The left side faces out towards Moby Dick Beach on the far side and is the more scenic of the two sides – if you prefer that sort of thing – which I do. There are probably less features on the left side and the water drops off more quickly, but it always seemed to be good for a fish or two if they were in the area. The other great thing about the Third Point is that both sides have lovely beach areas and in the warm, September sun it did give that feeling of being on holiday as well as fishing.

It was around this time that I was going through a tiger nut stage. I had used them as far back as my very first trip, but they weren't as effective as peanuts back then – at least not for me. But now that the fish had grown accustomed to them, they had become a really successful bait, probably accounting for more fish than any other bait for those in the know. I say 'those in the know' as there were a lot of people who had yet to discover them and although English anglers had been using tiger nuts for several years by then, there were plenty of anglers from other countries who didn't yet know of their potential.

There were a few people about in the North Arm but the Third Point was free and so that was where we headed. The first day passed by without anything of any note happening, although if I remember rightly, I did catch a roach of about 8oz! Just how the roach had the audacity to pick up my carefully-laid trap I don't know, but I suppose that was a feature of those earlier days, the smaller species were more prolific than they are now and they all seemed to take a liking to our offerings. Tench, bream and chub used to turn up with some regularity – but a roach was taking the biscuit!

It was just after getting the rod back out that I noticed a little boat heading our way. This normally meant some inquisitive holiday-makers or the inevitable pike anglers, who seemed to always target the areas where my lines were when spinning for their dinner. I did my best not to catch their attention but they kept coming and pulled in just around the other side of a large reed bed. There was some rustling in the reeds before they parted and out came two very familiar faces in the shape of Roger Smith and Kerry Barringer. Roger and Kerry were both 'old hands' on Cassien and were among the early English travellers to the lake. In fact, Rod Hutchinson's articles relaying the times he and Roger had fished the lake some years earlier, remain some of my all-time favourite pieces of writing and they were a big inspiration for me to start travelling down to Cassien in the first place.

"It's nice here isn't it?" said Roger in his own unique way.

"Well it looks nice" I replied "but I've only caught a roach so far!"

"Ooh that's not so good – have you seen any fish yet?"

I explained that I hadn't really seen much so far, although I had heard a couple of fish jump in the night but they were some distance away, but anyway it was early days yet. However, Kerry's reply stopped me in my tracks.

"Well we counted over sixty fish jump in front of us by 10 o'clock last night and we managed to catch four."

"What!!!" My next question was, of course, the obvious one – "Where are you fishing?"

They explained that they were fishing 'their beach' which was a bit of a code name for a swim that they had fished on many occasions. Actually 'swim' is hardly the correct name to use for this area, as it was right amongst a heavily wooded stretch, positioned virtually on a cliff face! So well were they hidden away, that I hadn't even realised that anyone was over there at all. It was a part of the lake that I'd never seen anyone fish before, partly due to the extreme nature of the bank side, but also due to the fact that the water dropped off very quickly over there and most people considered that it wasn't really worth the bother of fishing – well apart from the two people that I was now talking to, that is! It's always funny though that once you know someone has caught fish from an area it's always easier to see the potential of it. To me it now looked one of the best areas in the North Arm. It was virtually a safe haven for the fish, as most other swims had seen some sort of pressure

A familiar sight during the summer months.

over the previous few years, but as Roger pointed out, their swim was the only fishable spot in over one kilometre of bank on that side of the lake and it was virtually un-fished. Besides all of that, it was also a good vantage point to see what was going on in the rest of the North Arm and with their binoculars they had seen us arrive and set up the previous day.

It was still early days and I wanted to give the Third Point a decent try and I was still quite confident that something was going to happen, but needless to say the thought of what Roger and Kerry had told me earlier was going around in my head. The next couple of days were very pleasant, but also fishless and the confidence of the earlier days was now being replaced by the realisation that we were going to struggle here, and the Third Point wasn't looking like such a good choice this time around. That's nothing unusual with fishing Cassien, the vast majority of my trips have involved moving swims once or twice – sometimes several times before I've made contact with any carp. It was time to do something about it, so early the next morning I took to the boat and proceeded to row further up the arm in search of a new area. I didn't want to leave the North Arm as it was the part of the lake I enjoyed fishing most and we'd enjoyed Roger and Kerry's company, so we wanted to stay in touch with them if possible for the rest of their stay, which would be another week or so. We still had about another week on top of that so there was plenty of time for us to get things right, which I was sure I would do sooner or later. As I'd learned in the past, if things didn't feel right, it was generally better to move rather than just sit it out and wait for the fish to arrive, which could well be later rather than sooner.

There were a number of areas free, as only a few people were fishing the North Arm at that time – certainly something that wouldn't be expected these days where the lake is far busier around September time. I stopped at each likely-looking swim and just got out of the boat and had a look around trying to get a feel for the swims. I'd stopped at all the spots along the left side of the arm going up but nothing really took my fancy and so I rowed over to the other side for some inspiration. Towards the entrance to the dam, was the far end of the steep bank area. It was a long way from where Roger and Kerry were, but still on the same side of the lake, so I decided that it should be checked out. I'd never looked at any of those areas before with any intention of fishing, but after hearing of Roger and Kerry's results, all of a sudden these wilder areas looked a lot more appealing. One corner of the bank had a pathway running down to it through the woods and although it wasn't really visible from the water, there was just about enough room to put a bivvy up and get the rods out. It looked spot on and really my mind was made up straight away, but I rowed up to Roger and Kerry to ask their thoughts. We couldn't even see each other from the two respective swims, but I felt it was only right to check it with them first. Even though we weren't going to move in close to them, the idea to fish there came from their original thinking and I felt slightly uncomfortable about it for that reason.

Roger and Kerry thought nothing of it, they knew the swim well from previous sessions and were soon pointing out what they thought were the best spots. Actually, it was testament to how careful they were with the surroundings that the swim looked virtually un-fished. Mind you, the swim that they were in looked even more incredible! They both had umbrellas tucked up in the trees, some twenty feet above the water. It really looked like one false move would have sent them tumbling down the bank and into the lake, and tumbling down the bank was basically what they had to do in the event of a run as the rods were obviously right down at the waters edge. I could now see why I had failed to work out where they were fishing before as they were almost completely obscured by trees and there were just a few branches tied back so that they could make their way up and down. The only

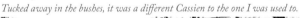
Tucked away in the bushes, it was a different Cassien to the one I was used to.

giveaway was the boat, but even that could be tucked away in a small bay to their right. They recounted a few stories of how, at times, people had passed within a few yards of them on their way down the lake, without even realising that anyone was fishing there, or how others had been given quite a shock when they did spot them peering through the branches. But it wasn't just the anglers that were caught out by Roger and Kerry's hidey-hole, the carp were fooled by it too and I was told how the carp would often start showing just around dark but would move in very close to the bank, sometimes throwing themselves clear of the water almost under the rod tips!

This was Cassien fishing, but with a big difference! Until now I'd always been of the opinion that it was all about fishing on the ledges and plateau from comfortable swims in the sunshine. But in these areas it was all about being tucked away out of sight and alone with nature, and with the carp of course. Just the thought of that gave me a terrific 'buzz' and I couldn't wait to get back and get the boat loaded and give the new swim a try. Thankfully, Joan liked the idea as well, I wasn't quite sure how she would react to moving away from the sandy beach and the sunshine, but she was as keen as I was and to be honest she thinks the same way as me for much of the time anyway.

The difference in atmosphere between our two swims couldn't have been more apparent. The Third Point is a quiet, peaceful swim – or at least I thought it was until now, as this new area was almost silent and I'm sure that you really could have heard a pin drop. One of the things I was looking forward to most was fishing at close range, it's always the way I like fishing if possible and although much of the fishing is like that on Cassien, this would be real margin stuff in comparison. A quick look out in the boat with the echo sounder showed that the bottom dropped off at what seemed like a 45 degree angle right down to around 100 feet. There were no obvious spots that stood out from the rest but I fancied 40ft as the starting depth as that had always been a good depth previously for that time of year. I dropped a couple of markers at the chosen depth and went back to the bank for a look and had to giggle to myself as I could virtually cast to the markers underarm and couldn't believe that at that short range it was already 40 feet deep. No wonder the fish would come in so close - they would have to if they wanted to find any food!

While the markers were in place I baited the area liberally with tiger nuts. My plan was to bait roughly around the area and then just cast the hook baits into place before removing the markers afterwards. That way the markers had no chance of spooking any fish or getting in the way while I was playing any fish – and the other thing was that they wouldn't be there for other anglers to spot. If I had to recast at any stage then as it was only just a flick from the bank, I was fairly sure that I would be landing more or less in the right areas. People have different ideas on how to use tiger nuts on the rig. Some people just prefer to use a boilie hook bait over the top or a bunch of several tigers; some people say that just one tiger nut on the hair is the best way to go. All of those methods will work on their day,

The fish were in 40 feet – but that wasn't far out!

but my own preferred way is to use two tiger nuts and a small 10mm cork ball on the top of them to balance the bait so that it sits as a snowman hook bait would. In reality, the cork balls weren't really needed as there are numerous cork oak trees growing on the banks of Cassien and many of them have small chunks of bark missing where anglers have taken advantage of this natural resource over the years. But for me, a little round cork ball looked more neat and tidy and fitted in nicely with the appearance of the two tiger nuts. To the carp it probably didn't make too much difference, but we have to feel right about the things we use in our own heads don't we?

Roger had already told us that he and Kerry would be up to see us the following day. Most of their action was coming during the hours of darkness and as they didn't want to pressure the fish too much, they figured that a few hours every day with the lines out of the water would only help their cause, and of course it would give them the chance to see how we were doing in our new swim. It was the chance to have a little social too. The difference with the new area was obvious to see straight away as, even in the middle of the day as we were setting up, some fish were rolling out in the middle over very deep water. It gave me the confidence that was lacking before and I felt sure that it wouldn't take long for the fish to move in closer, once they realised that the food was there.

The night passed quietly and I must admit that I was a little disappointed not to have got off the mark. In fact the activity had quietened down if anything during the night, but by daylight fish were starting to show again. At around midday the little white boat appeared from around the corner and a voice called across "We've brought some beers!" Joan always wants to feed everyone, so she'd already planned everything so that there was enough food for all four of us, which our two guests were not expecting, but the look on their faces told us that they were more than pleased to hear it. Just as Kerry was getting out of the boat, one of my rods burst into life out of the blue!

"That was good timing" I remarked, and after a brief battle my first fish of the trip was in the net. It was 'only' a small, but very pretty mirror of mid-doubles, but as ever I was so pleased to get off the mark.

"There's a lot of people on this lake that would like to be holding that fish right now" said Roger – and he was right.

I hadn't seen much happening elsewhere and the lake can seem very difficult when you're not on the fish, as I'd found the previous few days, but it looked like I was on them now and the meal that followed went down very nice with a few beers.

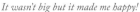
It wasn't big but it made me happy!

It was interesting to hear that again Roger and Kerry had received action during the night. The days for them were very quiet but the swim would come alive at night. For me it seemed like the opposite was happening and I was intrigued by the fact that two similar areas along the same stretch of bank, albeit some distance apart, could be so different. Either there was one group of fish that were moving between our two areas, or we had a totally different group in front of each of us. The first reason seemed to be the most likely to us all and as long as we could all catch fish, it didn't matter too much. Roger and Kerry had already landed plenty of decent fish including personal best commons for both of them of 37lb plus. Commons of that size were still a rarity back then and for them both to catch one was an even less likely event.

Later that afternoon the two well-fed anglers headed back off to their swim, keen to get the rods out again for the night ahead. I sat back in the knowledge that I'd at least got off the mark and sure that I had a few more to come yet. One thing that we soon noticed about being on that side of the lake were the amount of wild boars living around us. During the day there would be no sign of them but as darkness arrived they would soon start appearing. I suppose they were left alone more in the dense woodland and the softer, damp ground was a lot easier to root

Roger and Kerry head back to their swim after stopping for dinner.

through as they searched for food. As ever, the wild boars didn't bother us at all, in fact we went out of our way to look for them, so a few visits from them during the night was all part of the excitement as far as we were concerned. The only problem with our swim was much the same as Roger and Kerry's really in that it was quite a slope down to the waters edge from our set up. I liked the idea of being hidden away, but at the same time I like to be able to see my rods whenever possible and the bottom of the slope was obscured from view and also not particularly easy to negotiate in the dark. I decided that the rods would be better placed about halfway up the slope. The lines were at such a steep angle anyway that it didn't seem to make much difference and the rods were much easier to reach quickly. And of course once a fish was hooked I could then make my way to the waters edge without the initial panic that always occurs when I get a run!

The action was getting more consistent.

I love it when a plan works and by midday the next day I'd landed a couple of 20lb mirrors. It did seem very snaggy out in front, but I was able to land the fish from the bank without any major difficulties, the main thing seemed to be getting them under control as quickly as possible. However good I thought the idea was, though, Kerry didn't see it quite the same way and the following day as the two arrived he said nothing, but gave both the rods and me a disdainful look. I tried my best to explain but he obviously thought it was a bit of a 'Noddy' set up – at least it wasn't all on view for the whole lake to see.

The sun had made way for rain and we all ate dinner under the cover of umbrellas that day. It didn't make too much difference in the new swim, as we didn't get to see much of the sun on that side anyway, it was just a bit wetter than before. The one thing rainy conditions normally do, though, is to change the feeding times of the fish. If anything they tend to feed a little earlier than they might normally. Roger was keen to get going a bit sooner, mainly because of the weather. We had an afternoon with little to do so we decided to have a few games of cards to pass an hour. A few hands later, and there was a flier on one of the rods. I went down to do battle and wondered why Joan was taking so long? Little did I know that she was pulling a fast one with the cards, arranging them so that she could win the next hand! Everything went without a hitch and another 20lb mirror was soon being held up for the camera. With the fish returned and the rod back out, it was back to the cards and I couldn't believe my luck when I was dealt the best hand of cards that I've ever seen! Joan had got it the wrong way around and given me the set of cards that she'd sorted out for herself, of course she couldn't let on – well not for a while anyway. What's that saying – 'Cheats never prosper'?

Cheats never prosper!

It was still drizzling the next morning when the next run occurred. I couldn't make much headway with the fish so we both went out in the boat. For a while I really thought that I had a big fish on as I just couldn't budge it above a certain depth. There was an old French guy out for the day in his boat and he was watching everything intently. After about ten minutes it dawned on me what was happening. The fish that I'd hooked had become entangled in someone's lost line and although it felt as if the fish could move freely it would only come up so far before locking up. I tried for probably about another 15 minutes to free the fish but eventually it just shed the hook and I was able to pull for a break. The Frenchman had watched throughout and it was only a couple of days later when I returned to Pierre's for some supplies that people started coming up to me and asking me about this huge battle that I'd had with some unseen monster that had eventually beaten me. Somehow the Frenchman's story seemed a lot more exciting than the truth!

The story doing the rounds was that I'd lost a monster!

It was quite strange that while the rain had brought a decent spell of action for me, Roger and Kerry's swim had totally switched off and they'd not had a run from the time since they'd left the previous day. That is the way Cassien can work, though, and it can be very moody at times. There are no hard and fast rules where those fish are concerned. The good news for them, though, was that the sun was starting to appear again through gaps in the cloud. That night brought the best fish of the trip for me so far, at just under 30lb, hardly a monster by today's standards, but it was a different situation in those days and in fact I later went on to catch some of the same fish on future trips at much bigger weights, but at the time just catching some Cassien carp was good enough for all of us.

It was like being perched on the side of a cliff.

One thing I did notice, though, was that where the fish had been rolling around the whole area in front of me at various times, they had now stopped showing to my right. I still caught that day, but the next day they had stopped jumping in front of me and it looked as though the fish were moving out. When Roger and Kerry arrived for dinner they told me that for the first time since they started fishing they had seen fish showing in the daytime and it was now apparent that we had been fishing for entirely different groups of fish, the problem for me was that my group had now disappeared off down the lake. The good thing for me was that Roger and Kerry would have to be off in the next day or two and they kindly suggested that we should move in after them. As they pointed out, their action hadn't gone unnoticed by then and if we didn't move in then someone else was sure to. It sounded like the perfect idea to me and after another fishless night we were more than pleased to have a chance of fishing an area which never looked fishable before – but now looked like the best swim on the lake!

It was definitely worth making the move.

It's always a shame to see friends leave but they had run out of time and we'd at least had some good days together and some good fish. They both explained that the fish were still showing well in front of them and I was looking forward to that experience for sure. We bid our farewells to the pair of them as they set off for home and we were left with the job of getting everything sorted. If I thought that the last swim was precarious, then this was even worse. From the only spot where we could wedge a bivvy in, it meant a similar run down the slope but then there was a drop of about four feet down to the rods with just a rock sticking out to form a step. How they'd coped without breaking any bones was anyone's guess, but I literally had to tie rope between the trees to get up and down, so severe was the incline. At the bottom was just one area the size of a 45-inch umbrella where all the rods had to go and the only flat spot for us to sit – and that was only because the water had receded during the last few days. However, the area out in front looked much better than in our previous swim. It dropped off just as quick but it just levelled out slightly right at the forty feet mark, which looked spot on. There were also far less snags and all fish could be played fairly safely from the bank.

I sat there in the evenings just watching the rod tips.

That evening was one I'll never forget. As promised, the first fish showed just on dark, then another and another, there were loads of them and they were getting closer all the time. We sat there behind the bushes hardly daring to breathe, as just the other side, a few yards away, big fish were throwing themselves clear of the water. It was one of those times when it's just a matter of 'when' you catch and not 'if'. Sure enough, by morning I'd caught three fish, the best of which was a 29lb common. I'd not caught a common from the previous swim and as Roger and Kerry had caught more than a few in their total, this just reinforced my view that this was a separate group of fish altogether. Unlike the previous occupants, though, I didn't intend on resting the swim for the time we had left. That may or may not have been a good idea, but we had around five days left and this was an opportunity that I wanted to make the most of. This was carp fishing at its most exciting. Being so quiet, there were no distractions and, sitting in our little area at the bottom amongst the rods, it was impossible not to sit there watching the rod tips with the expectancy that one would pull over at any second. At 5pm just as we were catching the sun for the short time that it reached that area, one of the tips nodded and pulled over. I was on it after one bleep and soon locked in battle with a 28lb mirror. It was hard to imagine anything better, it was almost like barbel fishing but for carp instead. Just as darkness was closing in another rod tip jerked and arched over, this time I was on it before the alarm could sound but the power was just amazing. It ripped several yards of line off down to the right before kiting through the entire swim until it reached the bank around to the left margin and it simply couldn't go any further. Then it just plugged away for ages in the deep margins before Joan could finally put the net under it. It was a pristine common of 33lb 4oz – a personal best common at the time, which meant that three of us had all landed PB commons from the swim in the space of two weeks.

It was one of those sessions that I really didn't want to end, but all good things do have to come to an end sometime and the way that I always look at it is that no matter how quick the time has gone, at least I've been there and done it and gone away with the memories – and they will last forever! I continued to catch fish right up until the end, in

A nice mirror that decided to feed in the afternoon.

We'd all caught our biggest commons in the space of a couple of weeks.

fact with everything but the rods packed up on the final morning, one last run brought yet another common, not so big this time but a fitting end to the trip and well worth a picture, I thought. But the fish clearly had other ideas and managed to throw a 'wobbler', soaking me in the process and getting away without having its photo taken. We both saw the funny side of that and I carried on packing away the last of the remaining rods before heading back to Pierre's and ultimately back to England.

That would be the end of this chapter but there is one little piece to add. We returned the following year at around the same time and sure enough, Roger and Kerry were back in 'their' swim, only this time they weren't hidden from view as they had been before and we could clearly see all of their set up from some distance away. As we got closer we could see that the surrounding trees and bushes had been massacred by someone who'd obviously thought that they would have a go in the swim, but wanted all the comforts and the view of a 'normal' swim. An area had even been dug out and flattened to take a bivvy more easily. The tone in Roger's voice said it all as he exclaimed "In the last two years we had over fifty fish from this swim and this time we've had one!" Bearing in mind they had been there for almost two weeks and were due to leave soon, it was obvious what effect the 'improvements' had on the fishing. The fish showing at close range were now only a distant memory and it was now just another swim which was being fished regularly.

In reality it wasn't the end of the swim and many fish do still get caught from there, but normally from further out than those early trips. I've fished it several times since and have gone on to land fish to just under 50lb from there, but it will never be the same as it once was. Most countries have different names for the swim now and it is regularly fished all year-round, but to me it will always be that little hidey-hole in the trees and it will always be Roger and Kerry's swim.

I did go on to catch some bigger fish from the swim – but it was never quite the same.

Cassien – The Early Years

Something a Little Different

Cassien had always been the place for a summer trip. Enjoying the long, sunny days and swimming in the clear blue water were all very much part of the equation when visiting that lovely part of France. It was very easy to see why so many people with money chose to holiday, or even live down there. Of course, I couldn't live the lifestyle of those people, but I could enjoy much of what it had to offer in my own way by spending a week or two with the rods out! In the early years of me fishing the lake, a two-week summer trip was about as much as I could manage. I was still working full-time then, and any trip away would have to come out of what little holiday time I had owing. So back then it seemed that summer was the obvious time to go away. In those days there were a lot less visitors to Cassien, no night fishing was allowed as such, and that put a lot of people off going and the summers provided everything I was looking for – plenty of sun, carp and space.

But in 1994 there were drastic changes taking place and for the first time ever on Cassien, night fishing was to be allowed through the whole year. At first this seemed like a great step forward in the whole scheme of things. We had always been able to 'sneak' the odd night here and there, but we always had to be very careful and we could never really fish comfortably without bivvies and bedchairs, which was the way we had to go about it then, in fact it was the only way to do it until that point. But now we could literally take virtually anything we wanted and stay on the bank without having to look over our shoulders all the time.

We moved onto Chantecoq and straight into the Church swim.

It all sounded great and I was soon organising a trip for the early part of the year, around May. However, on arriving at the lake, it was immediately obvious just what an impact the new ruling had. All around the banks, which were normally devoid of anglers for much of the time, there were now bivvies – and lots of them! I just had a feeling of disappointment, somehow the lake seemed different. I started fishing how I normally would have before that, by staying a day or two in one swim and then moving if nothing had happened, but everywhere that I fancied moving to already had someone bivvied up in there, and it looked like they would be there for some time. It had changed the atmosphere of the lake and I was struggling to settle into it. In the end I actually packed up and left the lake early, the only time that I've ever done that over the years. Cassien had changed and had become a lot busier almost overnight and I wasn't really sure what to do about it.

Later that summer I started looking at a few other waters in the hope that I could find somewhere else to fill the gap. In those days there weren't so many waters known to us and two very large and very obvious lakes to try were the Orient and Chantecoq. Both of those were far bigger than even Cassien, but it was the sort of fishing I was looking for, and besides, they were both a lot closer to home. I had stopped off and looked at both of them before when driving home from Cassien, and out of the two it was really the Orient which attracted me most, the main reason being that it was known to hold far less fish than Chantecoq, but they were known to grow much bigger, up to 70lb and more.

The weather changed and the fish turned on!

I organised a trip for myself and Pete Jones in the September of 1994 for a ten-day session, but on arrival at the Orient we found that most of the areas were already taken. As big as the Orient was, it only had relatively small areas open to night fishing and as we found, they soon filled up. We did fish just one night around at Geraudot, but it didn't look or feel right at all and rather than stay somewhere we weren't really happy with, we both chose to load the gear up and see what Chantecoq had to offer. Well we got lucky and managed to move straight in next to the famous Church Swim after two Dutch guys had recently gone home. The expanse of water in front of us was huge. It was something like five miles to the opposite bank, by far the biggest water that I'd ever fished and that got the adrenalin pumping more than normal. We also got lucky with the weather as, after a warm, dry spell, it all changed quite rapidly and as the wind picked up, the rain began to fall and the fish, which had been quiet until then, started to feed! We both had loads of action; there were obviously a lot of fish in the lake and when they went on the munch it was 'fill yer boots' time! It was very hard work, though, more because of the conditions in which we had to fish and because of the great distances that I had to row out every time, generally against a strong wind. Despite all of that, we ended up catching loads of fish with the best of 41lb 8oz, falling to my rods. It was exciting enough for me to want to go back for more, and a month later I went back for another ten days with Joan, although we fished the far side of the lake at Port de Nuisement that time around.

I decided to experiment with some really big baits.

The best of my fish from the first trip at 41lb 12oz.

I caught even more fish on the second trip – loads of them! I don't think that the area had been open to fishing long and it seemed to be just full of hungry carp. With the two of us there, we could've had eight rods out, but in the end I was only using three. The water was much lower now and getting through the mud just to play the fish and get out in the boat was too much, especially when all of the rods could go off in an hour or two when it all 'kicked off'. In the end I was just putting three rods out in the afternoon/evening, and once I'd caught three carp that was enough for the night. I could have caught stacks more, but I'd caught stacks as it was, up to 41lb 12oz. They were lovely carp I have to say, but it was just too easy and I didn't find it quite so enjoyable just looking at one similar fish after another without really having to try too hard to catch them. The one thing I did notice from that trip was that the bigger fish did tend to go for the bigger baits. I had made up some real whoppers for that trip, boilies which were 45mm or even 50mm diameter and, almost without fail, the biggest fish each night did fall to the rod with the biggest bait on.

The fishing was just mad. A huge lake which was just full of hungry carp!

The big problem was of course the mud!

I suppose, looking back, that it was very good fishing really, but there was something missing. Perhaps it was the challenge, as I needed to feel that I'd achieved something by catching the fish and not just stacking up a list of weights, and anyhow, whichever way we looked at it, there was no way that it matched up to being at Cassien.

I was missing the place already, but I didn't like the idea of the crowds that had been there earlier in the year. I just knew that I wanted to be back there, but summer was already gone and I wasn't quite sure of exactly what I wanted to do. The more I thought about it, the more I got confused until the possibility of a winter trip dawned on me. I'd never really fancied the prospect of Cassien in the winter before, as for me it was always about being there in the summer, but the more I thought about it, the more it made sense, after all, few other people had ever

considered fishing through the winter on Cassien, so the chances were that even if it was colder, it should be a lot quieter too! Plus the fact that, around Christmas time, I would have some spare time – and Joan would too, as she would get a break from running the bar at Farlows Lake, giving us the opportunity to return to our favourite place!

They were lovely fish but it all seemed too easy.

It was a trek from the bivvy just to get to the waters edge.

We couldn't make it down until just after Christmas as we'd already agreed to go down to Pete and Jean Jones for Christmas and Boxing Day. I certainly didn't realise it at the time, but that was to be the last Christmas Day that we would spend in England! It was December 28th when we made our way down to the ferry port. Crossings were a little cheaper at that time of year as obviously not so many people wanted to travel across the channel in the winter. It had a much different feel to it altogether. Instead of heading off to France in the warm sunshine, it was cold and grey outside and quite choppy too. I wondered just what we were heading towards, although I do remember being more than just a little excited at the prospect of another Cassien session when I'd normally be stuck at home. The drive down was very different too. By late afternoon it was already dark and getting colder, but with the heater on in the car it made everything feel a little better. All around we could definitely tell that it was the festive period, with Christmas lights everywhere and fireworks going off every now and then, it really made the long journey pass by a lot more quickly. We only stopped for fuel and one or two of their 'rocket fuel' coffees on the way. It's not the nicest coffee you'll ever taste but it does have the same effect as someone giving you a slap around the face!

It was sometime in the early hours when we finally pulled off the motorway at Les Adrets and drove the last couple of kilometres down the winding roads to the start of the South Arm. I strained my eyes to get a glimpse of the lake but it was far too dark to see anything. We drove past the restaurants, they all had their gates locked, and were effectively shut for the winter period. Most of their trade was obviously with

The drive south in December was certainly a lot different to how I'd known it before!

summer tourists and it was hardly worth staying open for the few visitors who might pass by at that time of year. We pulled up at the bridge which, besides being a central area of the lake, also has a car park either side at the far end and by then all I wanted to do was to pull in somewhere and have a few hours sleep. I remember stepping outside of the car to see how it felt. I suppose I was hoping that it would be much warmer than it had been across the rest of France, but I was wrong, and all around was a thick, white frost and it felt bitterly cold after being in the warmth of the car. So there was nothing to do other than jump back into the warmth quickly and worry about everything else a bit later on when in was light.

I awoke some hours later and tried to peer out of the windows, but they were all thick with frost. It was light by then and the nearby road was busy with cars as people made their way to work in the early morning. Coils of mist made their way slowly across the water; the lake had a much different look about it altogether. The water had a grey-look to it now, instead of the usual blue in the warmer months. I wandered down to the margins. The water felt cold to the touch and it looked 'dead', actually that's probably not the right word to describe it, but normally the margins would be alive with small fish, the small and colourful Rainbow Perch normally, but there were none to be seen, in fact there was no life to be seen anywhere.

While I was crouching there, the sun started to appear over the distant hills to the east. As soon as it appeared, it began to feel very different. The frost on the car began melting straight away and the warm rays beaming down felt very nice. It wasn't all that long before it was warm enough to walk around in just a tee shirt! What a difference an hour made, the sun obviously still had a lot more strength in that part of the world and it made the whole place look a whole lot more appealing.

With the restaurants closed, we had the problem of where to leave the car. Although I'd never had a problem before with leaving my car anywhere, this would be a little different as it would have to be left in quite a public area, with some of our gear still in it. The good thing was that the bridge area itself was known as a decent area carp-wise. I had always given it a wide berth before, as it was always so busy in the summer. But now it was almost deserted and looked to be a much better prospect, and I would be able to leave the car just above where we would be set up.

I knew that I wouldn't be able to store baits anywhere this time around so the baits I took with me were suited to the situation I was in. I had made all the boilies myself and then air-dried them at home for some time before the trip, which would preserve them for the duration of the session. This was the bait that I went with:

10oz Milk Mix (Carp Company)

6oz Dairy Mix (Solar)

8ml Sweet Plum (SBS)

3ml Dairy Sense Appeal (Hutchinson)

6ml Sweetener

12 large eggs

Air-dried for two weeks

I made some slightly larger baits for hook baits, they were around 25mm to 30mm diameter, not quite the huge 'donkey chokers' that I'd used at Chantecoq, but big enough to deal with any pests that were around such as bream or crayfish, which of course were prolific in the warmer months, but I had no idea how active they would be now. The freebies were 18mm's but I didn't have loads of them, and so to make up the bulk of the free offerings I'd planned to just use a mixture of hemp and tigers, both of which had proved themselves before.

It looked the right spot to be.

The biggest problem I had now was just how to approach the fishing at that time of year. I didn't actually know anyone who'd been there in the winter, so I had no real idea of the habits of the fish. With such a vast area of water in front of me, it could pose all sorts of problems. To start with, for all I knew, the fish might well have all shoaled up together and gone to one area of the lake to over-winter. And then there were the depths; I had already learned, over time, at which depths I was likely to find the fish in September or October – but in December I didn't have a clue! There were no signs of any fish showing anywhere, and I suppose that didn't surprise me really, so all I could do was a bit of 'trial and error' to start with and just hope that there wasn't too much 'error' involved.

Out in front of the main bridge swim is a large plateau towards the third pillar of the bridge. It was a famous feature even back then, probably the most well known feature on the lake. The water level was down somewhat and the top of the plateau itself looked a little too shallow to really be worth a go, but over quite an area, the plateau gradually dropped off all around, giving a variety of different options. In those days only three rods were allowed and so three hook baits were placed at various depths between ten and forty feet.

Before long it was getting dark again. The days might have been a little warmer, at least while the sun was shining, but they were also a lot shorter, and by 4.30pm the sun was disappearing and I was reaching for a jumper – and a coat. To be fair, that night wasn't quite as cold as I expected it to be. A fairly strong westerly wind had sprung up and it had a slightly milder feel to it. In our position by the bridge, we were more sheltered from the wind anyway, so it wasn't too uncomfortable.

The night passed by quietly and after the long, dark hours, it was good to see the sun rise in front of us again. Soon after, we had a visitor. It was a young German carp angler, who explained that he was fishing in the South Arm with a few friends. He went on to say that he knew of a couple more German guys fishing in the North Arm and some more were due. He was surprised to see an English angler on Cassien in the winter and after that I became labelled as 'the Englishman' as everyone else on the lake was German. He hadn't caught anything up to that point but was hopeful enough that something would happen.

He went on his way and left me to ponder what I needed to do to catch one. I had another good look around in the boat that day and re-positioned all the rods on different spots and in different depths, just to see if I could find some sort of a clue. But again I had nothing to show for my efforts by the following morning. It was still early days so I certainly wasn't getting impatient or anything like that, and in a way I just had that feeling that it was going to be tough going whatever the conditions. Joan went off for her usual wander and came back a while later and said that it looked quite nice over the other side of the bridge. I had of course seen that piece of bank several times over the years, but never during the wintertime, so it had to be worth a little look.

It did look good! With the water down a little, there was room to put the bivvy on a sandy strip down at the waters edge and not only that, it was possible to get the car right behind us. Besides all of that, the area of water out in front also looked very good. I could just make out a couple of bivvies on the far side of the lake, which were probably the German guys that I'd heard about, but other than that there was no one about, which gave me plenty of room to mess about with. After two nights with no action and no sightings to go on, it seemed like a good idea to move around and at least give it a go for a few days. Soon after setting up, a little van pulled up behind us and Pierre from Chez Pierres fame got out with that familiar big smile on his face. He had just been down to the restaurant to feed the guard dogs, which were always left there, and had spotted us while driving across the bridge. It was always good to see Pierre, he was-and is, very much a part of Cassien. He was heading back home for his dinner but just wanted to stop in and wish us the best of luck before heading off. Pierre always had that way of making you feel at home and it was good to see him again.

Out to the left of the swim is what is now known as the First Point, although unbelievably looking back now, I had yet to ever see anyone fish there. But I did know that there were some big features coming out from the bank around the First Point. My only problem was that for some reason my echo sounder had packed up and no matter what I tried there was no way it was going to work again. On a place the size of Cassien an echo sounder is a vital piece of kit for just saving time when looking for depths and features. Luckily I had a rough idea of what was out there and I just had to improvise a little. I had taken a little spinning rod with me, and digging around in my rucksack I found a few different spools of line of various colours. So I set about tying different bits of line together, all five feet in length but varying in colour. That way, when I dropped a lead down to the bottom, I could tell fairly accurately how deep it was. It worked surprisingly well and I soon had a couple of markers in what looked like decent areas. As a matter of fact they were both on the nearest of the features to my left, one in 25 feet and one further down the ledge in 35 feet. The third rod was just put straight out in front of me in 20 feet. With that done it was soon time for dinner and then there was no other option than to get in the bag as, although the wind had dropped, the skies were clear and it was already getting cold. Our gear was still quite basic then, and there were none of the home comforts we now take for granted, such as bivvy heaters and portable DVD players, just a few candles for light and to keep the cold at bay a little.

Another quiet night followed and I couldn't really see the point of keep chopping and changing around with the baits, so I decided to leave them where they were. It was obvious that the crayfish and other nuisance species just weren't going to be a problem, in fact they were noticeable by their absence. Every bait that I had reeled in had been un-touched so far, so I didn't see the need to move anything and figured that it might actually improve my chances just to leave everything in placc.

It was the first time we'd met the talented Marcus Lamprecht.

That evening a different German guy came to visit, called Marcus. It was our first meeting, but he would go on to become a good friend in the following years. We had a few beers and chatted for some time. He was amazed at how deep I was fishing. He was fishing at a maximum of two metres, with one or two of his baits in just one metre of water. He figured that it was where the food would be and where the fish would come to feed after dark. It was interesting talking to Marcus, and I did wonder if what he was saying was true. Perhaps I had all of my baits too deep? But looking at the shallows, they just didn't look appealing to me, so I kept the faith, as it were, and told him that I was quite confident that I would catch sooner or later. Marcus and his friend were moving every day or two and were just on their way around to fish on Ellis Point, but Marcus had stopped off for a chat first. We said our goodbyes and wished each other luck before he disappeared off into the darkness to go and get his rods out. I remember thinking that I didn't envy him having to do it all at that time of night in those temperatures, but Marcus, besides being a great bloke and good angler, was always as mad as a bag of snakes!

I'd got my first winter carp!

After another good sleep, the sun once again did its bit and began to warm us up. As it shone through the door, I laid back and just made the most of it. I was beginning to wonder if anything was ever going to happen when, all of a sudden, I heard what sounded like a spool ticking away. I sat up sharply and Joan thought I was dreaming, but as I looked out to the rods I could see one of the tips bent over, and the indicator jumping up and down. Somehow I had left the alarm switched off, something I've done quite a few times and thankfully I was awake when something finally happened. I was on it in a flash. It was the bait in 35 feet that had been taken and the fish kited right towards even deeper water. This was just what I wanted as that was a safer place to play the fish, and I was soon in the boat following it out into the lake. It was flat calm and with the sun shining, it was lovely to feel a fish on at last. In the clear water I could see it down below the boat, even at quite a depth. It twisted and turned and every now and then plumes of bubbles would rise to the surface, but it edged closer and closer and was soon lying in the bottom of the net. It looked smaller than I'd expected but was still a chunky mirror of 30lb 4oz. I remember thinking how much smaller it looked compared with the Chantecoq carp of the same weight. The Cassien carp are definitely more compact and chunky but all I knew was that I was pleased to see one of them – my first Cassien winter carp!

At last I knew that I was doing something right. Even though I still hadn't seen a sign of anything, there were obviously some fish out there and even if they weren't as active as in the summer, at least there was a chance of a fish or two. I had to put that rod back out and the others had now been out for two days, so I decided that I might as well do the lot. I kept one bait on the spot where I'd just caught from of course, but I knew that further out in the same direction the features went out further and shallower from the bank. My little feature-finding rod confirmed what I thought and, quite some way from the bank, I found a little flat spot in 25 feet that looked really good. A polystyrene marker was dropped on the spot and soon afterwards it was getting a good sprinkling of hemp and tigers, along with a fresh hook bait.

Two mornings later, after nothing of any note had happened, I awoke a little earlier than usual. It looked bitterly cold outside, the ground was covered in frost and a thick, heavy mist hung over the lake. The water that had collected in the bottom of my boat was frozen solid and I figured that the best thing I could do was just to stay in bed and watch the day unfold from there. I couldn't help reaching down for my camera and taking a picture or two of the dawn. It looked nice enough out there; I just knew that I didn't want to be out there, though!

As I peered out in the freezing dawn, the middle tip pulled over.

I had just put the camera back in its bag when I heard a bleep. I looked up to see the middle tip pulling down. Another bleep and the line pulled out of the clip, but the tip just kept on pulling down. There was obviously something not quite right and I leapt from my bed and down to the rod as quickly as I could. It was so cold that the spool was frozen to the reel and a few panicky seconds followed while I tried to free everything. Thankfully, a bit of twisting on the spool did the trick and the spool screamed as by now it was under such tension from the fish, which had been doing its best to take me water skiing! I leaned into the fish expecting to turn it towards the deep water as with the other fish, but everything just felt solid. It had already found a snag and there was nothing else I could do but get in the boat asap. It was an eerie feeling being pulled out into the cold mist – and it really was cold, my fingers started to hurt where they were holding on to the frozen rod, but I still couldn't feel the fish on the other end. After what seemed like ages, I finally drifted past the marker. The fish hadn't travelled all that far – I just hoped and prayed that it was still on there. As I got above the spot where the line was jammed, I felt something give and then felt that very reassuring pull on the tip, meaning that I was thankfully still attached to the fish. It didn't go shooting off but rather just held itself down in the water. For a while it was a bit of a stalemate as it didn't go very far but I couldn't gain any line. Then the fish wandered off around ten yards before going deeper and pulling the rod tip down into the water. I had no option but to give line. It was an incredibly powerful fish, just in the way it could hold itself down in the depths. I was feeling cold all over but my hands and feet were starting to feel numb and I just hoped that the fish would give up soon, but it just showed no signs of doing so. This must have gone on for half an hour. Literally, the fish was just towing the two of us around in the boat as it pleased, and I was beginning to wonder if I'd hooked some sort of monster. Eventually, after what seemed like forever, I caught a glimpse of it and to be honest I expected it to look a lot bigger than it was. I suspected that it was probably about forty-five minutes from the time of that first bleep to the time when Joan finally lifted the net around it. I just dropped the rod and clasped my hands together. The pain from the cold was unbelievable, but at least I had the fish! At that moment I just wanted to get back to the bank and warm up with a cup of tea. I had to weigh the fish first, though, and once back on dry land, I quickly rummaged around in the bags for the scales and the sling. Against the white, frosty background, the fish really stood out. It had a lovely dark brown colour and was in superb condition, as all of the Cassien carp were. I settled for a weight of 47lb 4oz and quickly just sacked the fish in the margins so that I could get some life back into my hands.

It was bitterly cold but I was one happy chappy!

The kettle went on straight away, and in no time I was clasping a hot, steaming cup of tea. As I warmed up I could at last begin to appreciate the fish that I'd just landed. It was certainly my best winter carp by a long, long way although I suppose that winters have been a good time for me in the past. A short time later the suns rays started to make their way up the hillsides. The frost particles glistened like small jewels over everything and even the landing net, which had only recently been used, had already become frozen solid. But everything now began to thaw and within fifteen minutes it looked totally different. It was almost like a different day, the frost melted and the mist lifted, and once again the warmth of the early morning sun started to filter through.

Once the tea was finished it was time to get the fish out for a few pictures. It looked glorious in the sunshine. My initial thoughts when I had seen it down in the water were ones of slight disappointment. The fish had fought so hard that my mind had begun filling with all sorts of ideas of huge carp. But once everything had calmed down, I realised that this was a very special fish – and a fairly big one too. Everything about the capture made it so memorable, from that first bleep to the moment when I finally watched it swimming away into the crystal clear depths.

At 47lb 4oz it was the highlight of the session.

With a couple of days left, nothing else happened. It was the end of our first winter trip, but only the start of our winter fishing on Cassien. From then on it was to become a regular fixture and although it could be very tough at times, generally there was a chance of a better fish or two. Of course, it wasn't long before more people started to catch on to the winter fishing and, as ever, the numbers of people arriving during the winter started to increase. But as with anything that is good, it's hard to keep quiet and of course I have written about my fishing for many years, so I was as guilty as anyone else of spreading the word, the period around Christmas is now actually one of the busiest times of the year on Cassien, believe it or not. But I've continued to enjoy my fishing on the great lake. Sure, I was disappointed earlier that year when I had arrived to find bivvies dotted all around the lake, but I knew deep down that I loved Cassien too much not to go there any more. So, all I did was to find another way of going about it and it was probably the best thing I could have ever done.

New Challenges

New Challenges

Lake Raduta

1998 was a good year for me. I remember picking up the phone one day and it was Rod Hutchinson on the other end to ask me if I'd be interested in joining a new team he was putting together called the 'Dream Team'. This would be with a view to working with his company – Rod Hutchinson Fishing Developments - using, promoting and helping to design new baits and products. For me it was a dream come true to be able to work alongside someone who'd been an inspiration to me for so many years. I'd also be joining forces with Simon Crow, Rob Hughes and Martin Clarke. Martin I'd been friends with for quite some time, I'd not met with Rob or Simon previously but it would be something that would have a great bearing on my future over the years to come, as we all forged a strong friendship that would see us work and fish alongside each other in the subsequent years. Also in 1998 I was lucky enough to win the Classic Carp of the year award with my first English forty, a stunning linear that I'd been after for some time. I'd been present when the previous years winning fish was caught, and remarked at the time that the following year I'd like to catch the linear and be in with a chance of winning – not realising at the time that it would all come true! Besides all of that, it was also the year that I first started writing regularly for Carp Talk, something which I've managed to keep doing ever since and something which I still enjoy immensely.

So as you can see, quite a lot happened in 1998, but there was something else that came about, which for me, was just as important as all the rest – and that was the discovery of a new monster carp water, over in Romania of all places. Lake Sarulesti, or 'Lake Raduta' as it became more widely known to most people, was discovered almost by accident. The valley running through the Sarulesti area had been damned and flooded in an attempt to create a waterway connecting the city

The snags at Raduta were like nothing I'd ever seen before – this used to be an orchard before the flooding!

of Bucharest to the Black Sea. The waterway was never actually finished, but Robert Raduta, who now owned Lake Sarulesti, was a keen angler and stocked the lake first with zander, and then with grass carp in an attempt to rid the lake of weed. The addition of the grass carp worked very well and gradually most of the weed was cleared.

The story goes that there was a carp farm present in the valley before the flooding occurred, and when the flooding took place the carp all escaped into the main body of water. Robert Raduta preferred fishing for zander, but one day outside the lakeside hotel that he'd had built, a number of these carp were spotted spawning. Apparently armed with just one rod and some maize, he thought he'd give it a go and ended up catching one of the world's largest carp at the time, a beautifully-scaled mirror of 78lb! The carp being left to grow on unhindered had reached massive proportions. Unfortunately, the fish was killed as carp had little value at the time, and Robert wanted the fish set up to be displayed in the hotel. For some reason the fish was sent to a taxidermist in Austria to be set up, and the guy who was given the job just happened to know some carp anglers – and the rest, as they say, is history! A remarkable sequence of events for sure, and if things had gone slightly differently this fantastic water might have remained 'undiscovered' to this day.

A sad end for such an impressive fish, but it alerted the world to what the lake held.

When I heard the news and saw the picture of the big mirror, my chin nearly hit the floor! I loved Cassien for sure but was also longing for a new big-fish challenge and surely this was it. If Robert could catch one fish like that in a few hours fishing, then what else did the lake hold? Without a doubt there were sure to be other carp of similar sizes swimming about in that vast water. How true that was! In no time, other anglers had made their way out to fish the lake and had caught some truly massive carp. Both mirror and common carp over 70lb had been banked in a relatively short time, but topping the lot was the news that a new world record mirror had been captured by Austrian angler, Christian Baldemair, at 82lb 3oz.

Little did I know at the time, but I narrowly missed out on being amongst that first group of English anglers to venture out to Lake Raduta in the May of 1998. I had already planned a trip to Portugal with my good mate Pete Jones for the same time based around some information of big fish being caught in some of the large reservoirs (which actually turned out to be untrue) in the south of the country. It was only afterwards, when I spoke to Rod and Simon, that they said that I could have gone with them to Raduta – if only I could have turned the clock back! In the end, Portugal was hard work but quite an enjoyable trip, but all the time I was thinking about the boys out in Romania and wondering how they were doing. I can remember my excitement as the copy of Carp Talk fell through the letter box, knowing that it would contain a full write up of how the trip had gone. It had proved to be a tougher trip than expected, at least for the big fish. Most of the anglers had caught some fish, mainly around the low to mid-twenty bracket, but Rob

Hughes had landed a nice common of over 45lb and Simon Crow had done best of all by landing a stunning personal best common of 52lb! The story was all about this huge, wild and windswept lake, which was full of snags that ranged from sunken trees, to literally whole villages! It was obvious, at that early stage, that there weren't vast amounts of carp present either, and all of these things put together made it look a really tough challenge – but one that I really wanted to take on. Thankfully, there were three other trips organised for that year and I made sure that I was on all of them!

The whole valley was flooded and everything had to be left behind.

Rob Marsh gets a helping hand from some of the local gypsy kids.

The first trip was in the August of '98. Little did I know that August is probably the worst possible time to fish Raduta. I was paired up with the very talented Rob Marsh, in the Gypsy Village area. I had two main aims, one was to catch my first grass carp and the other was to catch a 40lb common. It was apparent that most of the Raduta stock was made up of commons, many of them being of a good size, so it was a reasonable target. The grass carp came easily. During the first morning I had two or three and I remember Rob having one that was about 30lb, but we soon realised that we didn't particularly want too many more of them – to put it bluntly the grass carp would become pests more than anything, and they didn't smell too nice either! The carp proved much more elusive with only six being caught that trip amongst the entire group of ten anglers. The big news was that one of those carp weighed 61lb, captured by Paul Jones, which at the time was the biggest common ever caught by a British angler. The weather on that first trip was close to unbearable, with temperatures topping 40 degrees every day and only the lightest of breezes to cool us down. Then, of course, there was the Gypsy village itself. I'm not a great fan of kids particularly, and every day we had a swim full of them, but you couldn't help but like them. They had nothing and had lived a very basic life, so we were almost like a circus turning up in town, with alarms that bleeped and flashed, and binoculars that they could spy on their mates with. Everything we owned seemed to fascinate them in some way. They were good kids, really, and never stole anything, but peaceful it certainly wasn't. Despite all of these things, Lake Raduta held a real attraction for me and I couldn't get back there fast enough.

It was like going back in time.

If anything, that first trip was just a good insight as to how to fish the place. I thought I'd fished snaggy waters before, but none of them came close to this place. In several areas you could see trees, parts of buildings, concrete pylons etc. all protruding from the surface and if that wasn't enough, everything was coated in a thick layer of zebra mussels, even the lake bed itself. Tackle needed to be seriously upgraded to stand any chance of landing these fish. I clearly remember the first indication from a fish that I had there. I was using bow string as a leader, which had been the strongest gear that I'd ever had to use anywhere else, but a drop-back at first light saw me reel in a totally slack line. The leader had cut through like cotton without me feeling the fish at all. This was a whole new ball game to what had gone before and it had me searching around for materials that would cope with the sort of fishing that I was now faced with. In fairness, it wasn't too difficult to find the right gear. 45lb Quicksilver would be okay for the hook lengths and a leader material from Berkley, which I'd never heard of before, called Fireline, in the 80lb version, was perfect for the job. Leads would have to be bigger too. I was used to using 4oz weights on average, but the mud on the lake bed was more slippery than most waters and they simply weren't holding still, so for the first time I started looking at 6oz and 7oz leads. I remember someone remarking that it was more like sea fishing gear, and perhaps it was, but then the carp we were fishing for were bigger than many of the fish which sea anglers fish for with similar gear! As far as I'm concerned, you do what you have to do.

My first Raduta carp came at the start of the second week.

Armed with a more suitable set up, I returned about four weeks after the first trip, this time in the company of Pete Jones. Somehow we managed to secure the area where Paul Jones had caught the 61lb common on the previous trip and hoped that it might be an area for the better stamp of fish. The change in weather was very noticeable from the start. We were dropped off just on dark and there was a decent breeze blowing into us, with a slight drizzle. It was certainly cooler than August had been. Two other anglers were dropped off just around the corner from us and basically would be fishing to the same sort of areas as us, which didn't help matters, but it was one of the features of fishing Raduta, you often got dropped in places that you didn't necessarily want to fish. In fact, if I remember right, we actually had chosen the Pylon Swim originally, which was about a mile away, and somehow Martin Clarke and Xavier Paolozzi ended up in there! But we were happy enough with our swim.

This was the normal way of getting to the swim – although I didn't always end up in the right one!

It was a bit of a toss up whether to fish that first night or not. Pete decided to wait until morning but I couldn't resist just casting a couple of rods out – although that proved to be quite an ordeal with the extra-strong gear that I was now using. I don't suppose I managed to get the baits much further than about 50 yards out into the murky darkness. It was

obviously good enough, though, as I received three runs that night. The first fell off after a few seconds, while the other two produced commons of 21lb and 25lb. Not the Raduta monsters for sure, but they were my first carp from the lake and I was very pleased to see them. In the end, I was grateful that I'd made the effort as the rest of the week was quiet for us after that, I did manage one other double figure common and of course several grass carp. The snags weren't as bad there as they were in the Gypsy Village Swim, but the gear had stood up to the challenge well anyway. Once again there had been a good fish landed, though. Rob Marsh, my partner from the first trip had fished alone this time, moving constantly, and he was rewarded for his efforts with a 60lb common from the entrance to the Barrage section. From memory it was his only carp of the week – but what a carp!

October saw me back again with Pete for the final session of the year. We had started off in World Record Bay with the rest of the guys on the trip, but after a few days of no action we all decided to look elsewhere. Pete and I went back to the Gypsy Village area, but further along from where I'd fished before. With only a few days left we both managed to get a few fish up to just over 30lb from around a large plateau, out in front of us. One thing that stuck in my mind was seeing several fish rolling in an area fairly close into the right of Pete. For some reason he didn't put a bait there at the time, but it was an area that would serve me well on a future session. For once there wasn't a massive carp landed by any of the group, the biggest one we saw was landed by Mick Gudgeon, who'd fished on his own all week and landed a 41lb common near the end of the trip.

Gradually I started to get amongst the better fish.

Three trips had passed and I have to say that they were expensive trips too, and I'd only managed carp to just over 30lb. Looking back, it was certainly no easy water and big fish were only a possibility if you did everything right, and had a bit of luck on your side. A few people questioned why I wanted to keep fishing there, but it was already in my blood and I couldn't think about much else. At the time, commons over 40lb were still few and far between anywhere around the world, let alone anything over 50lb or 60lb. It wasn't just the size of the fish, though, it was also how they looked. They were absolutely stunning fish, deep bodied and scale perfect and I really don't think that I've ever seen better commons anywhere in the world. Apart from the fish, as barren and as primitive as it was in that part of the world, it was a very different experience and also very addictive.

The first really good trip happened the following year in May 1999. It was the first time that a two week trip had been organised, which would give us that extra time to settle into some sort of routine. One week trips seemed to be over all too quickly. Simon Crow was leading the group out and, for him, disaster struck when his hand luggage bag was accidentally placed on the conveyor belt without being checked in at Heathrow airport. The bag contained his camera, mobile phone, bite alarms, reels, echo sounder, amongst many other things. Simon was sure that it would be lost and was proved to be right when, at Bucharest airport, there was no sign of it. He was obviously not happy, thinking that his trip was over before it had begun, but between the group we managed to sort him out with most of the gear he needed. Pete and I had taken spare reels and alarms, so suggested to Simon that we fish as a threesome, which he accepted gratefully. That was the first time I really had the experience of seeing what Simon takes with him on a trip away. His rucksack, that looked full of carp gear, was actually full of biscuits, milk and pasta and everything else was to be borrowed from us. Mind you, we all had our 'little' home comforts that we had to take away with us. I seem to remember that Pete and I had a carrier bag full of chocolate bars that weighed seven kilos! The thing was that the food we were given was just about as basic as it could get, and I'm not joking when I say that often we couldn't even guess what it was! So Simon had got it exactly right and had all the gear necessary to at least eat properly throughout the trip.

It hadn't been fishable before but now the Shepherds Cottage was a great swim.

Anyway, after the usual scenario of being dumped off in darkness at some obscure location, we had a good nights kip, and in the morning after an action free night, Simon suggested that we move over to the old Church Bay area, which was devoid of any anglers. It sounded good to us so off we rowed. At first Simon was disappointed as he looked around. There were old tree stumps dotted all around us and it was obvious that a lot of the snags had been removed over the winter. He figured that it might ruin the fishing, but to me it looked great as further down the bank it now opened up another area that had previously been more or less unfishable. This was the area that eventually became known as the Shepherds Cottage stretch and it looked exactly the sort of place that we wanted to be in.

A quick scout about in the boat revealed that not all snags had been taken out. In the murky water, long dark fingers of old trees could be seen reaching up to just below the surface, most of which were at about 90 yards range, close to a long ridge that ran fairly parallel to the bank. I figured that this was probably the old river bank, before the valley was flooded, and sure enough on the other side of the ridge it did drop down into the old river bed, where it was anywhere between 20 and 28 feet deep. It was the area in front of the ridge that looked most promising, though, with depths ranging down to 9 feet, with the obvious holding features of the snags just beyond.

We had to bulk out the bait as best we could.

The bait that we had available to us then was still fairly basic stuff. Back then, we weren't able to send anything over in advance and we had to rely on maize supplied at the lake, along with any extra bait that we could fit in our luggage. At the time, our allowance was only 30kg and that covered virtually everything we needed to take, so I did well to squeeze a 5kg bag of boilies in. Maize was still fairly effective at the time, but of course we could have done with 50kg or even 100kg or so of bait to really make any sort of impact and we only used to get one bucket of maize per day. Nevertheless, the sight of fish showing over our areas made us all feel very confident. If anything, there were more showing in front of Simon, but it was the first time that I'd seen fish showing in numbers anywhere on the lake and it was a lovely feeling to be sitting back behind the rods, expectantly waiting for something to happen.

We didn't have to wait too long. I think Simon had the first action with fish to upper twenties and I wasn't far behind with three fish to 20lb, including my first mirror from the lake. The weather that first day had been quite warm and sunny and as the sun began to drop over the horizon it was easy to see fish showing on the flat, calm surface. The night time was surprisingly quiet, which wasn't such a bad thing, if we could get action during the day it would be easier to deal with. By the following morning the weather had changed dramatically, the clear skies had been filled with cloud, and rain was starting to fall sporadically. Conditions looked better than ever and I wasn't surprised when my left hand bait, in 5ft of water, was picked up. The tip whacked over and the clutch screamed, straight away I knew this was a better fish and a more exciting battle commenced. Luckily, that close-in rod was the furthest from any snags and I soon had the fish under control and Pete was able to scoop the fish up in the waiting net. It looked a 40 but at 38lb 12oz it was still my biggest common at that point, by a few ounces, and reason to celebrate – mind you celebrating out there meant sticking the kettle on for a cup of tea and breaking out the Kit-Kats, there were certainly no luxuries!

A forty each for Pete Jones and me within minutes of each other.

The wind had got up a little and was blowing straight into us. It looked good, so I got the rod straight back out while Pete took care of the tea. We'd only just sat down with the cups of tea and a chocolate bar each, when the same rod was away again. It felt very similar to the first fish and I remember standing in the margins with the waves lapping against my legs and just thinking how this time I felt we'd got it right. Pete did another great job with the net and this time it did go over the magical mark at 40lb 8oz – Yeesss!! But no sooner had we got the fish weighed than one of Pete's rods was away and I quickly sacked the fish up so that I could give him a hand. It was all a bit hectic but more than worth it as Pete's fish turned out to be another common of exactly the same size. After both of us trying for a 40lb common for so long we'd both achieved the target within minutes of each other!

A nice start to a very hectic day where I had 25 runs on one rod alone!

It was really kicking off and I could see Simon also playing a fish further up the bank, and in between our fish I did my best to run up and photograph his fish too, as of course he had no camera. At one point he called for our help and we ran up to find him with one fish in the net that looked close to 50lb and struggling with another hooked fish, which had snagged him up. From the boat he managed to free it, and then land the fish of 28lb. The one we were looking after was weighed at 48lb 12oz. After the struggles of the previous trips I couldn't believe what was going on, but it was our first insight as to just how good the late April/early May time could be on the lake.

Many of the snags were removed but there was still plenty out there.

Mind you, if we thought we were doing okay it was nothing compared with the results being experienced around the rest of the lake. Simon was there to make a video and he was spending more and more time whizzing off around the lake to see what could only be described as monstrous fish. Across at the Water Tower, a young German guy landed a 60lb common, but over in Record Bay, Henk von Dorn landed the record mirror at 77lb 15oz, an amazing fish, but little did we know at the time that it would be the last time it would ever be seen. Just what happened to the fish after that is not known, but it almost certainly died at some stage.

A fine Shepherds Cottage brace during a really productive session.

The Shepherds Cottage swim was maybe not producing the largest fish, but it was one of the nicest areas that I had fished on the lake. It was away from the main villages and the only people we saw were either when our meals were delivered by boat twice a day, or when the shepherd walked by with his sheep and goats, going off to the grazing grounds over the back of the lake. The shepherd certainly led a very basic life and, come rain or shine, would wander past at the same time, wearing the same clothes, and even in the hot, sunny weather he would still wear his thick, heavy coat and woolly hat. There were also plenty of dogs around and although they looked scruffy and wild, they were invariably timid and very hungry, so of course we made a few doggy friends quite quickly. The two main ones were called Dietzer and Novak, Dietzer being the smaller of the two but definitely the boss. They would hang around most days but would always be there when the food arrived! The Raduta food was never all that great and there was always something going spare, plus they always gave us more than enough bread, which the dogs seemed to prefer as it filled them up quicker. They didn't take long in making themselves at home and I remember one day when we had to go out in the boat to play a fish, just after breakfast had arrived, and I recall looking back to see the two dogs fighting over our food and, once they'd eaten it, they then laid down on our bed chairs for a rest – what a cheek! We couldn't be too angry as they were a constant source of amusement and good company, and if the

Storms were frequent and often quite savage, but they always got the fish feeding.

Many times we just had no idea what it was.

Romanian people had a tough life, then it was nothing compared with how the dogs had to live. It was an amazing place, it was like looking back 100 or 200 years ago to how life must have been for us at some stage, and yet the lake itself was right at the forefront of world carp fishing.

One evening, after dark, we saw the boat which normally brought our food, going up and down for what seemed like ages in front of the shepherds' cottage, with bright torches shining all around the area. We had no idea what was going on, but in the morning all we could hear was screaming and wailing coming from the cottage. It was a horrible sound and we knew something bad had happened. As it turned out, the shepherds' father used to work in the fields on the opposite side of the lake, and every evening the shepherd would go across in a small boat and pick him up. Well that day, for some reason, he was late getting back and rather than wait, the father tried to swim across the lake with dire consequences. He had disappeared and couldn't be found anywhere. Sadly, he had drowned and a few days later they did find his body. This all happened just a few yards from where we were fishing and it almost felt wrong to be there fishing at a time like that, but life goes on and we spoke with most of the shepherds' family, who really didn't mind us being there. We just got on with what we were doing and kept out of their way for a while.

We were still receiving incredible action, it has to be said, and Simon returned with his video camera the next day just in time to film two fish of 39lb and 32lb 4oz which I'd just landed. In between all his running around he had lost, right at the net, what he still describes to this day as the biggest fish he'd ever hooked. But he had started to land more and more grass carp, which made him decide that he wanted to move swims and he went off to the Pylon area with Mick Gudgeon and Sandy Hough. It was certainly a good move for Sandy as, during that first night, he landed a PB mirror of 46lb and after that, a simply enormous common of 72lb, which turned out to be the fish which Paul Jones had landed at 62lb during my first trip. Simon, Sandy and Mick actually made the journey all the way up to us at around 2am to tell us the news. It seemed as though every big fish

There were some good fish out there like this 42 pounder.

Pete Jones with a cracker of 46lb from the Shepherds Cottage.

in the lake was feeding after the long, cold winter and at the time it was the most incredible sequence of big fish captures that any of us had known.

Sandy had done remarkably well, but I suspect that Simon regretted his move from Church Bay when some Austrians moved in and proceeded to whack out some good fish up to 60lb 4oz. I must admit that the rest of the session did go by in a bit of a blur. We were catching an absolute stack of fish but the average size was small at around 20lb, although I still landed some more upper 30's and a 42lb common. Pete did better towards the end and had a real old-looking original mirror of 37lb and the best fish from our swim, and new PB common of 46lb. I know between us we'd had something like 150 fish and were absolutely shattered, but went away relatively happy. We'd longed for some proper action and we had got it, but at the same time I couldn't help feeling that a real chance of one of the big fish had passed us by.

Moving on

In 2000 I returned to the Shepherds Cottage swim for another try. It turned out to be a very similar session to the previous year with an absolute stack of action. The best of the fish was a 41lb common with several decent back-up 30's. If anything it seemed to be a passing through area; a junction between the main Gypsy Village Bay and the channel leading down to the Pylon Swim and Hotel Bay. Undoubtedly, good fish would pass through at some stage, but there were simply too many small fish to put up with – I can remember one day when I received twenty five runs on one rod alone and after starting with a couple of good 30's the fish gradually got smaller and smaller, leaving me exhausted by the end of the day.

So, in April 2001 I decided not to fish the Shepherds Cottage again. I had only just come away from hospital, where I'd had quite a serious operation a couple of days before the trip and really shouldn't have been there at all but, as ever, I couldn't bear the thought of missing out on a bit of fishing and I had explained to everyone concerned that I would just be sitting back, relaxing for a couple of weeks with little to do, and it would be a good rest for me. Somehow the doctors believed me and I was able to go, although I must admit that a few times on the journey I was thinking that I'd made the wrong decision.

I knew that the last thing I needed was constant action from small fish. Simon Crow had saved the Shepherds Cottage swim for me, which was good of him, but I explained that I would rather fish the opposite side of the lake at the end of the Gypsy Village, where I'd fished with Pete in 1998. Tim Paisley, who was on his first trip to the lake, went into the Shepherds Cottage instead. This time around I was with another friend, Paul Sanders, otherwise known as 'Glum'. Glum had questioned my sanity when I first started going to Raduta, but in the end couldn't resist the temptation himself, and he came along to see what it was all about.

I always seemed to acquire a 'pet' for the trip.

I went on the right of the swim as I really wanted to fish one spot, where I remembered seeing fish showing when I was with Pete previously. But, although he was on the right back then, he hadn't fished there for some reason. Looking out in the boat with the sounder it looked perfect. Out in front of the swim was a huge plateau which gradually dropped off in the distance. The top of the plateau was fairly flat and around 10 feet deep, before dropping sharply down to around 26 or 27 feet on the right. There was a slightly rounded area on the plateau, just before the drop-off, which looked to me like a big dinner plate for the carp and the perfect place to present a bait.

The whole area was certainly quieter than the Shepherds Cottage and the first night we were only disturbed by some small carp that were spawning close in and constantly giving us liners. It was 5pm the next day before I received the first proper run of the trip from a mid-double common. Glum was always good company and there was always a friendly rivalry between us when fishing, so even though it was only a small fish I still got a few 'choice' words thrown my way for getting the first one. The second day went much the same way, although I think we both caught one small fish. On the third day, however, a strong wind swung round and started blowing straight into us, it made getting the rods out a lot more difficult, but it looked perfect! Again, at 5pm I landed an upper double from the

It was worth all the abuse for this 45lb common.

dinner plate spot. I dropped the rod straight back on the spot and it was away again, literally within seconds. This time the longer fight told the story and it was a much better fish of 41lb. On seeing the fish, Glum congratulated me by saying,

"You jammy ****** you would get a ****** forty, you ********!" I just laughed, Glum always said exactly what he was thinking, but I know he was pleased to see the fish (I think).

The wind still blew and at 7.30am the next day the same rod was away again. With the line cutting away down the margin and the waves crashing into the bank, I stood on the high bank behind the swim to avoid the marginal snags, which were the main danger. I knew it was another decent fish and from the high vantage point, I could see it before Glum netted it.

The following day I finally got my Raduta 50 at 53lb.

"You ******! It's bigger than the other ****** one, you lucky good-for-nothing *********! Mind you, what a lovely fish."

At 45lb 12oz it was lovely and a new PB common for me. This was just about perfect for me, only one or two runs per day but a better stamp of fish and so much better than the constant action from small fish at the Shepherds Cottage.

The following morning was one of those times which will stay etched in my memory forever. I was awake at around 6.45am but it was windy and drizzly so I stayed in the bag just looking out. Raduta could be a very bleak place when it was like that, and besides, it was nice and warm where I was. At 7am I saw my rod tip jerk round sharply without giving a bleep, then the tip pulled around more deliberately and the line 'pinged' out of the clip.

"You're in Steve," came the call from Glum, but I was already on my way. The fish just powered away from me, taking line in the process. Glum looked at the reel and then at me, not saying a word, but both of us knew that it was another good fish. I clambered up the higher bank again once the fish had stopped its initial run and I started to gain line slowly. It was quite strange to play a fish from such a high point, but it did keep the line out of the way of most of the sharp, marginal snags. In the murky water it was difficult to see the fish until it was ready for the net. Glum did an expert job amongst the waves, scooping the fish up first time. I knew what was coming.

"You jammy ****** it's even bigger than the others, this ones got to be a ******* 50, you jammy ****!"

I started to move away from the maize and on to more quality baits.

This time we both carried the fish back to the mat and tied the scales to one of the boat oars so that we could lift up the fish between us and get a proper reading. 53lb exactly – another personal best and my first 50 from the lake, and a fantastic moment from start to finish. The weather was horrible so I just popped the fish into the sack for a while until things looked a little better.

My old mate 'Glum' had plenty to smile about this time with a 41lb 8oz common.

Within the hour the skies had started to clear and the wind dropped. It looked and felt nicer, but we both knew that it wouldn't do the fishing any good and we were right. The magic moment had definitely passed and although we carried on catching fish, they were the smaller ones and you could feel that the big fish had gone on their way elsewhere. Maybe over to the Shepherds Cottage, actually, as news came through a couple days later that Tim Paisley had caught Sandy's Common from there, weighing a massive 73lb 13oz! In fact, many people had caught good fish this time and we had plenty to celebrate in the hotel on the final evening. Glum had missed out on the bigger fish on that occasion, but I did have a further two trips with him, one fishing from Hotel Point and one where we moved several times. On these trips he did get amongst some nice fish including one original mirror and a few PB commons up to 41lb 8oz, so I was able to return the favour and call him a few names. They were good times and I enjoyed fishing with Glum.

The Barrage

The bait made all the difference – thankfully Simon had enough for both of us.

The next, very memorable session came in October 2002, although it was one of those times when it was close to being a disastrous trip. The first thing that really stands out was that it was the first time that we'd been able to use any amount of decent bait. That was all mainly due to Simon Crow who'd made sure to get plenty of air-dried 24mm MC/Addicted baits sorted via The Bait and Feed Company. Crowy was leading the group out from Heathrow and somehow managed to wangle it, saying that the bait was to be shared amongst the group and in that way he got away without paying any excess baggage – always a shrewd mover that Crowy!

At the lake, Simon and I chose to fish the Barrage Swim, which we'd not fished before, but it had always been on the list of possible swims, should it be free, which it was this time. As we got dropped off it was the first time we had noticed just how atrocious the weather was. The sky was just a sheet of grey and there was a bitterly cold wind blowing. Along with the constant drizzle it didn't look nice at all. Apparently, it was a weather front coming across from Russia – and it certainly felt like it!

The areas were easy enough to sort out. There was a really large, barren expanse of water out in front of us with very little in the way of features. That was until we got close to the river bed. Then there were several snags in the form of old trees, where the depth began to drop off. It didn't take a brain surgeon to work out where we should be fishing, so we set about getting the baits in place. Simon went on the right where the river bed was closer, and I was on the left. The wind blew stronger through the night and it just looked horrible as I peered out in the morning. I could see that Simon's right bank stick had fallen over and the two rods were just lying on the floor. Nothing looked to be happening, so presuming that it was just the wind that was responsible, I let Simon sleep on. When he did eventually rise, he saw what had happened and went over to the rods. To our surprise there was actually a fish on one of them and that may have been responsible for pulling the rods over, but unbelievably it had hardly moved anywhere and was not even snagged. I ran out to help with the netting. The fight was over in no time and in the net was a fish that I recognised as my first ever 40 from the lake, which I had landed from the Shepherds Cottage, this time it was slightly heavier at 43lb 8oz. Over the next couple of days Simon had two more very good fish of 46lb and 48lb 4oz, the 48 being a very recognisable fish that had been over 50lb previously. By this time I'd had a few fish too, but they were only smaller ones up to around 24lb. It was much more difficult on the left of the swim, the range I had to fish wasn't helping and neither was the angle in which the river bed ran. It meant that as I was pulling the fish towards me, if they kited right, then they could always reach the snags on the edge of the river bed and I had lost a couple of fish already.

It was horrible out there but Simon was into a fish!

I ended up with a real banger of a migraine for the next two or three days. Simon's antics didn't help things (as many of Simon's friends who have been 'Crowied' before will know) but it all ended with me becoming a right miserable old git – and it wasn't helped by Simon constantly singing "Don't worry, be happy!" To this day, Simon still believes that it was

Simon had some good fish that first week including this very-recognisable fish of 48lb.

because he had caught the bigger fish that I was unhappy and I suppose I'll never convince him otherwise – but many of us have been 'Crowied' at some stage and will know different.

What kept our sanity intact was having a chess competition. Simon had brought along a set of 'travel chess' and he just hates to be beaten at anything. Mind you so do I, so it made for some real 'do or die' games. The competition was relentless and my favourite moment was when Simon thought he had me in checkmate with his queen, only to have over-looked the fact that I could take his queen with another piece and then go on to win the game. Simon went from jumping around outside punching the air with joy, to complete despondency within a few seconds and I increased my lead over him, giggling away like a pathetic little kid as I finished the game off. We still talk about those chess games now and, incidentally, by the end of the session it had ended with us winning sixteen games each, I think we called it a day then as neither of us could bear to lose.

It looked a bit crude but things needed to be tough.

Somewhere in between all of this, Simon had suggested that I move my baits closer to his. We had left a big gap in between our baits and there was plenty of room to move over, perhaps sixty or seventy yards to the right, and still be around forty yards from his nearest bait. It made sense to me as there were obviously a group of big fish around the area and it meant that I was able to fish at a much closer range due to the angle of the river bed. By now we were into the second week and time was starting to run out. I was actually considering a move of swims for the remainder of the trip as so little had happened. The next morning was the start of the ninth day out of the twelve that we had on the lake. I unzipped a small section of the bivvy door and peered out. It looked as dreadful as ever. A thick fog had descended and the only movement came from the many mice that were trying to take refuge in my bivvy. It was impossible to keep the little blighters out and I was constantly searching for them amongst my bags, I even got bitten on the finger inside my sleeping bag one evening!

It looked grim out there but it was all about to happen.

I peered out into the gloom and then I noticed one of my tips slowly pull over and the clutch started ticking. The bivvy door was ripped open and I was quickly on to it, but it had already found one of the snags by then. Simon was up too and although the boat was half full with water, we both jumped in and made our way out to the fish. Once over the top of the snag, the fish came free fairly easily and we just drifted over the river bed to play the fish in relative safety. It felt good to know that there was a good fish on the end at last and it was great being able to do everything without panicking, whilst over the deep, snag-free water of the old river. I took my time and let the fish just tire itself out. Simon did the honours and told me that it was a decent fish, and at 45lb 4oz it was enough to put a smile back on my face after all the doom and gloom.

It made a change from playing chess!

I re-baited all rods with renewed confidence, with the expectancy of more fish to come – it's amazing what a difference one fish can make! At 5am the following morning, one of the other rods was away. Although it was still pitch black it was a lovely morning. It was still cloudy, but flat calm and it had warmed up considerably. As I made my way out alone in the darkness, it struck me how quiet it was. There literally wasn't a sound coming from anywhere and, in the eerie silence, I slowly pulled my way out to the fish. I couldn't feel too much going on, just a solid weight on the other end. Then I nearly fell over as I went straight past the fish, which was lying almost sideways on the surface. I did a quick about-turn and had little trouble netting the fish first time. Back on the bank the fish turned out to be bigger than I'd expected at 47lb 12oz. I didn't get Simon up, but sacked the fish up and put the kettle on. I'll always remember sitting there in that warm, silent darkness, drinking several cups of tea. The only sound, in all that time, coming from one old truck which made its way across the dam wall as someone made their way to work, the hum of the engine seemingly taking for ages to disappear in the distance. Atmospheric stuff.

It was one of the nicest big commons I've caught and a morning to remember.

Over the last couple of days I had a further three fish up to high 30's. Simon actually failed to get a single run during the second half of the session, but dared not complain after ribbing me for so long. In the end it turned out to be a good session for both of us, the good quality baits had made a big difference and, although we didn't have many fish,

The weather finally changed – just before we had to leave!

we did land five 40's between us and despite the hardships of that trip, we both look back on it with fond memories.

Knowing what a difference the bait had made, I was determined to go back and give the lake a proper assault the following May. I was there for two weeks, but Simon had already been out the previous week with his friend, Derek Fell. Rob Hughes, on the other hand, wasn't due down until my second week and as there was an odd number on the group, which I had led out, I decided to fish alone for the first week and then Rob could join me when he arrived. The swim I chose was opposite the Water Tower Bay and although it didn't have a name as such, we ended up calling it the 'Nice Swim' because that's just what it was – very nice!

I was dropped off in darkness (as ever) and the sky lit up constantly with flashes of lightning. Thunder rumbled overhead as I hastily got everything set up. It all looked very good but the first night and day only produced a couple of small commons. That first

Heavy baiting with quality bait definitely made a big difference.

afternoon did enable me to have a good look around, however, and there were some very interesting features to be found at around 80 or 90 yards from the bank. I figured that these features were where some old pylons used to stand before they were removed by Robert Raduta at some stage. They stood out like big, rocky mounds from the rest of the surrounding lake bed, which was predictably fairly flat and muddy. It looked an obvious fish-holding area and I proceeded to spread 10kg of boilies and 15kg of pellets all around the area. I was full of confidence that the bait would pull some of the big fish into the area, so I was a little disappointed when the first run was from a grass carp. But later that evening two 'proper' carp of 27lb 12oz and 35lb 4oz did come my way. The night time seemed to be the best time as the next day only produced another couple of grassies to just over 30lb, but the night produced commons of 15lb, 17lb, 30lb 12oz and 43lb 4oz.

A definite pattern was emerging, where the fish would come in for the bait and feed heavily and then the action would drop away again after the bait had been virtually cleared. Replenishing the bait would see a sharp rise in the action once again. Also I noticed that

Rob Hughes moved in next to me and soon started catching.

a strong wind from the Water Tower would certainly help the situation and bring more fish in. By the following Saturday morning, when Rob arrived, I'd taken several more fish and even had a 42lb 12oz common waiting for him in the sack, which pleased him as he was putting together a new series called 'The Carp Show' for Sky TV, so he was able to get one on film straight away.

I had already decided to let Rob have the left side of the swim, which I considered to be the best side, as I'd already had some good fish and I wanted him to get some too. I told him how I'd baited up heavily and reaped the rewards and he agreed to do the same thing. I remember him remarking how odd it felt putting out so much bait in one go and I know what he meant, but it was the right thing to do for sure and that was confirmed when his first carp also weighed 42lb 12oz – "Ching Ching!" as Rob would say.

Actually, the next couple of days were quiet for me as I struggled to establish the bait on the right side of the swim and find the right spots. I found one small spot that rose sharply from the lake bed and, although it was only 6ft across, it was dead flat and rock hard on top. Maybe it was the base for one of the old pylons? I wasn't sure, but I placed a bait on top of it anyway and I was pleased I had when it roared off the next morning. Rob and I took to the boat, as it had gone around the back of the rocky features, and that was the start of a real to and fro battle. After a while I saw the unmistakeable scaling of a good mirror below the boat. The original mirrors were few and far between in the lake and it had been one of my ambitions to get one of the better ones from there, if I could. As the fish sunk into the bottom of the net, my ambition was realised. At 44lb it was a good enough reason to order a few beers for that evening! The action was increasing all the time and it seemed like the more bait we put out, the more action we received. We were sacking the better fish up for filming in the mornings and we were just looking at the sack pole, giggling sometimes as it looked more like a spiders' web, with all the cords coming from it. The following two days produced a further two forties, four thirties and a stack of twenties for me, while Rob was virtually matching me fish for fish!

With a couple of days to go, the wind changed and started blowing strongly from the Shepherds Cottage area. We thought it might be a good wind for us, but in fact it only helped to push the fish away from us and around the corner towards the Barrage. Our action slowed down, but we could hardly complain with a stack of action, eight forties between us and a TV programme more than completed – a NICE session in a NICE swim – just NICE really!

I finally got one of the original Raduta mirrors at 44lb.

The Hotel Point

In 2003 there had been some changes taking place at the lake. Many were improvements really, with the food undoubtedly getting better, but as with many waters, it seemed as if the best years had already been and gone. The big common that became known to most of the English as Sandy's Common, had died and of course the Record Mirror had also not been seen since 1999. There were some really good fish still in the lake for sure, but it was also becoming a lot more popular and swims which had been rested for long periods previously were now getting consistently pressured. When Simon and I arrived in the

The Danube Delta was a wild and wonderful place.

October of 2003 we found more anglers present than ever before. There was one area free, known as The White House, but after a couple of days it just didn't feel right and luckily enough we were able to spend the remainder of our time at the Danube Delta, which turned out to be a really pleasant session, even if it didn't produce the stamp of fish that the lake was known for.

The Danube carp were typical wild river fish.

As nice as the Delta was, we felt like we'd lost out on an opportunity for another good fish or two from Raduta and we planned on putting that right in the May of 2004. Another change at the time was that we were able to book up and reserve swims in advance – at a price of course. We figured that it would be a good idea to reserve the Barrage Swim, although I must say that it wasn't my first choice for that time of year. Hotel Bay or World Record Bay seemed a better option but I'd enjoyed fishing in the Barrage Swim so agreed with Simon to fish it with him.

However, in April 2004 disaster struck in the shape of a massive fish-kill. In 2003 quite a few fish had died, but the stories coming back from the anglers present told us that this time around it was potentially much worse. Some people tried to play down how bad the kill had been, and we just hoped that it wasn't too bad. It was already too late to do anything about it, anyway, as we were on our way. It appeared that most of the fish now being caught were the stockies that had been put in from the Danube Delta over the previous few months. Why anyone thought that these fish needed putting in at all is beyond me. The lake was already one of the best in the world, certainly when it came to large common carp. But it was too late to think about that now, we just had to hope that some, maybe many, of the big fish were still left alive.

We settled into the Barrage Swim and it looked every bit as nice as I'd remembered it, although the weather was a lot more pleasant than the previous session there. At around 5am I was awoken by a car door slamming behind me. I thought it was a strange time for someone to be driving around the lake, but figured that whoever it was would be gone soon. But I heard more and more doors slamming and people talking and then what sounded like people casting out. In no time all my alarms were sounding and I looked out to be amazed by what I saw. There must have been at least 50 people either side of us, all with three or four rods, casting all over the place – but mainly into our swim! We got on the phone to Marius, the fishery manager, to see what the hell was going on. Apparently, in an attempt to get rid of the many bream in the lake, they had opened up sections for people to fish for 7 euros a day. This was obviously very popular with the Romanians, the trouble was that we were slap bang in the middle of one of these sections and of course they just presumed that we had already picked the best spot and they all wanted to fish it too!

The point opposite the hotel was definitely the nicest of all the swims I fished there.

Simon took it worse than me and had steam coming out of his ears. Looking back, we should have moved there and then, but decided to brave it out in the hope of some good fish at some stage. Things weren't looking good, though, and after a few days the indicators remained motionless – apart from when they were being dragged around by bream anglers! Even when a really nice, warm breeze blew in our direction it didn't change anything. As ever, we'd acquired two young dogs as pets for the week, or at least I had, as Simon wasn't so keen on them. Unfortunately, some of the dead carp had been buried behind our swim and the little doggies took great delight in digging them up and leaving the odd rotten carps head outside Simon's bivvy. I'm sure they were doing it as some kind of friendship offering, but Simon was not impressed. One afternoon I landed one rather large grass carp and, for a while, we hoped that things would pick up. But they didn't and Simon was getting more and more frustrated – we both were. Eventually, Simon lost his cool. He had Hungarian anglers rowing all around his markers, Romanian bream anglers deep in conversation behind his bivvy in the early hours, and the doggies were always leaving carp heads in his doorway. Simon let them all have it! There were people, dogs and boats scattering in all directions.

"I think it's time for a move mate" I said, and a very cross-looking Simon agreed – I thought about a rendition of 'Don't worry, be happy' but I dared not!

Back at the hotel, in the shade and with a cold beer in front of us, the world seemed a better place. We had two reasonable choices open to us, we could go to World Record Bay, which was a consistent swim, but as I looked across to the point opposite the hotel, I knew that it was where I wanted to be. The young willow trees which had been planted around the area had grown on well and it looked lovely and shady. Besides that, it was always an area which I'd wanted to fish since Simon had caught his 52lb common from there back in 1998. So our choice was made and for once I even won the coin-toss for choice of sides, so I would fish the left side of the point.

"It's our boat and you're not having it!"

On arrival in the swim there was even an extra boat waiting for us, meaning we could have a boat each. The whole session seemed to be looking a lot more promising. A couple of hours had passed when a young gypsy lad came down and pointed to one of the boats. We thought he was trying to take one of them away and there was no way that was happening, so he got sent on his way. We remarked to each other how cheeky some of them were, and how annoyed Robert Raduta would've been if we'd just given one of his boats away. A while later, the lad returned with a bowl of cherries and was trying to exchange them for the boat. Rob Hughes, who'd joined us by then, laughed, but with a stern look, again told him in no uncertain terms that he wasn't going to be taking one of our boats away. Some hours later the speed boat arrived with our dinner, and even a couple of chairs, which made everything a little more comfortable for us. It normally took the boat around an hour to drop everyone's food off around the lake. As we were opposite the hotel, we were first to get our dinner and by the time we could hear the speed boat coming back it was starting to get dark. As we looked up we could clearly see that there was now an extra person in the boat and, undoubtedly, it was the young guy who had tried to take 'our' boat earlier. Only then did it begin to dawn on us that the 'extra' boat might have actually been his in the first place and as we were to find out the next day, he'd used it to get across the lake to do his days work picking cherries in the field behind us. He was being as nice as he could in his efforts to tell us of the situation, but it had all fallen on deaf ears and he nearly had to spend the night in the field because we thought he was just a boat thief – whoops!

Crowy had a few straight away, but they were mainly the Danube fish.

I finally got off the mark properly at last, during the night, with a 25lb common, Simon on the other hand fared much better, taking five fish up to mid 30's. At least we had got on some fish at last, although as Simon pointed out, they were mainly the Danube fish, which didn't quite mean the same as catching the old originals. That day a good storm sprang up, as they tended to do at Raduta, in fact the storms there could come from virtually nowhere and be quite fierce, but they all had one thing in common, and that was they got the fish going! That night I had around four or five fish and Simon the same, but in the morning Simon looked absolutely knackered.

"What's up?" I said and he replied that his alarms had kept going off all night but half of the time nothing was happening and for a few days that kept happening until one morning he finally twigged that his sounder box was tuned into my alarms as well as his, so he was getting up for all my runs as well as his and as I wasn't using a sounder box I was none the wiser. Now, what're the chances of that happening, eh? Laugh – I nearly cracked my ribs!

The lovely thing about this area was that it was all close range work. The depth dropped off very quickly from the edge and it was just a case of placing the baits along the ledge in various spots. Along to my left was a nice overhanging bush, with about 7 to 9 feet of water just by it, which looked really good. But just to my right was a small, clear plateau in between some snags. I just had to have a bait on that as I knew it was the spot where many good fish had come from in the past, in particular Sandy Hough's 72lb common in 1999, when he was fishing from the Pylon Swim on the other bank. All the spots were baited (as ever) with a good sprinkling of 24mm MC/Addicted baits and the action just kept coming.

"Yes – I've done it!"

By the next morning the storms had long gone but the skies were still cloudy. At around 7am I had a fish apiece on my two right-hand rods, both small commons, so I had already been out in the boat and replaced both baits with an extra top-up of freebies. Simon arose some time later and enquired as to when the kettle was going on or something. Just then, one of the rods was away again. Simon asked what it felt like and I shrugged my shoulders and said "Don't know mate" as it didn't feel anything special. As it came closer, it went around the other line and I had to pass the rod under and over until it was free. As I tightened up to the fish again, it surfaced and I could see that it was a mirror – and quite a good one, too!

I didn't say anything to Simon and just carried on playing the fish. It didn't really go anywhere and just plodded up and down the margins in front of me for awhile and I managed to relax enough to just take my time with what was obviously a very good fish. Eventually, I just netted the fish already knowing which one it was.

"What you got there, mate?" he asked.

"Oh, it's just that big mirror," I replied.

"Yeah, right," he said, wandering over to have a look. Upon seeing it his eyes nearly popped out –

"It's the big mirror! It could be 60lb!" he said excitedly.

It really was a magnificent fish and one of the original mirrors that I'd really wanted for some time. I'd seen pictures of it before and it was always on the list of fish that I'd like to get my hands on one day, although after many of the fish dying, it had seemed like it was never going to happen. The scales gave a reading of 56lb 12oz and I cannot describe how happy that made me feel. With all of the fish deaths and all of the things going wrong, I'd finally caught a 25kg Raduta carp, when, in all probability, it was the only one left in the lake at that moment! I felt honoured to be holding such a fish up for the cameras.

56lb 12oz of original Raduta mirror – it was almost certainly the biggest fish in the lake.

With another three days fishing left, we both caught more fish, mainly the Danube stock fish, but also some which were definitely originals up to mid 30's. In the six years, since the lake had been discovered and opened up to carp fishing, so much had happened at Lake Raduta. From being totally unknown to the outside world, it had suddenly become the main focus of attention for the big fish hunters from several countries. It held the world record for some time with that marvellous big mirror, but Raduta was just as popular with most people for holding more big commons than any other water that I've ever known. And then, in the matter of a few short weeks it was all gone - the vast majority of those wonderful fish that we all so longed to hold had all perished. For me, it was the end of a short, but very prolific era in carp fishing. Today the lake is starting to rebuild itself and good fish are starting to come through again. Rob Hughes kept faith in the lake and continued running trips there, through his company, Angling International, and today there is still plenty of interest from anglers wishing to sample what the lake has to offer.

I really do hope, in years to come, that Lake Raduta can return to somewhere near its former glory. Many lakes have had to regenerate and rebuild over the years – just look at Cassien for instance, it's always been a great water, but the stock of carp in there now is almost entirely different to what was in there when I first started fishing it. So I could never say that I won't go back to Raduta again, but what I do know is that it would be difficult – no, impossible to recreate the magic of those few wonderful years.

New Challenges

An African Adventure

The spread of carp fishing since I first started travelling abroad has been phenomenal. In that relatively short period of time it would seem that anywhere in the world that holds carp has now been visited by someone trying to catch them. It all started, of course, with France, but it wasn't long before many people started to look further afield. It seemed like everyone was trying to push back the boundaries and discover new waters in far away places. Most other countries seemed to hold big carp so they were all interesting in one way or another, but one day South Africa was mentioned and that got my attention straight away. It was a place that I'd always wanted to visit, although I never really thought that I would get the chance. Well, not only did that chance now look possible – it looked like I could fish for carp while I was out there.

We could always hear the lions roaring in the distance.

Now, carp fishing wasn't entirely new to South Africa and certainly people had been there long before I had even considered it. Going right back to the days when I fished Fox Pool, which was in the late 1980's there was a guy who fished there named Terry 'The Wedge', so called because he was a yacht designer or some such thing and was known for being absolutely loaded – or so the story went. Anyway, to be honest, after taking one look at the gear that he used for his fishing it would have been easy to think that he didn't have two pennies to rub together. I remember one time the pole on his umbrella just snapping in half for no other reason than it was just so old! But Terry was a real character and a really nice bloke and among the stories that he told me at different times, one was about a time when he had travelled to South Africa on holiday, and whilst he was exploring the countryside he came across a river. Being an angler he of course took an interest in what the river might hold and, lo and behold, on one large bend he saw carp jumping! He was, of course, more than a little surprised to see carp in such a situation but, unfortunately, had no fishing gear with him whatsoever. But the thoughts of seeing those carp jumping stayed with him and he made up his mind that one day he would return and try to catch one or two of them. Well, Terry did return some time later with his carp gear – and guess what? The carp were still there at the bend in the river and, if I remember rightly, he went on to catch some of them up to 28lb.

I thought that was a really nice little story and a true bit of pioneering for sure. However, it showed how far and wide carp were spread. There was also a mention of South African carp fishing in the fourth BCSG book which was published in 1983. In there a guy called Don Wittich was fishing at Hartbeespoort Dam, although it didn't go into much depth about it. In 1983 I was still only fishing my local waters and South Africa was just somewhere that I saw on the TV, or read about in the papers, little did I know at that time that one day I would actually drive past Hartbeespoort Dam and see it for myself!

Step forward into the late 1990's and carp fishing in South Africa was not only becoming more popular but a company had started up organising carp fishing trips. That company was African Gold, which had been formed by Martin Davidson, along with Norman and Mary Smith, with a view to offering people the chance of a lifetime to see the sights that the country has to offer, and to catch a few carp along the way. The carp in South Africa were more widespread than I'd ever imagined. By all accounts they had been introduced some years earlier by the Dutch migrants and, as ever, they had adapted well and spread far and wide. Carp fishing had become popular, although the South African's very much had their own way of fishing for them. Rods were 13ft and 14ft one-piece jobs that they had to strap to their roof racks on their cars, and the main form of fishing was with what they called 'mealy bombs', which were basically balls of groundbait fished in the way that we know of as method fishing. Surprisingly, most of the carp weren't that big and their carp fishing was more match orientated, and it was more about how many they could catch rather than how big they were. But the guys at African Gold had done their homework and had found two or three waters that held a good stamp of fish and, in a bid to promote and spread the word on what they had to offer, we received an invite to go over there and fish. Needless to say it was an offer that I wasn't going to refuse, even without the fishing it would be a great place to visit but with the chance to catch some carp too it was literally the chance of a lifetime.

Who would've thought I'd end up carp fishing in Africa?

It was at the time when I was part of the Hutchinson team, so to start with it involved me, Simon Crow, Rob Hughes and Xavier Paolozzi, who was the French member of the team, and a little later our friend Sandy Hough and Glyn Leach, who is editor of Boxing Monthly magazine, also decided to join us. The water we were going to fish was Klaserie Dam, one which was fairly new to carp anglers but was the biggest and the wildest of all the African Gold waters. It is set deep in the African bush and that appealed to all of us – none more so than me! A big part of fishing for me, and particularly when I travel away, is to see the wildlife. I know many people who cannot handle the idea of anything creepy crawly, let alone anything bigger and furry! But I love all that and it would be a disappointment if I didn't see anything whilst I was there. I loved looking for the wild boars down at Cassien but, in all truth, wild boars sounded pretty tame to what we could expect to find out in Africa. We were assured that we weren't likely to see any lions or hippos, at least not around the lake, but there were a variety of animals that we could bump into such as baboons, porcupines, leopards, monitor lizards, all sorts of snakes and honey badgers. Now the last one on that list sounded quite nice, almost cute and cuddly. Well, we were soon put right on that, in fact they could be the most dangerous of the lot and when cornered they had a habit of latching onto the genitals of whatever had cornered them, and spinning around until they had ripped them off – ouch!

If anything, though, it was the small things that we really had to watch out for, in particular ticks and mosquitoes, both of which could ruin anyone's trip. Of course malaria was a big concern and so we all embarked on a course of malaria tablets, which started two weeks before the trip and they were revolting things it has to be said, but as the mozzies have always had a liking for my blood there was no other choice.

We were taken back to the fabulous lodge for the first night.

January arrived and it was time for us all to meet up at Heathrow airport, as a matter of fact that was the other thing which we all found so appealing about this trip. While it was the depths of winter back home in England, it was of course summer time in South Africa and the chance to get out in some warm sunshine was something we were all looking forward to. The flight itself was pretty dreadful. I'm not a big fan of flying as I hate being crammed into a seat that's designed for a stick insect and eating food that's failed to make the grade for dog food. Also, I would rather feel a bit more in control, which is why I never mind driving anywhere, but the one big plus with flying is that it gets you to where you want to go quickly, although I use the word 'quickly' here as a relative term, as the flight was twelve hours of uncomfortable, sleepless boredom!

We stepped out into the warm Johannesburg sunshine with a sigh of relief. My eyes were just slits with big bags underneath from lack of sleep and, thankfully, the trip through arrivals and customs was straight forward enough. Waiting for us at the main exit was Martin Davidson. Martin's an ex-pat who has a wicked sense of humour and doesn't hold back with anything and his opening line to me was,

"Christ, you look like Rab C Nesbitt!"

I couldn't help but laugh (as everyone else did anyway) but we knew straight away that we were in for a good time. The plan was that we would go back to the lodge for the first night as it wasn't too far from the airport and there we could prepare for what lay ahead. The lake was a drive of something like six or seven hours away so, after the flight, we all needed to relax a little and chill out. The lodge was perfect for that with plenty of food and drink and even a swimming pool which Martin somehow arranged for us all to get thrown into, fully clothed. Martin's right-hand man was a South African called Gilbert, a much more sensible bloke than his mate and actually a really nice guy. He filled us in on what to expect and what to look out for. Apparently, it was difficult to use boilies as the lake held a lot of catfish which loved them. These were different catfish to the ones we had seen before and although they did grow to quite a size, most were between 10lb and 30lb and could be a real pain. But we had no worries as everything was prepared for us and tiger nuts and mixed particles were all awaiting us, as well as boilies should we want to use them. Norman and Mary Smith were back at the lake, getting everything ready for us at that end. All in all it was a very well organised set up and we were all more than impressed with what we'd seen so far.

It was a long drive but the scenery was spectacular.

After a good kip I started to look more 'normal' again and once we'd polished off a decent breakfast we all set off in convoy to go and do a bit of fishing. The surrounding countryside was far greener than I imagined and reminded me a lot of England.

"This is just the boring bit," said Martin, and he was right. The further we drove the better the scenery became until we found ourselves up in the Drakensburg mountains, which were just breathtaking. It was certainly a lot different to how I'd imagined it to be after seeing so many TV programmes, but then Africa is an absolutely massive place and obviously varies a great deal throughout its entirety.

Eventually, we came to a barrier where the small building had the name 'Klaserie Dam' emblazoned on it, and we had arrived. Most of the lake was indeed fairly wild but part of it was more civilised towards the dam end, with a camping area and shower block - thankfully we were based in the wild part closer to the inlet at the top end. Base camp was just as I'd expected it to be, with a big tent set up as a social and dining area. They had a guy called Peter working for them who was an absolute star and had already been busy setting up tents for us in the various swims. We would fish in pairs and only had to decide where to fish. I'd already teamed up with Sandy Hough and we chose what was a new swim, some 200 metres or so from the base camp. Simon and Rob chose to fish the base camp swim, as one fish had been lost there the day before. It would turn out to be a very good choice for them.

We had arrived!

For some reason we were all feeling friendly and Sandy and I decided to share runs and so too did Rob and Simon. I think it was probably the fact that none of the gear was our own and we all just wanted to have a good time and to catch a few fish – well at least that was the plan for two easy-going blokes like Sandy and me. For Rob and Simon it was probably the worst thing they could have done as, at times, we thought world war three was breaking out!

Our section of the lake was more like a big channel, with the opposite bank being some 150 to 200 metres away and completely overgrown. There was an old river bed which ran right through the middle but it was the far margin which looked to be the best bet and that was where we planned to concentrate our efforts. The only swim which was different was the base camp swim, which had quite a large bay on the opposite side and the inlet up to the right.

The bush camp was exactly how I'd imagined it.

With everything in place we all met up at the base camp for the evening meal. At last we could relax and I have to say that it was the point when I realised just what a fantastic place this was. We gathered around the fire and dined on Impala steaks and other local delicacies. The sky was the clearest that I've ever seen it and I really never knew there were that many stars up there!

Despite being clear, it was still warm and no problem to sit out in shorts and tee shirts, the fire keeping any unwanted visitors away. The night-time sounds were incredible and it was some of the smaller things which made the most noise. Tiny little frogs competed with the crickets to be heard and at times it was almost deafening, but every now and then we could clearly hear a distant roar. I'd watched enough films and documentaries to know what was making those sounds and it was definitely lions, but we were assured that they were a great distance away and wouldn't be visiting us in the night. It was one of the most enchanting and atmospheric moments in all of my carp fishing – and I had to remind myself that we there to catch carp, but this was a far cry from most of the fishing that I'd done previously. The only sound that wasn't all that enchanting was the sound of Sandy heaving up outside the bivvy later on. He'd been keen to get a tan and had ended up getting sunstroke instead! Thankfully for poor old Sandy, it was something he soon recovered from.

The rest of the night passed by uneventfully, although I think we may have had our first encounter with a catfish or two at some stage. By morning, it had been quiet for most of us, except Rob and Simon who had caught one or two but already there were the rumblings of discontent over whose run it was next and who should have had which fish etc. At least we had the chance to see our first African carp on the bank, anyway, and very nice they were too. In fact, Rob and Simon continued to catch fish and they were the only carp we were seeing as it appeared that most of the fish were congregated in front of them. The most exciting thing to happen in our swim was when we got up one morning to find animal

The paw prints around the bivvy showed that we had been visited in the night!

prints all around the bivvy, prints which were definitely from a rather large cat! A local guide who visited us every day told us that the prints were from a leopard and her cub, which were known to be in the area at the time. To think that we'd been sleeping only inches away, oblivious to what was just outside the door. It was a shame not to see them, anyway.

All the other entertainment came from Rob and Simon who, by now, were drawing up battle plans. They had drawn up a list of what constituted a run. More than three consecutive bleeps meant a fish had picked up the bait and if nothing else occurred it was the other anglers turn for a run.

"In a court of law it would be legally binding," Rob had said, whereas Simon just wanted as much of the action as possible. (Allegedly) Simon went out for a screaming one-toner one night and returned some time later after losing the fish and claimed that it was just a liner so that he could get the next run. Every now and then we'd get a visit from Rob who'd say,

"He's getting on my nerves," and then Simon would come up and say,

"He's doing my head in!"

It was amusing for us, but a nightmare for poor Norman and Mary who were camped right next to them and had to listen to it day and night.

With nothing to show for our efforts, me, Sandy and Xavier decided to move further up to our left for the remaining days, to a point which overlooked the main body of water. It was just our luck when Sandy was reeling in one of the remaining rods with what he thought was a ball of weed on the end, only to find that it was in fact a 33lb mirror! After trying hard for a few days I couldn't believe that when we finally decided that there were no carp in front of us, one decided to turn up right out of the blue. We were, of course, pleased but it didn't make any difference, we had already moved the rest of our gear by then and so carried on with the plan. At least we were off the

Got one! My first African carp goes into the net.

mark and now it was my turn, which meant I had six rods at my disposal. However, the weather was starting to change. We had seen several flashes of lightning during the evenings and now the sunny skies had been replaced by clouds, with a bit of the wet stuff falling every now and then. The move did at least pay off for us as I eventually hooked into, and landed my first African carp, a mirror of 24lb, and Xavier also caught one of 27lb. Nothing exceptional, but at least we'd all caught.

A brace of twenties for me and Xavier Paolozzi.

The rain began to fall harder and harder and in some areas they had been getting it severely for some time, causing all sorts of problems. We were getting news relayed to us that several areas had experienced severe flooding and, indeed, the water level at the lake was rising all the time, but we didn't have much time left and the last day of the trip was due to be spent at the Kruger National Park so I didn't think it would affect us too much. However, Martin just dropped something into the conversation over breakfast that would make a big difference to my side of the trip. He said that, if I liked, I could stay on for another week as the following week the lake would be totally empty! I knew that I could do it and answered "Yes" straight away. Sandy could also stay, but none of the others could, due to work commitments. All of this meant one very important thing – that Sandy and I could move straight into the base camp swim where, undoubtedly, most of the fish were. Rob and Simon had caught plenty by then, including a new PB for Simon of 55lb, which was a fish that we'd all seen pictures of and would all have liked to have caught, especially as it had only been captured once before.

Klaserie Dam was a lake full of mystery and character.

The day at the Kruger Park was just amazing. It was our own little safari and although it was quite gloomy all day, we saw most of the animals that we'd hoped to see. We've all seen them in zoos but to see them all roaming in the wild was totally different. We didn't see any rhinos or buffalos but we saw the rest and we did get chased down the road by an elephant – and I do mean chased down the road! I don't know what we did to upset him but he did have the hump with us. It was all part of the experience, though, and it was exciting, but all the time I had it in the back of my mind that when we returned after the day out we would be in amongst the fish for the first time and then, for me and Sandy, the trip would really begin!

We arrived back at base camp in darkness with the rain falling heavily. Even in the gloom we could see that it looked a lot different to when we had left earlier in the day. The rainfall had increased and the water level had risen by a couple of feet. The area where Rob and Simon had been bivvied up was now underwater and, to go with that, there was a bigger problem. Where the extra water had been rushing down the inlet it had brought all manner of things down with it, mainly parts of trees and various bushes, not

We had a great day in the Kruger National Park – but I couldn't wait to get back.

just a few but masses of them, so much so that the amount that had settled in front of the swim meant that there was no way that we could get the rods out that night. All we could do was sleep in one of the bivvies, which had been set up further back, and see what we could do once daylight arrived.

Morning arrived and it wasn't a pretty sight. For at least 40 metres out in front of the swim it was just a mass of branches, logs, bushes and reed beds that had drifted in and there was so much water coming into the lake that there was now a flow of water going through the middle of the lake, which was bringing more debris through all the time. The other guys now had to leave for the airport, so they wished us all the best and went on their way, while Sandy and I had to work out what to do. Most of the action had been at night so we figured that we at least had all day to try and clear a reasonable path through. We both put waders on and pulled out what we could by hand, but after an hour we'd hardly made a dent in it. The rest we could only reach by boat, but to try and pull it out by hand from the boat would have just been too much of a job, but then I had another idea. The inflatable did have a petrol engine and I had noticed that when the boat was turned in a sharp circle it caused quite a wake and the theory was that it might be possible to move all the debris that way out into the flow of water, where it would be carried away further down the lake. It was a long shot but it was the only option that I could see that we had.

Well, it took most of the day and it was hard work, but eventually we had enough clear water in front of us to get all of the rods out. We had no idea how quickly the debris would return, or if all the lines would just be wiped out by what was coming down in the flow, but at least we now had a chance, otherwise we just couldn't have fished and it would have been a waste of time staying on. Although we were taking turns on the runs, we still put our own set of three rods out. I took the left side of the swim and Sandy went on the right and we split the far bay sort of down the middle. This meant that we could have rods on both sides of it as well as one or two in the middle section where the old river bed was. We figured that the carp had congregated in this area because of the influx of fresh water coming in, and no doubt because of all the food items that were also coming in through the inlet. There wasn't really much of a variation in depth, it was around twelve or thirteen feet in the river bed but I could still find between eight and ten feet close to the bank across in the bay. Right at the entrance to the bay there were some very large, round rocks with some bushes that overhung the margins. It looked an ideal spot as it dropped straight off to eleven feet to a flattish firm bottom. All the baits were the same, double tiger nuts with a 10mm cork ball to balance them, and then with a few handfuls of tigers and mixed particles around the area.

To say we were confident was, as they say, an understatement – we just knew that we were going to catch. It was Sandy's turn for the first run and that came soon after darkness, but unfortunately for him the hook fell out a short time into the fight. He wasn't overly worried as we both knew there would be more to come. We were both still up chatting to a local South African guy who'd come down to fish for a couple of days when the next run occurred. It was the rod that I'd put near the rocks at the mouth of the bay. Sandy picked up the rod as I was messing about with something and then he passed it over to me, but by the time I took up the strain, whatever was on the end had already become snagged on something. We both jumped in the boat, Sandy grabbing the net on the way, and we made our way out in the darkness. As we got to the snag I realised that it was nothing more than a few old reeds and the line was easily freed. I took up the strain and heaved and all of a sudden the shape of a big fish came straight up to the surface! Sandy did no more than scoop it into the landing net and that was literally it. But if the fight wasn't exciting, the sight of what was lying in the net certainly was. I recognised the fish straight away as the fish Simon had caught at 55lb just a few days earlier! We made our way back to the bank and told the South African guy what we had and he thought we were joking until he saw it. It was slightly lighter this time around at 54lb 8oz, and was the fish that I most wanted to catch but never expected to see it again so soon. This was only the third capture of this fish but two of those captures had now been in the space of a week.

It was the end of the action for that night and by the morning the swim was just full up with floating rubbish again. We reeled in all the rods and all the rigs were tangled up in all sorts of chod and weren't presented well enough to catch us anything, anyway. The hard work from the day before had done the job though and I had banked the fish that I had most wanted to catch, and to think that by the time that had all happened, the other guys were still only on the plane home. What a good decision it was to stay on! Mind you, we would have to repeat the whole swim-clearing process in order to fish again the next night, but as strange as it sounds it was actually quite good fun doing it, even if it was

First fish from the Bush Camp swim and it was the big one at 54lb 8oz!

extremely tiring. The fact that the days didn't really fish anyway, and we knew that it would get us some more action, made the whole job worthwhile.

After all the hard work during the day, that next night produced just one fish of 24lb 8oz for Sandy, but it was another fish on the bank and it made the effort worthwhile. The thing I remember most from that night was feeling my skin tickling as I laid on my bed in the darkness. I couldn't work out what it was until I put the light on to see that I was absolutely covered in ants! Obviously, they didn't like the wet weather and had found a nice, warm new home during the day in the shape of my bed! Luckily they weren't the biting sort, but there were millions of them. Even if they didn't like it, they were soon back outside amongst the wet stuff.

The wildlife around us was just amazing. I remember having to step over a python one night as we went to go out in the boat for a fish. It wasn't a big python but it was a real one! Somehow, we just got used to things like that. One of the strangest things we saw were some bushbabies in the trees above us at night. We could hear something up there and in the torch light their eyes were just massive. There were always monkeys and baboons jumping around. There was a fig tree further up the path and they used to eat the ripe ones and get drunk on them and then act up like uncontrollable teenagers, shouting and fighting with each other. One morning Peter brought us back a tortoise to look at which he'd found wandering up the path one day. You name it and really we saw it there! In the end we just ignored the massive spiders, centipedes and beetles that always seemed to be around. Actually, there was one thing that freaked Sandy out one day. He was just coming past the boat when I heard "Bloody hellfire!" I actually saw the boat move as this huge monitor lizard shot out. It was obviously lying just out of sight in the shade and Sandy got a bit too close for comfort. It was around six feet in length and not so bad if you know it's there, but a bit of a shock when things like that just jump out on you.

The corner of the bay.

It was all part of the fishing and we wouldn't have had it any other way. I suppose it would've been different if we'd been bitten by something poisonous, but we were being cautious enough putting waders on every time that we got out for a fish. We just got into the routine and it was all working fine. The days, as ever, were spent clearing the swim and the nights were the main fishing time, or at least until the rigs became too clogged up with muck. But without exception we were catching fish every night and if anything the catch rate was improving as we got more used to what we were doing. The next couple of nights brought Sandy three fish up to 35lb, while I had three more up to 37lb 4oz. The majority of the fish were in the mid-20 range, as they had been for Rob and Simon, but with the odd better fish amongst them.

It wasn't until the last two nights that the floodwater started to relent a little. The water didn't drop by much, but by now there was less of a flow down the middle and less rubbish and debris being washed down. This, of course, made the fishing a little easier and also meant that we had more of a chance of fishing effectively right through to the morning.

The results showed the difference as, during the penultimate night, we landed eight fish between us, four each, with the best being a 38lb 2oz mirror for me. It was a shame to be coming to the end, now that we could almost fish properly again, but we knew deep down that it was only the conditions that we'd experienced which made the fishing so good in the first place and I don't think either of us would have changed anything. We both knew that we'd certainly earned all the fish we had caught.

It was hard work but the action made up for that.

With the last night upon us, all the rods were again in position and it was me who got the ball rolling at 11.30pm with a 24lb 8oz common, the only common that I caught. The next run was, of course, Sandy's and that came to the bait which he had been persevering with right in the middle of the opposite bay. The fish kited around into the reeds to our left so it was another boat job, which wasn't always necessary as we'd managed to land a lot of the fish from the bank if the muck wasn't too bad. Sandy soon freed the fish and, after a short battle, I managed to scoop up the fish from the murky water. We couldn't believe what we saw when we looked into the net – it was only the same big mirror again! We looked at each other and laughed, Sandy was well chuffed and rightly so. It had dropped weight again to 52lb 12oz but that didn't bother him one bit. Now, you might be thinking to yourselves "That sounds like a bit of a mug fish," well nothing could be further from the truth, in fact that fish was only ever caught seven times in total, it was just on a proper munch during the time that we were there, and three of those seven captures came in that two-week period – thankfully, the two-week period while we were there! We ended up landing six fish that night with one more being lost. The last fish came at 3am and was my second biggest of the trip at 42lb 12oz, a lovely looking mirror with a bit of length to it. During that final week we had landed twenty two fish between us and lost a further three. Considering the time that we actually had the rods in the water, and were fishing effectively, it was a result that we were more than happy with and we were so grateful to Martin and Norman for allowing us to stay on for the extra week and making it all possible.

Partner for the trip, Sandy Hough finished the session on a high with another capture of the big mirror.

Packing up was the easy bit as very little of the gear was our own so it was far easier than most times that I've been away, although getting home wasn't without its problems. As we got dropped off at the airport terminal I was approached by a guy who wanted to carry my bag, obviously for money, and as I only had one bag I refused his help. My ticket was inside my passport in my side trouser pocket, but by the time I had reached the ticket desk, only 50 metres away, the ticket was gone! We searched all around where I had just been but we never found it and it caused plenty of grief, which ended up with me having to buy another ticket and claim the money back almost one year later. I think I know what happened to the ticket but what could I do, the guy was of course nowhere to be seen.

It couldn't put the dampers on what had been a great trip, though. Klaserie Dam was an incredible place and we were so lucky to have fished it when we did. The flooding was undoubtedly terrible for some people but for us anglers it was just what was needed. A year or two later I was shown a picture of the bush camp swim and I couldn't recognise it as the same place for a while. The complete opposite had now happened and the flood conditions had been replaced by droughts and the whole area that we fished had become dry land with grass and bushes growing where, previously, carp had been feeding. The carp were still there, but they were confined to a section of the old riverbed further down the lake, which still just about had enough water in it. We did actually get invited back to fish Klaserie Dam again, but although it was one place that I will always have fond memories of, I didn't want to go back. My reason for that was that I knew that I'd been fortunate enough to fish there during a very good period and the fishing was not only superb but so was the wildlife, the scenery and just the whole experience really. We were also there right at the start and it had been fished a lot more in the time after our trip and I just knew that if I went back it would be almost impossible for it to match up to that initial trip, and the last thing I wanted to do was to spoil the wonderful images that are still so strong in my mind today. That wouldn't stop me fishing any of the other waters out there, of course, but I doubt that anything could match up to the magic and mystery of carp fishing in the African bush.

Last morning of the trip and a mirror of 42lb 12oz. to photograph.

New Challenges

Snagmere – Africa Revisited

Our first trip to Africa had been everything that we'd hoped and dreamed it would be. The atmosphere, the animals and the fishing had all been out of this world. But for reasons stated elsewhere in this book, I didn't want to go back to Klaserie Dam, the place we had fished on our first visit, as we didn't think that any trip could be better than that first one. But as ever, Martin Davidson and the team in South Africa had been searching around and had found another lake that sounded very interesting. By all accounts this new lake was full of sunken trees and snags, but had clear channels running through which could be fished easily enough and, indeed, Martin had already been on a few exploratory excursions and had caught enough fish to make us think that it was worthwhile us going over for a week or so. The lake quickly became known as Snagmere, for obvious reasons, and when we saw the photos of the place, Rob Hughes, Crowy and myself just knew that we would soon be jetting off once again to the southern hemisphere.

Snagmere was a daunting prospect.

'Davo', as Martin Davidson became known to us, picked us up from the airport once again and we went back to his house in Johannesburg, where he made us very welcome. Mind you, it brought home just what it was like to live over in South Africa, as the walls around his house were all very high and topped with barbed wire, while enormous guard dogs just strolled around, thankfully being quite friendly towards us, but I knew I wouldn't have wanted to get on the wrong side of them! Despite all of that, we always felt safe whilst we were there.

Snagmere was not such a long drive as it had been before to Klaserie Dam, something I think we were all grateful for as it was a bit of a slog after the 12-hour flight. We would meet up with Norman Smith with all the gear at the lake the next day. Davo kept us entertained, as ever, and although he had lived in South Africa a few years he still hadn't lost many of his old English traits. "Eh oop me duck," he would say to the wife every time she walked in. He made us all feel a little more at home – although you always had to be on your guard with him too as there was always a practical joke or a stitch-up not far away. He relayed a story or two of what he had done to people in the past and although it had us all laughing, I don't think it would've been too funny to be on the receiving end of one of Davo's pranks!

The following morning we were on our way, and a couple of hours later we met up with Norman at one end of the lake with all the gear, but from there we would have to load up the boats and go to the far end of the lake to where Davo had secured certain rights for us to fish. He pointed across to a couple of areas in the distance. "You can't fish those spots really, as the locals like to fish there and they won't like it if they find you in there, so it's best if you all go on to that little point and I will fish that swim, as I can deal with the locals if they come down." He pointed all this out as he would have to drive the car around to the far side and we would arrive there before him.

It was a dreadful night but this beauty made up for it.

We made our way across as the wind was picking up, in fact it looked quite stormy as the grey clouds gathered overhead. Norman agreed that a stormy night was definitely on the cards and we should get sorted as quickly as possible. We arrived at the far bank and Rob and Simon immediately started sorting their gear out. I looked across to Norman, who had a mountain of gear to unload, and I couldn't leave him to do it all on his own – how naïve I was. Norman was, of course, grateful for the help but as I walked back to our point I saw that Simon and Rob were already set up side by side, facing out to the main body of water down to our right. They had an oval brolly each and I looked around for mine, only to find a tiny 45-inch and some bright yellow waterproofs. "That's what friends are for," I thought. Mind you, someone had to end up with the short straw, I suppose, and I probably would have done the same thing. Our point was quite small really, and we were all grouped together but the rods could all go out in different directions at least. When I looked around I could see why Davo had told us not to go along the bank which was further to our left. This looked by far the best area, with clear water going right across to the far bank, where there were masses of sticks and branches sticking out of the water that just screamed carp. Davo knew that we would get there before him and had, without a doubt, pulled a fast one to secure the best swim for himself. I literally had to fish through a mass of sunken marginal trees before even finding any open water, which meant that I would have to take to the boat should I hook anything. Conditions certainly looked good for it anyway, with spots of rain starting to fall and waves rolling into our bank. By all accounts this lake also held lots of catfish, the same variety which we found at Klaserie, so it would be tiger nuts on all rods for sure. I went in with fairly strong gear for obvious reasons, with 35lb braid through to a 40lb mono leader. Quicksilver hook lengths and size 4 Hutchinson Precision hooks completed the set up. What did surprise us all was when we came across some rather strange looking beasts crawling along the bottom. They weren't the crayfish that I was used to dealing with, instead they were freshwater crabs! They looked just like the ones you'd find in the sea, but they were here crawling about in the lake and,

Freshwater crabs – I thought I'd seen it all!

by all accounts, they would eat baits when they came across them, but they could also snip through lighter lines quite easily, so it was another reason to use tough gear. Other than that, from what we could make out it didn't seem like there were too many sharp rocks and I couldn't see anything which was covered in mussels, so it was just a matter of keeping the fish away from the sunken trees, although on further inspection there were certainly more trees than just the ones we could see protruding from the surface.

It was a rush to get the baits out and they certainly weren't dropped too precisely, but the weather was closing in and we didn't know how bad it was going to get. Well, it certainly got worse and the wind increased, as did the rain, which was coming straight down the lake into me. I was copping the lot and as much as I tried to cover up with the brolly and the waterproofs, it was all to no avail and I was getting colder and wetter as time went on. Sleep was virtually impossible, not only because of the cold and the wet, but because I needed to have the rod tips up high and, with braided lines, the alarms were constantly bleeping. I was lying there with my eyes shut just making tunes from the regular bleeping ……. Beep ……beep …..beep …..beep …………..beeeeeeeeeeeeeeep.

All of a sudden, from nowhere, one of the rods just hammered off. I stood up with the rod arched over as the fish just tore line from the spool. Thankfully, Simon had heard it too and came over to help, which I was grateful for. After the initial run I started to gain line gradually but the line was grating around all manner of things so we took to the boat, which gave us the best chance of landing the fish. It was certainly no easy task in the pitch blackness, with foot-high waves battering us back all the time, but Simon did a good job of getting us out there. Thankfully once we were above the fish, the grating stopped and at last I had direct contact with whatever was on the end, I just hoped that it wasn't a catfish after all of that. A few more minutes and the fish was circling in front of us and, even in the gloom, I could now see that it was

We all had action during the first few days.

definitely a carp. Si did the honours and I had my first Snagmere carp. It was a real beauty too, a mirror of 33lb 12oz which was almost covered in huge plate-like scales down its flanks. It was a fish that I was really pleased with, not just because of how it looked, but because it made up for what was otherwise a truly awful night!

Rob with a 28lb mirror from just beyond the snags.

Sometime in the early hours the storm subsided and the skies cleared. I must have finally drifted off to sleep, but only briefly as the next thing I knew the sun was shining and Davo was looking down at me.

"You look like crap," he said.

"Thanks. As a matter of fact that's just how I feel!" I replied.

"Never mind, Norman's getting the Briar (South African for bar-be-que) going and you can all come down for breakfast, we've got steaks and sausages."

"Sounds good to me," I said "but we'd better take the pictures of this fish first." It turned out that Davo had also caught two or three fish, but only up to 27lb and me catching a bigger one certainly wasn't in the plan, but it was all good fun and at last something had gone in my favour.

Breakfast South African style is a sight to behold and it's no wonder that most of them over there are like man-mountains! It's not often that I've had steak for breakfast, in fact I'm sure that was a first, but they were big steaks too and, as for the sausages – well, they just became known as 'Crowy's todgers' for reasons I can't possibly go into here!

Norman called across

"Piece of steak for you Steve?"

"Yes please, mate," I replied.

"How about some Crowy's todger?"

"Ooh err, I think I'll give that a miss thanks." The sausages looked great but it was just the thought that put me off!

Simon stole all the tiger nuts and caught a fish or two.

A good fish on the bank, a huge breakfast and with the sun now shining, the whole world seemed a better place and I went from wondering what on earth I was doing at Snagmere, to actually starting to enjoy it. We all took the chance to have a better look around and soon found that there were more snags than we had first thought. If anything, from the spot where I had caught the fish it seemed I had done well to get it through all the stuff that was out there, but I figured that the fish must've had my name on it and I had deserved that one, whatever.

Rob and Simon came up with the ingenious idea to put a line of tape across the nearer branches that were protruding from the surface so that they could lay their lines across the top of the tape and keep them out of much of the danger. It seemed a good idea but I decided to try fishing closer instead, placing a couple of baits just beyond the trees in front of me with the plan that as soon as one went off, I would just jump in the boat, move out into the open water and play it from there. Well, the plan sounded good and I did get the run but the fish didn't go to the open water, much to my disappointment, and after a tussle amongst the snags the fish just shed the hook, leaving me attached to a rather large branch. Rob's plan did work, however, and when he did get his first action of the trip, he and Simon were soon out in the boat and, with less snags to worry about, he soon had the fish under control and netted, which was another mirror of 28lb. Simon, too, got in on the act soon after with a 28lb common, so at least we had all caught. Davo, of course, was receiving the lions share of the action and was in and out in the boat almost every time we looked up. The trouble was that he was losing the majority of them as he just couldn't keep them out of the snags for long enough, much to his frustration. I was fully expecting him, at any moment, to come around and say that he'd caught a forty or a fifty, but if he had hooked anything of that size then he had certainly lost it. We did have a good look around in the boat and in some areas we could see many of the fish. We saw plenty of catfish and plenty of carp but few of any real size, mainly twenties with a few thirties bunged in and the odd one that could be over forty. Davo assured us that there would certainly be fifties in the lake, but on the evidence it looked like anything over forty pounds would be a great result.

A blank night followed for all of us and in the morning Davo came over with the depressing news that some important work had come through which he would have to go back home to sort out, so we would all have to pack up as well and he came up with the

We had no choice but to use tiger nuts on all rods.

Basic but tough was the order of the day.

idea that we could spend the remaining days at Sun City, which is South Africa's answer to Las Vegas. None of us were that keen on the idea, least of all Crowy, who voiced his concerns that we had travelled all that way to fish and weren't happy at having to leave early. In reality, we didn't really have to leave as Norman could stay on with us and we could travel back with him at the end of week. So that was exactly what happened. I'm sure that Davo was more disappointed at having to leave us fishing while he went back to work more than anything, but besides now having a few 'extra' days at our disposal we would also have the opportunity of moving into where Davo had been fishing!

The area wasn't really big enough for the three of us, but Crowy had looked at another area, near to where we had first launched the boats from, and he fancied moving over to there with Norman for the remaining time. So that left me and Rob with three nights in

With Davo packed up, Rob and I were able to take over the better swim.

Davo's swim to try and catch one or two more before we had to leave. Rob went on the left and I took the right side. More action had come from the right side but Davo's friend, Gilbert, had fished a couple of nights on the left and had caught three fish between 27lb and 31lb so Rob fancied the chance of getting something a little larger than the 28lb mirror that he caught earlier.

Fishing this new swim was straight forward enough. It was a case of taking the baits across to the far side snags which were about 150 yards away, but the hard bit was getting the fish clear of the obstacles. I figured that the best way was to fish locked-up and then, as soon as a fish was hooked, just walk back with the rod under pressure and lead the fish into open water and take things from there. There was quite a clear pathway behind me, with enough room to walk back twenty or so metres, which should be enough, hopefully.

The next night came with an air of expectancy but only one run came our way, falling to my rods late in the evening. The tactics worked perfectly and I walked back as far as I could and the fish came away from the snags. But I didn't expect what happened next as the fish, far from trying to get back where it came from, headed at speed towards us and by the time Rob had the boat ready it was already snagged in the branches on our side of the lake! It all went okay, though, and once above the fish it came free and I soon had my second fish of the week on the bank, a common of 27lb 8oz.

Surprisingly, that was the only action of the night. We had certainly expected more, especially Rob, who seemed a little despondent at the lack of action. I knew how he felt, it wasn't as easy as we thought it might have been, but there was time to put things right and after my bad start I was starting to really enjoy it at Snagmere. There wasn't any of the wildlife that could be found at Klaserie, just the odd lizard here and there, but it was a stunning lake and the swim we were now fishing was far more comfortable than the point where we had started off, and there was plenty to keep us interested, in particular a huge fish eagle which chose to sit in an old dead tree on the far margin. It was the biggest bird of prey I'd ever seen by a long way and I imagine that it could take a fair sized fish when it was hungry. It was an impressive sight and every now and then would give one of those haunting cries.

Rob was rejuvenated by the time the evening approached once more. The days were virtually a lost cause and although I had left the rods out most of the time, the action never seemed to happen until darkness arrived, and that was the same this time around. Six runs came our way and, unfortunately for Rob, they all came to my rods again. The first one rattled off just after dark but it was only on for a few seconds before the hook popped out. That was always likely to happen under such pressure, but I didn't have to wait long for the next run. The walk back did the trick once again, although the fish did make contact with a few bits and pieces on the way through. Once in open water I just went out in the boat as usual and carried on the fight from there. It did feel a bit better than the rest, although all of the fish did fight very hard and almost certainly had never been hooked before. As it surfaced in the moonlight I could see that it was better than the run of the mill fish, possibly an upper thirty. Rob had the scales and sling ready for when I got back to shore. He agreed it looked upper thirties, but as I took up the weight, the needle swung around to 40lb 8oz. I called Rob across and we zeroed everything again and lifted it once more and sure enough 40lb 8oz was the weight! Not a massive fish in the whole scheme of things but in the circumstances it was the target weight I was aiming for and it was 'job done' as far as I was concerned.

The rest of the action only produced fish up to 24lb but at least things were happening. I just hoped that, with one more night remaining, Rob would get amongst them too as the bulk of the fish were definitely over my side of the swim. Well, the last night brought a

Most of the Snagmere mirrors were absolute stunners.

further two fish of 23lb 8oz and 22lb with another one lost. Just as the sun rose over the trees I heard a bleep and looked up to see one of Rob's rod tips bending over. At first there was no movement from Rob, he had heard it but thought it was one of mine again, but I called across and he sprang to life and landed himself a common of just over 20lb.

Every fish looked brand new.

Norman came across to pick us up and we were already packed up and waiting, as we knew that there would be no more action once the sun was high in the sky. Back at base, Crowy still had his rods out, hanging on for one last take which didn't materialize. He had

A forty at last – that was good enough for me.

caught a few fish since we had last seen him, though, but nothing of any great size, I think upper twenties was about the best. So, from a bad start, I had ended up with a result that I was quite pleased with. It certainly looked like it was going to be 'one of those trips' at the beginning, but the carp gods had smiled on me and given me a couple of decent fish amongst a few others. Snagmere was a lovely lake to fish, not easy for sure, but the sort of wild, rugged carp fishing that I love and the fish were gorgeous, the commons were almost like bars of gold and the heavily-scaled mirrors were just stunning. Davo kept plugging away at the lake and eventually he did indeed catch a fifty from the lake, which if I remember right did end up on the front cover of Carpworld. Snagmere became one of the African Gold waters on the list for people to visit and I'm sure many carp anglers will have enjoyed fishing such a lovely place. I wouldn't say that it was my favourite lake of all that I've fished through the years, but in its own way it was really quite special.

New Challenges

The World Carp Cup – Fishabil 2000

I was sitting indoors one evening watching the TV, with the usual cup of tea and tin of biscuits in front of me, when the phone rang.

"Now then fella!" which was always the announcement which meant that Tim Paisley was on the other end. "I've been thinking, the World Carp Cup is due at Fishabil soon – how do you fancy fishing it with me?"

"Well – err yes!" was my reply. It caught me on the hop a bit as it was the last thing I was expecting to hear, but it sounded good to me.

Actually, I liked the idea from the start, although I have to admit that I'm really no fan of carp matches! I've no doubt that they have a permanent and justified place in modern carp fishing, but they are not really my kind of thing. My ideal fishing situation is to be away from the crowds, enjoying the peace and quiet of some unspoilt water, attempting to catch quality carp rather than quantity of fish – everything that you don't normally find in a carp match. So, why on earth was I agreeing to take part in one? Well, I did have my reservations about the whole thing but the difference with the Fishabil match was that it had such a big profile and would be done on a grand scale compared with the others I had seen. I have to say that I was also interested because my good friends, Rob Hughes and Simon Crow, had won the previous World Cup to be held there in 1996. I'd spoken to them several times about the occasion and I could tell that they absolutely loved the whole thing from start to finish – especially the winning part, of course, as they were the original world champions.

Tim knew Fishabil very well, having taken part in many trips over the years, but I had never seen the place let alone fished it and, to be honest, it wasn't a place that I had ever taken that much interest in before then. But I did think that it would be an ideal venue for the event. I knew that the lake was very well stocked and that several swims would be in with a shout of winning, or at least competing for the top places. Tim reckoned that around a quarter of the swims could be potential winners, depending on who drew which swims and how they fished those swims. As ever, Tim was also well on the ball and very organised.

"There's another match on there soon which we can fish, and it will be good practice!" This match was a European event and certainly not on such a grand level but it would be good to get down there and to fish it just to see what it was all about.

Tim Paisley launches one to the far peninsula during the 'warm up' competition.

There were quite a few Fishabil regulars in attendance for this one so we would be up against it anyway but, as ever, hopes were very high before the start. We drew a swim right up in the back bay. There were a couple of fancied swims in that area but they seemed to be at either end of the bay whilst we were pegged more or less in the middle. Opposite us was a long, thin peninsula which led up to a couple of the swims on the other side. Tim reckoned that the margin of the peninsula would be one of the likely areas to pick up fish from. It looked the obvious spot but was a fair chuck across to the far side and, to be honest, long range casting for me is a bit like watching adult films (not that I do of course-cough!) I see what those blokes do and quite fancy the idea – but I know that I just haven't got the tools for the job! Still, with two rods each it at least gives the chance to experiment a little. To our right was an interesting stretch of bank, where it was quite overgrown and the next swim was around 100 metres away, so maybe a few options there.

Anyway, the match started and I remember catching our first fish, a 10lb mirror, which Tim refused to photograph for some reason, but we were up and running. I seem to remember that we caught three or four fish during the first 24 hours or so, which was okay but by then the better swims were already starting to pull away and the amount we were catching certainly wouldn't be enough to put us in the frame. A couple of times while walking past the bush directly to my right I had noticed a slight bit of movement close into the branches. I doubted really if it would be from carp but it got me interested anyway as I was set up on the right side of the swim. A couple of quiet hours passed so I thought "What the hell?" and decided to give the bush a try. Now, this was to be an important part of the whole sequence of events which followed, as what I decided to try was a PVA bag of pellets with a Hutchinson MC Mix boily flavoured with Monster Crab and Shellfish Sense Appeal. Nothing unusual there, you might think. But believe it or not, this was the first time in my life that I'd ever used a PVA bag! Don't ask me why I had never used one before as I don't really know, I think it was just the idea of using something which might possibly taint the bait in some way. Nevertheless, the bag was tied up and the cast was a little awkward as I had to flick the bait around the bush and sort of back behind me as well, as the swim jutted out from the bank. 'Sploosh!' went the bag, thankfully, just in the right spot, and I slackened off the line with the indicator just hanging loosely.

It must have been only a minute or so later when the line started twitching up and down, giving the odd bleeps. I knew they weren't pick ups but were liners from something taking an interest, but all of a sudden we were both very interested too! The lifts and bleeps continued for a few minutes before it absolutely belted off. I was expecting perhaps bream or something to be responsible but this was definitely a carp and we soon had another fish to be weighed. The first PVA bag I'd ever used had caught us a fish so, all of a sudden, something which before that moment I had no confidence in whatsoever, I was now full of confidence in! The bag went out again and, hey presto, it went off again with

Post match celebrations with Fishabil owner, Raphael Faraggi.

another carp. What it did was to give us another producing area, Tim was still picking off fish on the long range rods and we started to gradually creep up the leader board. We were never going to win but we were involved in our own little battles, trying to edge up one place at a time, which kept us working all the time. The bags were going so well that I ended up with them on both of my rods and, although it wasn't an area that was going to hold a vast amount of fish, it kept us ticking over for the rest of the competition – although it has to be said that I did also catch a fair few bream on the bags too, but in the situation it didn't matter as it was just nice to get something working. In the end I think we ended up seventh or something like that. Nothing outstanding, but we both felt that we had got the best we could out of the swim and it gave us both a very good insight into the lake and how to fish it for the main match which, by now, was just a few weeks away.

June arrived and we somehow found ourselves fishing at Etang de Margot for the week leading up to WCC. I think it was in some way a bit more practice and the chance to get a bend in the rods leading up to the event. I'd enjoyed fishing with Tim but I began to realise that the bloke just didn't like sleeping! He seemed to always be awake, day or night, apart from a daily snooze in the afternoon. Now that was fine by me but it also appeared that he didn't want me to be sleeping either. As anyone who knows me will tell you, I do like to get a good nights sleep under my belt, but it seemed like every time I dozed off I would get,

"You're not asleep again are you, Briggsy?"

I was already starting to feel exhausted and I had a 72 hour match to contend with yet. But we had a good time and caught a few fish along the way and, before we knew it, the time had come for us to make our way up to Fishabil.

Up at the lake Joan and Mary were already waiting for us at one of the chalets situated on the dam wall. In fact, it seemed as if the whole world was there. The place was packed with all sorts of people; there were plenty of familiar faces and friends as well as all sorts of people running around organising things and setting up stuff. It was a real reality check after the relative peace and quiet of Margot, this place was absolutely buzzing with activity.

Thankfully, we did have the chalet as most of the other competitors would have to bivvy up in a field across the road, which at least probably meant that half of them would end up as tired as me.

The calm before the storm! Swim 46 looked good enough but we had no idea of how it would fish.

Rafael Faraggi was the charismatic owner of Fishabil and he had plenty of things organised to make the whole event quite a spectacle. There was a fair at one end of the lake and an afternoon catwalk show where a bevy of local models displayed several items of clothing, as well as plenty of themselves too. You can imagine how well that went down with the place full of carp anglers! There were four or five Ferrari's on display, too, which were mainly Rafael's from what I could make out, and every now and then he would fly in and out in a blue helicopter for no other reason, it would seem, than to let everyone know that he had more money than the rest of us put together. To be fair, he did make the build-up really enjoyable for all of us, with a party or two along the way. The evening before the draw we were all taken to a hotel somewhere along the coast, where we would all have a sit down meal and register properly and also be given our clothing, as we all had to wear the official clothing given to us by the organisers. It was a very lavish affair with us all having to be suited and booted, something that made most of us feel a little out of place, but the intention was to make it a classy event rather than just any old fishing competition. It was to be a genuine World Cup ratified by FIPS, who set the rules and regulations for these things, so in my opinion it was the way it should be.

The draw took place back at the lake the next day, in a marquee in the Deer Park section. A few people remarked that I was very laid back about the whole thing but to be honest, after all the sleepless nights, I couldn't have been any other way by then. I was on the verge of learning how to sleep standing up with my eyes open. Again, it was all well organised and we were led in, country by country, to the sound of our national anthems. It was all getting closer by the hour and talk was of who would win and who were the main contenders. Rob Hughes and Simon Crow were, of course, defending champions and were looking to retain their crown, but were a little worried about us and some of the others. Ian Starmer and Mark Grygier were old hands at Fishabil and knew the lake inside out and were definitely among the favourites. The French hopes however, were pinned firmly on the shoulders of the Mahin brothers, two guys who had made quite a name for themselves over the years and, as far as the locals were concerned, no one else would match up to their angling ability. One by one the teams filed up on to the stage to draw their swim numbers out. I remember Ian Starmer picking the swim he really wanted in the back channel, giving him a real confidence booster. Then it was our turn and Tim stuck his left hand into the pot and pulled out number 46. That meant nothing to either of us at the time, our minds

We finally started catching and the tension was relieved a little.

went a bit blank during the whole ceremony. It was Rob Hughes, I think, who first came up and said

"You jammy gits, that's a great swim to pick – it's one of my favourites!"

As it happened, swim 46 was not far from the marquee in the Deer Park so we went for a look.

"Looks okay to me, Briggsy" said Tim.

"Yeah I quite fancy fishing here," was my reply, or something like that.

We quickly gathered all the info we could on the swim from whoever knew anything about it. Apparently, there was a snaggy area starting from around forty metres from the bank, which was the spot people normally tried to reach from other swims as, in normal times, there was no fishing allowed in the Deer Park area. The swim to our right was a fair distance away rather like it had been in the previous match, although the margin didn't look quite so inviting. Out in front of us in the middle of the lake was a huge scaffolding structure, erected just before our arrival, to display the relevant advertisements. We weren't sure how that would affect the fish although, as Tim said, carp are very inquisitive creatures normally. The swim to the left was quite close, though, and who should draw that? None other than the Mahin brothers – talk about putting ourselves under pressure, although I have to say that, really, I felt under no pressure at all. All the waiting was nearly over, and I was just looking forward to fishing. We would give it our best shot and just see where it went from there.

Each fish was gratefully accepted as we secured our place at the top of the leader board.

"How do you fancy fishing this swim then?" asked Tim. Well I was full of confidence in the PVA bag approach after what had gone before so suggested that I would like to fish to the snags on the left with bags on both rods. Tim seemed to like the idea too, and said that he would go on the right and fish further out, possibly around the recently constructed 'feature' out towards the middle. So, with tactics sorted we dragged our mountain of gear to the swim and began sorting everything out. We noticed that, to the right of our swim was one marshals bivvy, and to our left was the head marshals bivvy, both doorways pointing straight at our swim.

"Looks like they're taking a keen interest in us!" said Tim.

I don't quite know the reasoning for them being so close to us but it did make me feel a little uneasy. Jon 'Shoes' Jones came around to wish us good luck and take a few pictures. He had decided to come over and support our teams and help out as much as possible within the rules but also to photograph the event, which we were all grateful for as we all guessed, or rather hoped, that we would be too busy to be able to photograph everything going on and it would be a shame not to have some sort of record of the events. Each swim had tape around it and only official people were allowed inside at any time. Either one of us could leave the swim at any time, for whatever reason, as long as the remaining team member was there in charge of the four rods which were allowed per team. Thankfully, Joan and Mary were organising the food as ever, and at least we wouldn't have to worry about cooking meals over the coming days.

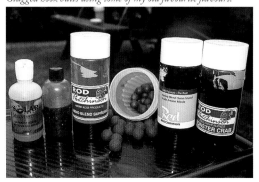

Glugged hook baits using some of my old favourite flavours.

The main thing for us was to get the tackle and bait in place ready for the start. This was really before the days of PVA mesh stocking so I couldn't tie loads of bags up in advance. I had bundles of Kryston's Melt-Ex bags, which were what I'd used before, but would have to tie them up as I was going along. We were allowed spare rods each so I could have a rod with a bag on all ready to go. I seem to remember that the pellets were Hinders Betaine pellets, which seemed to be doing great things at the time. I remember looking at the sack of them and wondering how many PVA bags it would take to use all of them. They weren't all to be used in the bags, as we would have a bucket of spod mix at the ready all the time, which we planned to keep topping the swim up with at regular intervals. Boilies, for me, were the ever-faithful MC Mix with Monster Crab and Shellfish Sense Appeal in 15mm and 18mm. But I

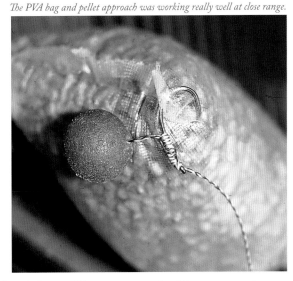

The PVA bag and pellet approach was working really well at close range.

also had some of them soaking in a tub for hook baits. They were soaked in a neat mixture of Monster Crab, Shellfish Sense Appeal and Amino Blend Swan Mussel. As you can imagine, they did chuck up a bit, but I had no doubt that if there were any carp in the area then they wouldn't be able to miss those little beauties!

Tim was going to be using Mainline Assassin-8 boilies along with the Betaine Pellets and Response Pellets and would get both out to the mark with spods and bait rockets. It was the Gardner Pocket Rockets that we had lined up for much of the work - they are light, easy to cast and drop the bait very well, ideal for most situations. But to get the boilies out at range Tim also had some more specialised boilie rockets, which really did get them out a long way. Wherever fish showed in the swim we were confident that we could fish to them effectively. Actually, there were no carp showing anywhere around the lake, from memory, so we had little idea if we had fish in front of us or not.

An hour before the 'off' we were allowed to have a cast about with the marker rods and put a bit of bait in. Well, my first chuck with the marker sailed out around fifty yards, where I got snagged up straight away, losing the lot.

"I've found the snags," was my rather obvious comment. After tying on another float and lead I cast a few yards closer and found that it was clear all the way to the bank. That was all I needed to know, in two casts I had found the snags and it required nothing more than about a forty yard chuck to get right on the edge of them. We didn't want to put too much bait out to start with, just a few spods to get them interested, but we were both worried about causing too much disturbance in an area that wasn't normally fished from this bank.

It seemed like we had plenty of time, but when the hooter sounded we were still running around trying to get things ready, which I have to say is always the case with me! But with two bags ready I cast the left one first.

'Badooosh!' It landed right on the money at about forty yards out and straight away the head marshal came over waving his finger. He was trying to say that we couldn't cast outside the line of our swim, but having been advised by Tim to read the rules thoroughly, I knew that it stated that the boundary was at the midway point between our swim and the next one, which meant that I was okay to cast where I had. He came back with a list of the rules and sure enough he had to concede that I was in the right, but I rather got the feeling at the start that, out of all the teams on the lake, it was us that were going to be kept under close scrutiny.

So the wait began. It's funny, but after all the build up and all the running around, when the rods have finally been cast out there is a real air of excitement and expectancy, but with nothing else to do but wait for something to happen. It was a feeling that soon wore off, however, and I sat back to await events. All around the lake the bombardment had begun with baits of all shapes, sizes and makes being launched towards the unsuspecting carp. Sometime soon after I heard an alarm sound, it wasn't ours and wasn't close by, but someone was into the first carp of the match. It turned out to be Rob and Simon, who were positioned right over the back from us. They didn't fancy their swim too much at all but they had caught the first carp of the competition.

Two or three more fish were caught from different sections and I wondered when it was going to be our turn as we were both confident that our turn would come. Then one of the bag rods rattled off and we were in! The old heart was pounding as usual and although I knew that it wasn't a monster on the end, every fish in a match is precious and especially the first one. Thankfully, nothing went wrong and soon the fish was netted and our marshal came over to do the weighing. All fish were weighed in kilos although I think that first one was just over 17lb in old money. We had made a start, it seemed to take ages to come but it was still only the first afternoon and there was a long way to go yet. However, that was the start of a little burst of action for us and over the next few hours we landed two or three more fish, and it was all starting to get a bit exciting. That night neither of us slept at all - normal for Tim but very unusual for me - but things were happening and we wanted to know everything that was going on. The PVA bag tactics looked to be spot on and the majority of the action was coming to the close in area. Thankfully, next door the Mahin brothers were using a totally different approach, just baiting lightly with boilies and sort of mid-range between the distances that Tim and I were fishing. That suited me fine as they weren't putting more pressure on the spots where our fish were coming from and they weren't getting amongst the fish themselves at that stage. We just kept the bait trickling in – not lots of it, but about half a dozen small spods of bait every hour, or after every fish, just to keep the swim topped up.

As the sun rose in the morning we'd landed eight carp, but we had no idea how anyone else had got on. As always in these situations you always think that one or two teams would have run away with it by then, and caught a stack of fish from one or two of the swims, which was more than possible at Fishabil as there could be groups of fish in all manner of areas. The good thing about this competition was, as I mentioned earlier, the organisation, and at regular intervals through the day we were due to get updated result sheets of how all the teams were doing. The first one was to show the results up to 8am that morning and was to be delivered some time around 9am or 10am. Of course, we couldn't wait to see that first sheet just to see how we were doing. We knew that we had done okay but when the result sheet finally arrived we were in for a bit of a shock. We weren't just doing okay – we were winning! We had caught eight fish for a total of 59.5kg. Not far behind us were a French team in swim 19 on the other side of the lake. They had also caught eight fish, but their total was slightly less at 51.9kg. The Mahin brothers next door had caught just one fish for 5.8kg and defending champs Simon and Rob, although catching the first fish of the competition, had only added one more to their total for 8.3kg. Twenty one of the fifty two teams had caught fish already though, so it showed how even everything could be. We might have been in the lead but it was only by a small margin and we figured that eight fish could be caught by any team in a relatively short space of time, so although we were in the position that every team wanted to be in, we felt far from relaxed, it has to be said.

But things were happening for us. The fish were obviously used to hanging around the snags and our careful approach wasn't spooking them it seemed. Once again though, as in the previous competition, the bream were showing their liking for the pellets and soaked boilies. For every carp we caught there must have also been at least two or three bream, probably four in fact. So it might have only been eight carp on our total, but that was out of something like twenty five or thirty bites already. The good thing was that the carp did keep coming in between the bream, and the next result sheet was due for everything caught up to 2pm. By then we had caught a further five carp for a total of thirteen weighing 86.7kg. Perhaps the most important thing

The man is just amazing! Tim with our biggest carp of the competition.

was that the second-placed team had only added one fish to their total and they were now on nine. All of the other teams had still only caught up to four fish and, for the first time, we did start to wonder if we could keep that sort of pace up. It was far too early to get over confident or anything like that. We had only been going for 24 hours now, one third of the way through, and anything could happen.

If anything our action was starting to become more consistent. We had struck on a formula that was working perfectly for us. Just as before, the fish absolutely loved the pellets and I don't think that the PVA

I'd never tied up so many PVA bags in my life –
but they were working and that was all that mattered.

bag method had been used to any great extent there before, in fact I'm sure it couldn't have with the way the fish were responding to it. It's fair to say that the main bulk of the fish were falling to this method, with only the odd fish coming from range but then, as evening started to draw in, Tim landed a cracking mirror of over 27lb, which came from close to the scaffolding structure. It might not sound anything extraordinary, but most of the fish had been from mid to upper doubles with a low twenty or two being about the best, so an upper twenty was almost like landing two at the same time and was sure to give us a little cushion.

By eight o'clock that evening we had moved on to seventeen fish and had broken through the 100kg barrier with 107.7kg. Perhaps, more importantly, the team in second place had failed to add another fish to their total, meaning that we now had over double the weight of fish compared to that of the second-placed team! Perhaps the main worry was that the Mahin brothers next door had

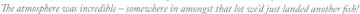

The atmosphere was incredible – somewhere in amongst that lot we'd just landed another fish!

seen enough of what was going on and they now started to fish at the same range as our rods on the left, and they also started to fish with PVA bags. It was probably too late for them to make a serious charge up the leader board, as they still only had one fish to their credit, but what bothered me most was that, with their extra lines and extra pressure on the area, it could start to push the fish out and the action could start to dry up.

After all of the excitement, the lack of sleep started to have all sorts of weird effects on us. The 'buzz' of what was going on was keeping me going but, inevitably, it all started to catch up on both of us. I don't remember going to sleep but I must have laid down for a few seconds and gone straight off into a deep sleep. I don't remember anything about what happened next but, apparently, one of my rods went off and when I didn't get up Tim sat up and shouted across to me that I had a run, at which point I apparently replied,

"You sort that one out Tim, I'm sleeping!" Tim did the honourable thing and did sort out the fish and even re-cast the rod while I snored away like a good 'un, just yards away. A short time later, oblivious to what had gone on before, I had another run which I did manage to get up for. This time Tim came staggering out and stood beside me, looking very puzzled.

"Where are we?" he said. He looked down at the swim marker and continued, "Are we in some sort of match or something?"

I smiled as I replied, "Yes we're in a match Tim – but it's better than that – we're winning!"

It was amazing how disorientated you can become just with lack of sleep and perhaps over-working yourself a bit and, believe me, it was hard work continuously tying up all of those bags. We were almost hallucinating at times. I remember playing one fish and thinking that I had to keep it clear of the big island in front of me – only there was no island anywhere in front of me. One thing we definitely weren't hallucinating about were the amount of spectators that were gathering around us, every time we had a fish. Rafael Faraggi had predicted that there would be around ninety thousand visitors for the duration of the event, and we thought that was all pie-in–the-sky stuff, but it was starting to look like he could have been right and we were glad that there were tapes around the swim, otherwise we could have been mobbed. Of course, the crowds came mainly during the day and it was an incredible sight to see so many people taking an interest in what we were doing. But we even had spectators during the night. I distinctly remember getting up for one run at around 3am, only to receive a round of applause from a whole family, including kids, who were standing behind us. Now, we were both asleep just prior to that in our bivvies, so that family must have just been standing there in the dark watching our 'empty' swim, waiting for something to happen, which it duly did much to their enjoyment. How bizarre!

By 8am the next morning we were on twenty five fish for 157.7kg and, looking back now, we were just stretching away all the time and had very little chance of being caught

The fish kept coming and at last we could start to relax and enjoy it, safe in the knowledge that we'd done enough.

by anyone. But at the time, when you want it so much you cannot help but fear the worst and our feeling was nothing more than we had a good lead and we'd both seen it before, in all manner of sports, where a good lead has been whittled away towards the end as someone makes a final charge. The worst thing was that the close range area was just starting to slow down a bit. The Mahin brothers had started to get amongst the fish and had added four to their total by morning, moving them from nineteenth place up into seventh, which was probably why our action was becoming slower. Well, I say slower but there was still constant action from the snags area, but it was coming more from the bream and less from the carp. I was quite happy to keep plugging away at the bags if it was going to keep getting us the odd carp, but by now I was starting to get perhaps seven or eight bream to every carp.

Carp-wise, that day was by far our slowest, and by the evening we had added just two more fish to our total and we feared the worst. It was definitely grinding to a halt and our only saving grace was that none of the other teams had made a significant move. Waiting for the result sheet that evening was nerve-wracking and we both breathed a sigh of relief when we saw that, somehow, we still had a reasonable cushion and all we had to do now was hold on until the next afternoon, when the whole thing would be over with.

However, by the next morning something started to happen. The fish, which had vacated the snags area, had done no more than move out to the middle section, in line with the scaffolding. We knew this as Tim's long-range rods started to liven up somewhat. Things had changed, but fish were still there to be caught. For the first time I actually brought in one of the bag rods and changed it over to a long range set up so that we now had three rods out at range and just one left on the snags. With around one fish an hour coming to our rods, we could at last start to relax a little. We now knew that if we just kept that going, the title would be ours. The party atmosphere was starting to kick in and the crowds were gathering more than ever. A few of the other guys actually packed up early to come around and join in the fun. Martin Locke and Lee Jackson cheered us on and passed a couple of beers over the tape, while various TV crews all hovered around filming the action. The two marshals that had us a little worried at the start turned out to be absolute stars and my initial thoughts were totally unfounded. They seemed to love being involved and didn't mind us waking them up any time, day or night, to weigh the fish. The head marshal kept singing "We are the champions" every time that he walked by, always with a big smile on his face.

The hooter finally sounded at 2pm and that was it – we had won! The tapes came down and everyone charged in. It was mayhem, but brilliant mayhem. Our final tally was 37 carp for a total of 225.4kg, over double that of the team in second place. Along the way we had broken the world records for the 48 hour stage and 72 hour stage of a World Cup. The Mahin brothers had shown their quality and had dragged themselves back from nowhere into fifth place. Ian Starmer and Mark Grygier finished a creditable fourth and defending champs Rob and Simon, from a poor swim, had still finished in the top ten in ninth place.

We only had an hour or so to get everything packed away before we would have to go for the presentation. But what a feeling it was as we walked along the

The hooter sounded and the champagne was cracked open – we'd done it!

And the crowd went wild!

dam wall to the marquee. All the English guys carried flags and banners and I have to say a massive thanks to all of them for making it so special. I couldn't believe the reaction from everyone, they cheered us all the way to the stage and I remember looking at the podium in front of us – the same podium that I had looked at before the match had started and I had wondered to myself just who would be standing on there at the end. Well, now we knew it was us! We sang the national anthem and picked up our prize and soaked everyone in champagne and drank a fair bit of it too. It was a magic moment.

Afterwards we walked right the way up into the local village for a celebratory meal. There were still crowds everywhere and they cheered and clapped all the way and cars tooted their horns. I had never expected any sort of reaction like that but after all of the intense feelings and hard work through the match, it was a fantastic way to finish. So, had this changed my attitude to carp competitions? Well no, not really. When I stand back and look at them they are still not my sort of thing, so much is down to the luck of the draw, although a lot still depends on how you fish the swim which you get.

The moment every team had dreamed of before the start – but for us it was real.

But I have to say that winning a competition like that is something that it is just not possible to experience in any other form of the sport. Catching a big fish is what I aim for and generally you only share that with a handful of people, maybe only one or two. Winning the WCC, we had shared it with literally thousands of people and the feelings were incredible, the highs, the lows, the lack of sleep, the countless bream that we had to wade through. And, of course, none of it would have happened without my fantastic partner and Captain, Tim Paisley. That man is just incredible! His motivation and drive is just amazing. Without a doubt it helped to bring the best out of both of us and we fished very well as a team. I know that the outcome would have been different if I'd fished with anyone else. Why he picked up the phone that evening to ask me to join him, I don't really know, but I was just glad that he had. We hadn't fished together much before that, but for that style of fishing something just 'clicked' and the result of all of that was that we were champions of the world!

There's no doubt we made a pretty good team!

The Colne Valley

The Colne Valley

Harefield

It only seems like yesterday, the Colne Valley had become the capital of carp fishing in England and it was where everyone wanted to be. The lure of it was very strong and I knew it would only be a matter of time before I headed that way too. Of all of the waters in the Valley, it was Savay Lake that was making all of the headlines, not just because of the fish that it held, but also for the people that were fishing there. Rod Hutchinson and Rob Maylin had written about the lake and made it a household name. But literally just across the road was another large lake, and although it had received its fair share of publicity over the years, it wasn't quite in the same league as Savay; the name of that lake was Harefield.

John Stent was the fishery manager at Boyer Leisure, the company who had control of Harefield, and I think it always got under his skin a little bit, knowing that the lake across the road was receiving most of the publicity and so he had some really forward thinking ideas of how to make Harefield a much better lake than it already was. Basically, what he did was to drain down two of their other waters, Rodney Meadow and Willow Pool, and put all of the good carp from those two lakes into Harefield and, all of a sudden, he had created a fantastic big-fish water that could rival the very best!

News travels fast on the carp grapevine and the lake was soon attracting a lot of interest from some of the well-known anglers around the country. By then, I had already become good friends with Rob Maylin and he was quick to see the potential of Harefield and had

already been there the previous year and helped himself to some very nice fish. It all sounded great, but I still had some unfinished business down at Johnsons Railway Lake in Kent where I had struggled for some time, but had finally started to get amongst the fish. I felt like I wanted to carry on and at least do the start of the next season on the Railway, while Rob, Pete and the rest of the gang had already made their minds up that it would be Harefield from then on.

I stayed on at Johnsons for the start of the season.

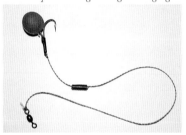

It was all plain sailing once I got the rig right.

As planned, I fished the start of the season down on the Railway and I was so pleased that I did, as it was a great week. I fished the End-of-the-Willows swim and ended up catching five carp and losing another three. I only lost those three fish by persisting with a hook pattern that people had advised me against, and being stubborn I used them anyway, and suffered three hook pulls on the trot! After changing hook patterns over to the long shank Drennan O'Shaugnessy's it was all plain sailing, as it were, and I landed more fish in that week than I had done over the previous couple of years on the lake. It was all down to little microwaved pop ups. The fish just loved those little fruity pop ups, after ignoring most other things that I had thrown their way. None of the Railway's big carp were amongst those fish – although having said that, I did land a common of around 24lb, which was the biggest common to come from the lake at the time. The Leather was the fish that everyone wanted back then and although there weren't many other fish caught that week, a guy fishing right up to my left in the corner had one run and it was the Leather at around 34lb. I was happy enough with what I'd caught, really. That one week satisfied my needs for the Railway and, although I could have carried on fishing, and I'm sure caught more fish, I was also now feeling a bit left out and I wanted to be up in the Colne Valley with the rest of the guys.

It was a great way to end my fishing on the Railway Lake.

However, fishing Harefield wasn't going to be at all straight forward. It was now the water to be on and of course tickets got snapped up quickly. Everyone else had got on there before the rush but, because I had stayed behind on the Railway, and for various other reasons, there wasn't now a ticket there for me. I didn't know what to do. I had set my mind on fishing there and all of my friends were on there, but it looked as though I wasn't going to be on there that year at all. But someone came up with a cunning plan! Each member was allowed to take one guest for a weekend session each year and as everyone else was already fishing there anyway, most of them didn't have anyone else in mind to take as a guest, so I asked all of them if they would mind guesting me for a weekend each, which of course they were more than happy to do. So that was it, somehow, one way or another I had found a way to fish Harefield. I'd never been so pleased to have all those friends – bless them all.

I already knew how I was going to approach the fishing once I got there. I had just had some real success on small pop ups, and indeed Rob Maylin had used similar tactics to good effect already at Harefield. But I wanted to go down a different route. A few years earlier I had formulated a fishmeal bait of my own, which had worked really well and caught me a lot of fish, especially back at Sutton Lakes near Dartford. The fishmeals seemed to work really well on the shallow gravel pits and Harefield seemed to me to be just a bigger version of the gravel pits that I had fished already, and I couldn't see anyway that they wouldn't work just as well there.

My Fishmeal Mix

4oz Capelin Meal

4oz Sand Eel Meal

3oz Sardine and Anchovy meal

3oz Sluis CLO

2oz 80 mesh casein

1oz Codliveine

Fish Feed Inducing oil

Geranium essential oil

Actually, the Harefield anglers seemed to almost be divided into two groups. You had the long-range anglers, and then the others who would fish at closer range over beds of bait. Care Bear and Frogger had been very successful fishing the latter method, but as I've said already, Rob Maylin and several others had also proved how effective the long-range casting with small baits could be. I wasn't much good at the long-range stuff and certainly couldn't compete with some of the others in that department, so I was more than happy to go down the baited-area and closer-range route.

Rob Maylin, a good friend and a great angler.

The tactics might have varied, but it felt very much like the anglers were one big group and it was a nice atmosphere on the lake. One thing most of them had in common was that, in the evening, they would reel in their rods and go for a 'social' just across the road at the infamous Horse and Barge pub. It was the meeting place for many of the anglers fishing through the Colne Valley and beyond, and I certainly wasn't going to miss out on a bit of that. It was all very much part of the Colne Valley scene in those days and we had some fun. You couldn't help but be influenced by Rob Maylin, he was the ring leader and normally party organiser and just brilliant company. It was never a dull moment when he was around and some of the nights with him would be unforgettable – if I could only remember them!

For my first weekend, I found myself up on the causeway, which divided Harefield from the massive Broadwater Lake behind. For me, it was the prettier of the two main banks of the lake. The Road Bank on the other side seemed a lot more barren, although I suppose in reality it was never the prettiest of lakes to look at, anyway. The one thing it most certainly did have going for it, in my eyes, were loads of gravel bars. It was a feature-finders dream and one of the things that immediately amazed me were how few people used marker floats there. The guys that were chucking out to the middle could have been landing in ten feet of water or ten inches and I wondered quite how they knew one way or the other. I've no doubt that they were doing it right, but I felt that by using a marker float I could get everything sorted exactly right and I would be able to fish very confidently. The first bar I found was quite close in – a little too close I thought, but there was another one around seventy to eighty yards range and that was where I baited. A few kilos of the fishmeals went out; the 18mm baits were easy to get out with the throwing stick, while I used a much bigger hook bait of around 25mm.

The following afternoon, out of the blue, one of the rods was away and I was into my first Harefield carp, however, I didn't have a direct line to the fish as it had gone at right angles to the bar and I could feel everything grating. I felt the fish for a while before that sickening feeling came of the hook pulling out. It was my first full day on the lake and I'd got my first run quickly, but I'd lost it – something which has actually happened to me a lot over the years, but although I was obviously unhappy to lose a fish, I also felt that I had got the tactics spot on and was fairly sure that it wouldn't be too long before I would have a fish or two on the bank.

Harefield Lake was busy but I found a swim – can you spot the 'Mexican riding a horse' tree?

Nothing else happened for the rest of that weekend so I packed up and went back home, and back to work for the following week. After coming so close to getting my first Harefield carp I was just counting the days away until I could get back there again. The following Friday afternoon I raced back along those same roads and in a way I was hoping that the same swim would be free, after all I had found some nice spots and figured that if I could get back in there then I would have a great chance. But I wasn't ready for what was waiting for me when I arrived. The car park was full, in fact the whole lake seemed to be full! All of the swims up the Causeway were already taken and on a lake of that size I couldn't believe how many bivvies I was seeing. It was a long walk around the top bank and then down the road bank and it was all a bit disappointing. I passed one small swim at the far end which I didn't fancy at all, but otherwise it appeared that nothing else was free. Then, just as I was approaching the end of the lake where the gate was, I came across an empty swim. Phil Harper was next door and he said he would put a chair in the swim to save it for me, while I got my gear, and I was so pleased he did as someone else arrived just after me who was also looking for somewhere to get the rods out.

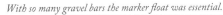

With so many gravel bars the marker float was essential.

With the swim secured, the first thing to do was get the marker rod out, of course, and find the bars – the only problem was that I couldn't find any. I was expecting to find bars in every swim, but in this one the bottom seemed to be flat and smooth. That threw me a little and I didn't feel quite so confident, but at least I had somewhere to fish. About three-quarters of the way across the bay it was around ten feet deep, so I figured that I would just bait up an area at that sort of range and

see what would happen. Phil was full of confidence in his ham-flavoured pop ups, which he always seemed to be using, he must have got a job lot of it cheap or something. We joked between us as to who had the best tactics and who would have the best chance. Phil was always up-beat about things and a great person to fish next to. Further down the bank was Travolta, who was also great company. As always, he had all the home comforts with him and fished the nearest swim to the gate. It was boxing that night with Chris Eubank versus Michael Watson, and Travolta had his portable TV with him. I had to miss the pub that night to watch the boxing. It was a sad outcome to the fight, but what a fight it was! Eubank was victorious and I was always a bit of a Eubank fan, whereas although Travolta was from Brighton, the same town as Chris Eubank, he didn't reckon him so much and wanted him to lose, so it added a bit of spice to the whole thing. By the time it was all over, the rest of the gang were already making their way back to get their rods out for the night and it was time for bed.

A great way to get off the mark – Small Pecs at 34lb 8oz.

The night passed by quietly and the next morning the sun rose over the trees and it looked like being quite a warm day. Joan had finished work for the week and came down to join me. She was manager of the bar and restaurant at Farlows back then and was glad to get a rest after working the long hours that were all part of the job there. It really didn't look too promising, I hadn't seen any real sign of a fish and nothing had happened along the bank either side of me and, with the temperature rising, I figured that the best chance of a fish would be during the hours of darkness. It got to about 11am and I lay back on my bed chair just happy to relax in the sun when, out of the blue, one of my rods just suddenly screamed off! I jumped up and grabbed the rod and immediately had no choice but to give line. Whatever was on the other end was really powerful and was trying to get as far away from me as possible. It could only go so far before running out of lake so, eventually, it slowed down and I was able to turn it. It was a really angry fish and was charging off in all directions and no sooner would I gain a little line than it would be wrenched from the reel again. Travolta, Phil and a couple of the other guys had heard the alarm go off and had gathered in the swim to watch events and by then the fish was not too far out in front of me, but with the water being quite murky due to it still being a working pit, it was impossible to see the fish. Eventually, the fish tired and as it came up to the net we could all see it was a good fish and, as Joan did the honours with the net, we all let out a big cheer, just to let everyone around the lake know that I had caught my first Harefield carp. It was a lovely looking mirror, dark brown in colour, but none of us had any idea which fish it was. Thankfully, one of the bailiffs, a chap called Rob Still, arrived at that moment and recognised the fish as one called Small Pecs, one of the fish from Rodney Meadow, which had the reputation for not being caught too often. It weighed 34lb 8oz and was a new English personal best – not bad for my first fish from the lake! Rob Still went on to tell us more and it just showed the quality of the fishing at Harefield. The date was July 17th and it was just one month into the season, as Harefield still stuck with the old close season dates, but this fish was already the 17th different fish to be caught over 30lb that season and one of the few that they were still waiting for. Needless to say I didn't miss the pub again that night!

What a great start to my Harefield campaign, in fact it had been a great start to the season with the fish from the Railway Lake just a few weeks earlier. I couldn't wait for the next weekend to come around and after what had happened I didn't really care where I fished on the lake as I felt that I would be confident enough in any of the swims. It's great when you get

Another of the great Harefield carp, the hard-fighting mirror known as 'Stripes'.

on a bit of a roll like that – it doesn't always happen of course, but when it does, you just feel like you're going to catch no matter what.

When I returned the following week I was quite keen to get back in the same area as where I'd caught Small Pecs from. Someone was already in that swim, but the next one up was free, so that was good enough for me and after a chat to the guy it turned out that he was only staying one night anyway, so if I wanted I could always move into there the next day. Richie MacDonald was in the next swim along the bank, and he'd had a long association with the lake, so it was good to see him again. He is a proper carp fishing character as well as being a great angler. With the marker float out, Richie told me that he was 'the nuts' with a throwing stick (as he would) and wanted to put some bait out for me.

"Cor these baits stink!" he said, "I wouldn't use these if you paid me!" I suppose they did smell a bit strange. I was using Geranium essential oil along with Fish Feed Inducing Oil from Premier Baits and it was like nothing I'd seen anyone else using, but the fish loved it everywhere that I'd used it so that was good enough for me. But with Richie curling his lip every time he picked some up, I could see that they weren't to everyone's taste!

There wasn't time to cast out as, of course, we all had to go across the road to the Horse and Barge and very good it was too. The way I prepared everything was to line up with an object on the horizon that I could line up with in the dark. Over on the workings was a tree that we called the 'Mexican riding a horse tree', a strange name indeed but when we saw it, that's what it reminded us of! With that to aim at, I then cast out to the desired distance either side of the marker float and then clipped the line into the line clip, before reeling in again and placing a fresh boilie on each rig. That meant that as soon as I returned there would be no messing about and I could get them out to the right spots straight away.

When the time came the baits went out perfectly, as I'd hoped they would, but it didn't do me any good, as by the morning nothing had happened for any of us. As promised, the guy next door started to pack up and I had a dilemma. Should I stick with the baited area that I had already created, or should I move to where I had caught Small Pecs from the week before? In the end, I decided on a move as I liked the next swim a little more than the one I was in. I could fish the same area out in the middle of the bay where I had caught the fish from the week before, but there was also a line of pads out in the centre of the bay, but further down to my right. Behind the pads looked an ideal area for the fish to patrol up and down, but there wasn't a swim where you could really fish that bit unless you cast right over the top of the pads, which no one was really going to do. However, from the swim I was now in I had the angle to cast across and get into the mouth of that channel, which gave me another area to have a go at, so I was happy that I had done the right thing by moving.

Richie Macdonald lends a hand as I hold Small Pecs for the second time in as many weeks.

Pub time came around and, one by one, everyone filed past me, but I fancied staying on the lake. With only the two nights a week at my disposal, I wanted to make the most of them and I felt that if I made the effort, then I could catch another fish or two. I liked the social, but not as much as I liked catching carp! Pete Jones stopped in for a chat and I said that I would be staying on the bank that night. He replied that he would go over for a while but return early to see how things were going. By 10pm nothing had happened and I was beginning to wonder if I should've gone over to the Horse and Barge with the others when, as promised, Pete came back over and the kettle went on. Just then, the right hand rod hammered off and Pete just burst out laughing, but I was a bit more tense, as I could feel the line grating around the pads. It was okay, though, as the fish soon became free but was pulling very hard again.

"Christ they all fight hard in here, don't they?" I said to Pete, "this was just how Small Pecs fought last week!"

Apart from the pads there was nothing else really to worry about where the fish could go, although that didn't make me any less nervous. At one point it did shoot along the margins to my right, where the trees overhung the bank but, by poking the rod tip under the surface, I was able to keep the line clear and gradually pump the fish back towards me. Pete waited with the net and, as the fish came up to the surface, he scooped it up first time.

"Bloody hell, no wonder it fought like Small Pecs – it is Small Pecs!" I said. That was the last fish I was expecting to catch after only banking it the week before from the same swim on the same bait! But sure enough that's what it was and it was even a bit heavier this time around, at 35lb.

"He's been eating a few of those baits, hasn't he?" said Pete. It obviously liked them, that was for sure. Soon afterwards, the other lads started to wander back and we relayed the story to them and they agreed to meet up in the morning for the pictures. Richie was convinced that it was all down to his baiting up with the throwing stick, but I had to remind him that I'd actually moved swims since he had done that!

Quiet descended on the swim and I cast the rod back in the general direction of where it had been earlier. With that done it was time for a few hours sleep. An hour or two later I sat bolt upright and looked at the rods. Nothing had moved and Joan said

"What's the matter?"

"I don't know" and with that the other rod in open water just ripped off! Even though I was already awake, I still managed to burst through the mesh door of my tent – I'm still like

Besides the mirrors there were plenty of good commons in Harefield too.

an over-excited little kid every time I get a run! There was no need to rush with the fish in open water, but I felt a lot happier with the rod in my hand. This fish fought quite hard too, but nothing like the scrap that I'd had with Small Pecs earlier and I wasn't at all surprised when it was a smaller, but very nice looking mirror of 25lb.

Everyone came down in the morning for the pictures and while the cameras clicked, Richie kindly helped out with the fish. I wouldn't exactly recommend brace shots with carp, especially big carp, as you can only control one fish at a time, really. But with plenty of people on hand to help out, I knew everything would be fine and a few minutes later both fish were swimming back off into the depths. That was, of course, just the start of my Harefield fishing and there would be many more happy times to come and many more fish to be banked, but few of them could match up to the memories of those few weekends when I got my Colne Valley campaign off to a flying start!

The Colne Valley

Summerleaze – The Forgotten Lake

Around the time when I first joined Harefield I bumped into a guy called Mat down at Farlows. He was a nice enough bloke and was often around, although I never saw him fishing any of the local waters. It turned out that he was fishing a lake a little bit further away at Maidenhead, and although the lake was very difficult, he had caught a few of the fish in there, including one that was over 40lb! He came down with the photo's of the fish and they were real beauties, some were very scaly and long and they all looked like the proper authentic Leney strain, which they were rumoured to be anyway. He had some really interesting stories about the place. One that really got my attention was when he was walking around the lake one morning. He was all alone, as usual, and on his way round he spotted a couple of fish moving under one of the overhanging trees. He climbed the tree and, as he watched, he saw a couple of the fish that he recognised come in and feed. One was the forty that he had already caught, but what happened next was a total shock as, from out of the depths, came this huge sandy-coloured fish that dwarfed everything else that he had seen in the lake! It shocked him so much that he actually fell out of the tree. He estimated the fish to be at least 50lb. Looking back now, it was just amazing that there weren't more people fishing there.

"Why don't you have a go up there?" I remember him saying, but with the prospect of fishing Harefield, I couldn't really think about anywhere else at the time and I sort of forgot all about the place, in fact it seemed like everyone did. At the time I just wasn't looking for a head banger of a lake to fish, when we all had a place to fish together, which was stacked full of good fish anyway.

But time went by and gradually everyone went off to do different things. I had got a bit more involved with the fishing abroad and put the English fishing on the back burner for awhile, and I'd even taken quite an interest in barbel fishing, which was brilliant, but the old urge for a proper bit of carp fishing soon returned, it was just a matter of finding a water which fitted the bill. Then news filtered through that the lake which I'd talked about, those few years earlier, was going to be forming a syndicate for twenty anglers and there was a place going if I was interested. Well, by then that was exactly what I was looking for! The idea of a big, difficult lake that offered a real challenge certainly got me going and I said straight away that I would be more than interested. There was, however, something that really worried us. There were rumours that there had been a fish-kill sometime previously and no one could be really sure if there were, in fact, any fish still in the lake or not. This obviously didn't help matters and it was probably why we hadn't heard anything of the lake for a while, but it didn't put any of us off and we all still fancied having a go at this strange but very interesting water.

Money was paid and tickets were sorted out, and once we got keys for the gates, I was keen to get down there and have a look around. In a way I could see perhaps why this lake hadn't attracted more attention in the past. It was big; estimated to be around sixty acres, although it didn't actually look that big to me, but it was still a working gravel pit and there were two other, smaller pits at the far end, which were joined to the main body of water. Right from the start it was quite clear that no one had fished there, or even been there for some time. There were no pathways leading to the edge of the lake and, all around, the grass was knee-deep. We literally had to flatten the grass and bushes as we went through, just to get to what had been the swims when it had been fished some time before. I could only guess that no one had been there for at least a couple of years, maybe longer!

The far end of the lake which was being worked was out-of-bounds, as lorries were going by all day long, although they didn't seem to go close to where I would have fished if I could have. Most of the bank on the left was also out-of-bounds. Where the workings ended, the boating club was situated and not only couldn't we fish over there, it also seemed to be the case that the lake was very much under the control of the boating people and we would have to fit in, and work around their activities. This didn't leave a great deal of the lake for us to fish. I should imagine we had about one quarter to one third of the bank space available to us. The only saving grace in all of this was the fact that a southerly or south-westerly wind would blow into the fishable areas, which made things feel a little better. So what about the fish? Well, of course we didn't know if there were any in there still but, going on what we knew from before, there appeared to be about seventeen original carp. That was all that was left from a stocking from several years earlier. Even if they had all survived, seventeen fish in sixty acres of water was going to be tough, especially with what

We only had access to one third of the bank and we always had to make way for the boats.

little water we could fish. It was quite possible that the fish wouldn't even enter the parts of the lake we could fish. A tough challenge – you bet!

A few of the guys in the syndicate were part of the Carp Company team, or were at least using their stuff. Carp Company were actually a Belgian company originally and their baits were being distributed in England by Bob Newman and Chris McKendry, before Bob took over on his own. They had a really great fishmeal mix back then, one that was really fine and full of good ingredients (this was the forerunner to the mixes that they sell today) and we all felt very confident that this was as good as any bait that we could use that year.

Summerleaze Fishmeal bait

1kg Carp Company fishmeal
10ml Premier Baits Salmon Oil
3ml Salmon flavour
1ml Solar Squid and Octopus flavour

I think it was around March when we first started on there. I felt that it was a little early perhaps, but often lakes do 'wake up' around that time. Harefield, for instance, was one water that didn't really fish in the winter but March always produced a few fish, so it had to be worth a go. In any case, we could use three rods so I decided to have one rod out for pike, which I suppose was a bit of a 'cop out' but there might not be a carp in there, so I might as well try to catch something. I think what surprised me was how clear the lake bed was everywhere. I had heard that it got ever so weedy, to the point where the sailing club were unable to use the lake at times. But there was no evidence of weed at all and most of it seemed to be fairly shallow and clear, so it was easy enough to see the bottom. We weren't really supposed to use boats, as the boat club had to pay to use theirs, and by all accounts they wouldn't be too happy if we were seen rowing around having not paid anything to do so. But an agreement was reached through the syndicate leader that we could use boats in moderation, so long as they were out of the water and were out of sight when the boating club were using the lake. That sounded sensible enough and with only twenty of us fishing the lake there shouldn't be any need for rules, as we should be able to sort everything out sensibly amongst ourselves (how naive I was!)

I was glad that I took the pike rod along as that relieved the boredom during those early sessions. The lake was barren and windswept enough anyway, but none of us saw or heard anything – apart from when one of my dead baits was picked up every now and then. The Summerleaze pike were quite sorry looking things really; long and skinny and always looking in need of a good meal. There was obviously not much in there for them to eat and I almost felt guilty catching them as I'm sure they thought it was like Christmas Day when they came across a nice, juicy sardine. But it was something to pass a few hours away.

The first glimmer of hope came a few weeks later. It was starting to warm up a little and the winds that were blowing down the lake into our bank at last had a slightly warmer feel to them. I remember thinking that if there were any carp in the lake then surely they would be on the move by now, but the only things that were on the move were the hundreds of birds that were always a bit of a pain. There were lots of swans, for some reason, but it was the tufties and coots which caused the most grief. In the shallow water our baits were easy pickings for them and it was a constant battle to keep them away. Early one morning I was awoken by a drop-back and looked out to see which bird it was, only there wasn't a bird out there and on the end was a fish! Not a carp mind you, but a tench of about 6lb. That alone got us all excited as it was the first run on a boilie, and it gave us hope!

After all the doubts about the lake it was great to put the first one on the bank.

Gradually, a few more tench started to show up and everyone was looking for the first carp. Some of it was getting a little silly as no one wanted to miss out and one or two people were so keen that if they rang my house and didn't get an answer, they would immediately load the gear in the car and drive straight to the lake in case they missed something. I didn't like that side of it as I just wanted to relax and enjoy the fishing, but we all knew that if something was going to happen, then it would probably happen quite soon.............then it did happen!

I got an excited call from one of the guys late one evening. "I've had one – a 22lb mirror – lovely old-looking fish and I've heard other fish jumping!"

That was what we had all been waiting for – the news that carp were still in the lake. I hadn't been fishing there for nothing after all. Now all I hoped was that all of the carp were still there, including the forty – and maybe even the elusive 'Sandy Fish', which I have to say was more than a bit of a mystery. I didn't doubt that Mat had told us the exact truth but I suppose the story of an uncaught carp weighing over 50lb was almost too good to be true. It was the stuff of dreams for sure.

A few days later I was back with Pete Jones. As we arrived through the gates I could see someone set up on the First Point. It was Richard, the syndicate leader, with his friend Dave. We stopped off for a chat and they were quite excited and said that they had seen fish, and even while we spoke I could see fish for myself. Forty or fifty yards out I could see the odd dark shapes cruising about, definitely carp but they weren't close enough to see just how big they were. We didn't want to crowd the areas out too much, so Pete and I went around to the car park corner. That was probably a bit of a mistake, as over the next couple of days, all I caught was three more tench and a few pike, which were now munching the boilies too. Looking back, we should have just gone in the next available swim to Richard, but at least things were looking good and although there had still only been the one carp out, surely it wouldn't be long before others would follow?

Once they started appearing the fish weren't too hard to spot.

So far I had done sixteen nights on the lake, with three nights being the most in one go. But now it seemed so obvious that something was on the cards that I just had to get down there for a longer session. I planned to do the next fourteen nights in the Second Point swim. By then, everyone had more or less settled for their own swim – at least the people who were fishing regularly. I arrived to find Chemo in his usual First Point, and Second Point was still free. By now the weed was starting to grow and although it was probably only around ten or twelve inches off the bottom at the time, it seemed to be coming up at a rate of knots. Being such a shallow lake, the weed had all been wiped out during the cold winter, but it was now coming back with a vengeance. It took awhile to find some decent clear spots with the marker float, but out in front was a fairly clear channel that was just slightly deeper than the surrounding area and the weed had yet to take hold there. More to my right I found a lovely clear, gravelly spot which looked really good. I also planned to fish one rod just in the margins to my left, which covered a nice little corner, where I was sure that some fish would pass around. But there was a bit of a spanner thrown in the works. Just a few yards to my right was another old swim, which hadn't been fished by anyone up to that point, although I had done one night in there but preferred the swim I was now in. Two other members, Gaylord and the Fossil had always fished at the far end of the syndicate bank up until then, but the Fossil had gone away on holiday and Gaylord had decided, for a change, to fish in the swim just to the right of me. I have to admit to feeling a bit disappointed to see him going in there, it cut the room down considerably and I now felt that I was 'piggy in the middle'. But I have to say that Gaylord was a great guy and there was no reason not for him to go next door, other than on such a big lake it was nice to have more space. It meant me moving my right-hand rod from the clear spot that I'd found, which was to have quite an effect on my results over the next few days.

The big fully-scaled mirror was just an outstanding fish.

The first couple of days passed by quietly, but then around the third evening a big southerly wind blew up as a new front moved in. Dark clouds whizzed by overhead and drizzle began to fall. It looked good......really good and in the early hours I wasn't surprised to be woken up by Chemo who had just landed a cracking fully-scaled mirror of 37lb. It was an awesome fish, there's no other way to describe it. The lake was coming to life before our eyes and it was all looking so different to the weeks leading up to that point. Pete was set up around the corner on the edge of what was the open field area. He couldn't stay too long but before he left, the following morning, he said that he had seen some fish jumping out in front of him at first light. As the bank he was on was at right angles to my bank, the fish that were out in front of Pete, would actually be out somewhere in front of us too.

Pete must have only got a few miles down the road when I heard one of Gaylord's alarms go off and he was already out in the lake in his waders by the time I got there. By the bend in the rod, and the slow, plodding movements, I could tell it was a good fish. A short time later it was in the net and the cheer went up. It was the forty that I'd seen in the pictures from a few years back, only it looked even bigger and better to see it in the flesh. We wondered just when that fish had last been on the bank. We settled on a weight of 43lb 8oz I think, although I can't remember the exact weight now, but it was the biggest fish that had ever been banked from Summerleaze, and there was only one fish that was thought to be possibly bigger, if it was still there, so it was good reason to celebrate.

I heard Colin 'Gaylord' Nash's alarm go off next door.   *The Summerleaze forty looked very impressive.*

Later that same day the same alarm sounded and Gaylord was in again! It was like a repeat performance of the first battle and indeed it was another big fish, this time going just over 39lb. It was a much lighter fish than the other one, but just as lovely, with scattered scaling along its flanks. It was all happening and there I was stuck in the middle wondering if I was going to miss out on such a great chance?

News was spreading fast about what was happening down at the 'forgotten lake' and Chris Ball stopped by to pay a visit. Of course he was always interested in the old English carp, especially the old Leney strain, so he was his usual enthusiastic self, and he kept us entertained, as only he can, with various stories from the past as we sat there listening, cups of tea in hand.

I walked around to the gate to let Chris out and his parting words were, "Don't worry, I know you're going to get one soon!" I could only hope that Chris was right because, after seeing those other fish, if I didn't get one now, I think I would have been pulling my hair out.

I went back to my swim and got in the bag, thinking all the time of what might be swimming around out there. At around midnight I was awoken by a screaming run – and at last it was one of mine! It was the margin rod on the left and it was belting out. I picked up the rod and just attempted to slow the fish down. It took several yards of line before I could turn it and, as is often the case with un-pressured fish, after that initial run it was almost a case of leading it slowly back to the bank. Gaylord had heard it and was waiting with the net by now and scooped it up first time.

And there before my eyes was the legendary 'Sandy Fish'.

"Well done" he said. I felt more relieved than anything else, but very, very happy. My first Summerleaze carp was on the bank! It clearly wasn't as big as the others I'd seen, but it was another fantastic looking mirror of 27lb 10oz.

The following day arrived and the weather had changed from cloud and rain to bright sunshine. I didn't know how that would affect the fish, but what it did was to make them a lot easier to see. All of a sudden they all came up to bask in the sun in what was referred to as 'no carp bay' (always the way isn't it?), and for the first time we were able to get a good look at most of the stock. Amongst them were the forty and the fully-scaled fish that I'd seen caught just days earlier, and then, right before our eyes it appeared – the Sandy Fish!!! No rumours, no hearsay, this was real! It was every bit as big as Mat had estimated some years before, although that was the only previous sighting of this fish - how incredible. It certainly was around 50lb, maybe a fair bit more. The other big fish were there for us to judge it by and it was considerably bigger than any of them. It actually stayed there for a couple of hours and I was able to go back and get my camera and take some pics and although it's never easy to judge from distant pictures, when you know which other fish were around it, you can tell the size of it.

Needless to say that got us all 'buzzing' and I went to bed every night just dreaming of that fish. The action slowed down a little, but a couple of days later I was in again. It was the same margin rod again and although I was hoping to see something big and sandy-coloured, it turned out to be a mirror of 22lb 12oz, which was the same fish which had been landed first, a month or so before. So it wasn't quite the start I was hoping for, but at least I was off the mark.

The place hadn't been fished for years, but they still took some catching!

As the following weeks went by, we kept seeing the fish, but it was getting tougher. The weed was now starting to get really thick and the fishable spots were dwindling almost by the day. I did fish one more longish session to make the most of it before it became unfishable. I fished for a couple of days back on the second point and caught another mirror of 20lb 8oz on a close in spot. Even then it was a struggle to get it in through the weed, but it was another fish to the tally.

I moved for the remainder of the session up to the far end of the bank as I was starting to see more fish there, but it only resulted in me catching two chub. Some of the Summerleaze chub were massive, the two I landed weighed 6lb and 6lb 6oz and were actually the smallest of the few that ever got caught there. I saw one at the far end one day that had to be around 10lb, which I thought was a small common to start with, but it was definitely a chub.

The weed was growing fast but there were still a few clear spots.

It got to the point where the weed was so thick that it was virtually impossible to fish. The others came out with the statement that they were all going off to fish Silvermere or somewhere, which left me with a dilemma. I only had Summerleaze or one other water to fish and at the time, I wasn't too keen on having a go there either, but it was that or nothing. Over the next couple of months I fished a bit here and there but without any real conviction. Summerleaze was still very much on my mind and towards the start of September I thought I would pay a visit just to see how it was looking. When I returned it looked like no one else had been there since I had last been down and the sight that greeted me in the Second Point came as quite a surprise. There was still a lot of weed about, but a lot of it had uprooted and was drifting about in huge clumps, but most importantly, there was a clear channel running right through the swim at around 60 yards range. As I stood there and watched I clearly saw a fish cruise down the channel from right to left before disappearing out of sight. It was all I needed to see, and plans were made to get back the following weekend.

On the Wednesday evening I went down and put some bait out in the channel and I also took my rods with me, so that I could cast them into the channel and clip the lines onto the spools at the right distance. The reason for that was because I knew that when I got back to the lake to set up, it would be dark and I wanted to just cast the hook baits into the channel with the minimum of fuss so as not to disturb the fish, which had definitely become more wary of leads and lines. Just clearing the weed that had collected in the margins was a mammoth job, but it was worth it as I now had a fishable swim.

The careful approach paid off when I returned to land this lovely mirror.

I returned, and three baits were cast into the channel. That old feeling came back to me once again and I remembered those big fish that I had seen in the bay earlier in the year, they would still be out there somewhere and hopefully a little more off-guard again by now. By morning I'd already had three pick-ups, all from tench, which seemed to be more active than ever, although I think that they were just using the channel for getting around. But the following morning I awoke to a one-toner that could only be from a carp. After a tense battle I was looking down at one of the prettiest carp I've ever seen; a near, fully-scaled mirror of 21lb 4oz. Not a monster but a capture that pleased me immensely as the plan had worked!

I packed up a happy man and planned to do the same thing the following week. Again I went down on the Wednesday and baited up in readiness, I had even left my bivvy up as it was clear no one else was going there. Friday came and I was off down there like a shot. No tench this time but another one-toner on the Saturday morning that resulted in the friendly mirror for me again, this time at 21lb 6oz. I was loving every minute of it and felt sure that a big fish would be on the cards before too long. But, just after putting the fish back, I saw a little van come through the gate. It was a couple of the other members and I got the impression that they weren't very happy that I was there fishing without them knowing, for some strange reason, and it was even worse when they spotted the wet mat. With the fish I'd just caught it now meant that I'd caught five and that was more than any of the other members, and even though I would have swapped them all for one of the big fish, it seemed to go down like a lead balloon with them. I knew that it was going to change from then on. I returned the following week and got back in the same swim, but word had been spread, and all of the swims either side of me became filled in no time. Two other anglers even arrived and asked me when I was leaving as they wanted to get in the swim. On a lake like Summerleaze it was just going to be the kiss of death, of that I was sure.

"When are you due back down?" One of them asked. "Well, I don't think it's going to be for the rest of this year now," I replied.

I knew that it was over for the moment, and really that was the end of the good times on Summerleaze. There were rumblings of discontent in the syndicate, which only got worse the next year. But the memories of that first year had been logged away and nothing could change that. It was an incredibly exciting time to fish this forgotten lake and to catch some of its jewels. Those last couple of weekends, when I was alone on the lake with Joan, were

Top rod for the year but I knew the fun was over.

some of my fondest memories of fishing there altogether, and I still reminisce about it sometimes. But perhaps the most vivid memory of all was seeing that great big Sandy Fish, sitting there as plain as day. It had never been banked and as far as I know it never has been to this day, but it was there - I saw it with my own eyes!

The Colne Valley

The Linear

For several years I had been a member of a club water in the Colne Valley. For some time it's had a no-publicity rule, so you'll have to forgive me for not giving the name or the exact location of this lake away, but although I had always kept my membership going, for probably six or seven years, I had only fished one session of note, when I caught a common of around 21lb. Apart from that, I had only fished the occasional night here and there without much success. The lake was much smaller than Summerleaze, where I had just stopped fishing, and it certainly held more carp, but it appeared to be every bit as much of a head-banger of a challenge. It was deep and weedy and few people seemed to have any real success, in fact three or four fish in a year seemed to be thought of as quite a result. So why on earth should I be interested in somewhere like that now? Well, for a start, it was somewhere to have a proper go at. It didn't see much angling pressure, especially during the week, and I was up for another challenge. But really it was some of the fish that made it most appealing. There were a few different strains of carp from various stockings over the years, but it was the originals (as always) which were the most sought-after. In particular there was one fantastic-looking linear mirror, which also happened to be the biggest fish in the lake. It had been caught every now and then at weights reaching high-thirties and it just looked magnificent. I clearly remember thinking to myself that I would love that fish to be my English personal best any day of the week! So, the only way I was going to catch that fish, or any of the others, was to get myself down there and fish for them, and now was as good a time as any, considering that I had few other options anyway.

The start of the season arrived and I picked what I thought was a decent swim down in one of the corners, in fact the swim where I had caught the common from a year or two earlier. But it wasn't a great choice and nothing happened of any note – at least not for me, but of the few fish that did get caught, The Linear was banked from the opposite side of the lake at 38lb 10oz! I went around and helped with the weighing. It was the first time I'd seen the fish in real life and I could just see it was full of character and history and I dearly wanted to hold it for myself.

After the opening week, most of the anglers went back to their everyday lives and apart from the weekends, it started to get fairly quiet. That didn't really change things much. The carp were as elusive as ever and just seeing one jump or roll was an event in itself. But I've

Runs were few and far between but this one took a liking to the bait.

always enjoyed peaceful fishing and that's just what it was and the lack of action was only a minor annoyance. One night I fished over on the field bank for a change. I remember that it was bitterly cold, with an east wind blowing, but thankfully it was blowing from behind and I had some cover from it. As with all lakes that are similar to this one, there was a fair bit of weed starting to come up all over the place, but with the marker rod I did find one nice, clear channel in the weed at around fifty yards range. I was still on the same Carp Company fishmeal bait that I had used at Summerleaze and although it was hardly the weather for it, I stuck about 300 baits out into the clear channel. Over the top of the baits, I carefully cast two white pop ups flavoured with Salmon and Squid and Octopus. I wasn't that hopeful, but around 6am a single bleep was followed by an absolute screamer and I soon landed one of the later stock fish of high doubles. It was a nice enough fish and I was pleased to at least get off the mark.

I moved around to the corner and fished the margins.

Chances over the next few weeks were very few and far between – in fact there were none! It really was quite a tough water to get to grips with. I did try concentrating on one swim and kept the bait going in consistently. Several kilos of hemp and boilies went in, but the only result was a few bream. Then one day, out of the blue, some fish started jumping further out to my left. One after the other came out of the water, but all within a twenty metre square area. I had seen that happen before on other lakes in the past and had caught fish by casting in amongst them. So I quickly reeled in one of my pop ups and launched it into the middle of where the fish were showing. It was only there for a few minutes before I saw the line tighten up – and I was into another fish. Again it wasn't big, a common of 19lb, but it was another fish, a chance capture rather than something I'd worked up to, but beggars can't be choosers, as they say.

It was all quiet again for a few weeks after that and, approaching the middle of July, I was back in the swim where I had caught the mirror from earlier, but with nothing happening, as usual. It was a nice enough day for a bit of fish spotting, so I reeled in and went for a wander. I looked hard and saw nothing for awhile, until I came to one corner that is, then I saw three or four fish, all cruising close into the edge. That was all I needed to see and I was soon packing down all of my gear to move around into the corner swim.

The fish were still there by the time I got everything sorted, but it was a matter of how to fish for them? In the clear water I could see that it was virtually wall to wall weed, the only spot that was clear was a marginal spot along to my right which didn't look all that promising as it was well away from where I'd seen the fish moving. There simply wasn't another clear spot to be had, so I had no choice other than to somehow present a bait in the weed. Over to my left, the weed did seem to be a little thinner up the marginal slope, so I flicked a bait across to about four feet from the edge and went around to have a look. It took a little while to spot but, sure enough, I could see the snowman bait just resting on the weed, and the rest of the rig seemed to be quite well hidden. I broke up a few boilies and scattered them around the hook bait, some of which sank out of sight, but a few of the others did come to rest on the weed where they looked quite enticing.

The hook bait was just between the weed bed and the pads.

But, however good it all looked, by the following morning nothing had happened. I peered over the edge of the swim and was quite shocked to see a big fish sitting down in the depths. I didn't know this fish at all but it looked big, and as it wandered off I reeled in the right-hand rod and replaced the hook bait with a zig-rigged pop up that sat just above the weed, in the hope that the fish would return – but it didn't.

As the sun rose higher it got warmer and flatter and by midday I was thinking that any chance was gone for the day. But then I noticed a dorsal fin just break the surface – and then another one not far away. "I wonder if they'll have a floater?" I remember thinking to myself. It was quite rare for these fish to take surface baits, but it had been known in the past and I quickly dug my little bag of mixers out from the bottom of my rucksack and fired some out in the general direction, then sat back to watch and wait. Shlurp! One mixer disappeared, and then another. Soon there were about five or six mouths going along the top, munching mixers with abandon. This was my chance, and I reeled in the zig-rig rod and started to try to assemble a floater rig. With hands shaking, it was almost impossible and I kept glancing up to see if they were still there, which they were.

The needle settled at 40lb 6oz.

Just then, my other rod, which was still out, burst into life! It seems strange now, but I remember thinking at the time that I didn't want this fish to disturb the ones that were taking the mixers and I thought it would only be one of the stock fish again, anyway. The fish shot out of the shallows and away from me. It must have taken around forty yards of line before it came to a grinding halt in a thick weed bed. I looked up and the other fish were still having the floaters, which I was still concerned about, but now I also had a fish bogged down in the weed. I leant into the fish as much as I dared and, ever so gradually, the whole lot began to inch towards me. As I got everything moving, some of the weed was falling away until, suddenly, the fish was free again and it did no more than kite across to the right where it just got stuck again. I repeated the procedure and once again it worked and everything began to move towards me. This time, with weed still around it, the fish seemed a little confused and just seemed to wallow under the surface. Yard by yard I eased the whole lot back to me until it was almost within netting range then, as I began to draw the fish over the net, some of the weed parted and I just saw this row of big scales. My jaw must have almost hit the floor as I immediately recognised exactly which fish it was – it was the Linear! "Yeeesssss!" The shout went up, although there was no one there to hear me.

I scrambled back up the bank with the fish and admired its beauty in the sunlight. It looked big to me but there was only one way to find out – into the sling it went and I hoisted the fish up and my jaw dropped again as the needle went past 40lb! Now I had a problem, I was alone on the lake and Joan was visiting relatives up in Newcastle. I not only needed someone to

It was without a doubt one of the best-looking forties in the country.

take some pictures, but I also wanted someone to witness the weight, as I knew that no one would believe me when I told them the weight. I thought about who I could call. I knew my good friend Paul was at work, but it was worth a try. Paul was in the middle of plastering a ceiling with Johnno, but bless 'em, they both dropped what they were doing and raced down to the lake straight away. Actually, by the time they arrived a couple of other friends had also been able to make it down. I constructed a makeshift tripod from some extra long bank sticks and for the first time we were able to weigh the fish properly. We all agreed on 40lb 6oz.

It was the perfect result!

It was a moment I'll never forget. To target a certain fish is never easy, but when you finally hold that fish in your arms, the feeling is very special. We all have aims and dreams and most of us want our first twenty, thirty or forty to be something a bit special. I don't believe at the time that there was a better fish in the country to catch as my first English forty. It was a stunning carp with history and undoubtedly one of the best-looking fish I've ever seen. It was the first time over forty for it too, and it got captured over that weight a few more times in subsequent seasons. Sadly, the fish is long gone now, but the memories burn brightly – what a fish it was.

The Colne Valley

Warty's Downfall

Ever since I moved up to the Colne Valley, at the start of the 1990's, I've had quite a strong affinity with the Boyer Leisure waters. It started, really, with Farlows in what was then the old close season. I had some brilliant times down there in a period when the rods would normally have been hung up for three months. Good company was never hard to come by, as the restaurant and bar were the general meeting place for most of the carp anglers in the area and it used to get very busy. When it wasn't busy, Rob Maylin was always there anyway, along with a few of the others such as Steve Newman, Ginger Steve and so on, and we would have pinball competitions in between fishing. It was all great fun and we caught loads of fish along the way, mostly doubles with a few twenties thrown in. There was one thirty in there at the time, known as the Pet, this was one of the fish taken from Rodney Meadow when that lake was drained down and the fish removed. I was lucky enough to catch the Pet from the front swim on Herons Point, at around 32lb. I say 'lucky' as, although the Pet did see its fair share of unhooking mats through the year, it was the only time that it ever got caught from the Herons Point area of Farlows, and as

Farlows biggest – the Pet at 31lb 8oz.

that was the only part of the lake we fished, it was a bit of a result at the time. I remember it being one of fourteen fish that I'd caught that weekend, on microwaved pop ups. They opened up a whole new world of possibilities and I went from catching one or two fish a weekend on single bottom baits to catching upwards of ten a weekend with the new little baits, all thanks to Joan, who bought me a microwave cooker as I couldn't afford one before then! I also remember one time in the winter when the lake was freezing up on the Sunday. Everyone was packing up to go home, but I had just packed in my job and had no reason to go anywhere so, rather than reel in, I just placed back leads in front of the rod tips and kept breaking the ice in the margins to keep the line free. Well, to cut a long story short, it was Thursday morning just as I put my breakfast down on the table that I saw one of the rod tips pull down and I was in! I managed to play the fish in through that little hole in the ice and although it wasn't a big fish, about 16lb I think, it was such a pleasing capture as I was the only one on the whole lake with a bait in the water and it was on the fifth day after casting out that the fish had picked up the bait. I had earned that one – although we weren't exactly 'roughing it' down at Farlows.

Playing a Farlows carp through a hole in the ice - the bait had been out for five days!

Pop Up Mix (one egg mix)
Carp Company Milk Mix *(no longer available)*
2ml of flavour: Solar Esterblend 12 or Richworth Blue Cheese or SBS Fruistraw or Richworth Tangerine
½ ml intense sweetener
Microwave on full power for 4 minutes, leave to cool then place in plastic bag and add 1½ ml of chosen flavour and ½ ml of intense sweetener.

Over time, I got to know a little more about some of the other lakes that Boyer Leisure had control of. Among them were Rodney Meadow, which had been restocked, Stockley which had a fair bit of history to it, and Colnbrook West. The last of those three I found particularly interesting as, although the lake was only around four acres in size, it did hold a fish that was known to come out at around 40lb. A 40lb carp in four acres of water seemed to be a good target to have a go at, although it's fair to say that, to begin with, the lake did hold a lot of carp during the first year or so that I fished there. I say 'to begin with' because later on the lakes flooded and many of the fish ended up escaping down the river. Most of the Colnbrook West fish were commons of around mid-doubles to low twenties with the occasional bigger fish approaching 30lb. There was also one other decent mirror in there known as 'Half Tail', which generally came out at around 30lb, but Warty was definitely the star of the lake.

To start with, I didn't fish Colnbrook West with any real conviction, it was a bit of fun in between the other fishing, with the chance of a good 'un. The fish were easy enough to come by and the first evening session with a floater rod produced four fish to high doubles, and after that a couple of over-night sessions brought me a few more in the same sort of weight bracket. It seemed I could catch fish any time down there and I have to say that I was enjoying it, they weren't big fish but that didn't bother me as there was always the chance that Warty would turn up in amongst them. However, Warty didn't turn up and after catching a lot of other fish it started to get under my skin a bit and I started to take it a little more seriously. One of my main

Colnbrook West was good fun and there were always a few carp to be caught.

problems was that I was fishing mainly at weekends, when it was very busy, and I was having to fish in the swims that were left and they were normally tucked away in the corners, out of the way. So I started to find myself a little more time during the week and, even if they were just quick overnight jaunts, at least the lake was quieter and I could get into some of the better swims. There are about twelve swims on the lake and, really, four or five of those give you good access to the main middle areas. Among those was the Plateau swim, which I had yet to fish, and don't ask me why but with a couple of days to play with I still found myself in one of the corner swims with the Plateau free. I still caught fish, as ever, two or three up to low twenties during the first night, but made the decision that I would be much better off with the central plateau swim as so much more water could be covered with the lake fairly quiet.

Evening in the Plateau swim.

I was still on the microwaved pop ups - Scopex and Esterfruit flavour - at that time and fishing those over various amounts of the MC Mix. One bait was placed just on the far edge of the plateau where it was only shallow, dropping off from about eighteen inches down to three or four feet. The other rod was used more as a roving rod, cast to any showing fish, of which there were normally plenty to have a go at. In fact, that was one of the great things about this lovely little lake, the fish would show themselves constantly and it always kept you interested.

I was always catching carp without getting amongst the big ones.

By the following morning I'd had a couple more fish and, as the sun climbed above the trees, I noticed a dorsal fin break the calm surface on the far side of the lake. Joan had joined me by then and I pointed out the fish to her as it was the first one of the day to break the surface. I sat there with a cup of tea and just watched as the fish swam a bit to the right and then back to the left, all the time with an inch or so of its back out of the water. Eventually, it started to edge its way slowly across the lake, still ambling from right to left and back again, until eventually it was not far away from the plateau. Closer and closer it came, until it was right above where my bait was and then for the first time, it disappeared from the surface. I looked at Joan and then looked at the rod as, literally a second or two later, the indicator lifted up as the fish took my little yellow pop up. It took around ten yards of line before becoming weeded. All seemed solid, but a bit of extra pressure got the whole lot moving and slowly but surely I brought it all towards me. Joan scooped everything up in the net and, as I parted the bundles of Canadian weed, there in the bottom was Warty! I was well chuffed, not just because it was the fish I wanted but because of the whole sequence of events. It was down a bit in weight, however, at 36lb 4oz having spawned well at the start of the season – actually, it was well down as it had been captured during the opening week of the season at 44lb 12oz but it was target achieved all the same.

That should have been it, I suppose, but as time passed by I kept hearing of Warty being captured at over 40lb and although I'd already caught it, and I'm not one for re-captures, I did feel for some reason that I wanted to get Warty over that magic mark. For that reason I started having a 'dabble' there again and, once again, I was catching plenty of fish but Warty was being more elusive, as before. It always seemed to get caught just before I arrived

Warty at last! But well down in weight after spawning.

or just after I'd left. I can remember one session vividly when I was in the Plateau swim again, in late autumn. I had the whole lake to myself and was catching well. The fish were getting their heads down on the baits and I'd landed something like fifteen fish up to mid-twenties already in three days, and I was sure that there would be a good chance Warty was not far away. Soon after, Colin Webb turned up for a day session and after a brief chat he went around the bank to my right, into the Bailiffs swim. Colin had caught Warty something like ten times over the years, and I did wonder why he still wanted to fish the lake after so many repeat captures. But each to their own, as they say, and I hardly had time to wonder about that as, a few minutes later, Colin was back in my swim. I thought he'd forgotten something at first but then he said,

He'd only been there a few minutes!

"Have you got any scales? I just cast my first rod out and it went straight away, with Warty on the end!"

I couldn't believe it, that fish certainly liked him. I went around to lend a hand. It certainly looked a fair bit heavier and indeed went 41lb 12oz. It looked lovely at that weight and it just made me want to catch it at over forty even more!

I had the 'odd dabble' on Orlitts Lake next door with some success.

A plan was formed. The season opened every year on May 1st and most years it seemed that Warty would get caught during that opening week. I figured that if there were about fifteen anglers there for the start and I could get a reasonable swim, then that would give me perhaps the best chance of catching Warty at the right weight that year. After all, if it was going to get caught I had at least a one in fifteen chance, which were probably better odds than the rest of the year when I seemed to miss the right times anyway.

The draw for the start arrived and there were plenty of people there hoping for a decent swim. I didn't let on too much, but I was hoping to get the Bailiffs swim where I'd photographed Colin Webb the previous autumn, but I figured that it would go fairly quick. Actually, Colin was there for the draw so I feared the worst once again. I knew some of the people there, my good friend and neighbour, Den for one and of course bailiffs Lal and Brian, good people. In fact that was one of the things I always liked about Colnbrook West, there was always a good, friendly atmosphere on there – apart from when one dickhead called 'Gums' was about, but that's another story.

The first tickets came out of the hat and mine wasn't amongst them. the First Point went and then the Plateau swim and the A4 Point and it was looking grim, and then a sigh of relief as my ticket came out and, thankfully, the Bailiffs swim was still vacant. I had plenty of 18mm MC Mix with me and the plan was to establish an area of bait somewhere near to the middle of the lake and hope that, over the coming days Warty would at some stage end up having a feed there. As ever, the hook baits would be my trusty microwaved pop ups. I had made a fresh batch for the start, this time flavoured with Esterfruit along with Amino Blend Swan Mussel, a weird combination but it just seemed to smell right when they were mixed together. This time I coloured the baits white, which was something I'd had a fair bit of success with over the years. I felt happier with pop ups for two reasons, one of course because I'd had so much success with them on other waters and on Colnbrook West before, but also because there was always a fair bit of weed present in the lake. It is a bit of a strange lake in that the margins are the deepest areas in most of the swims and the shallower spots are generally more towards the middle. Much of the deeper water could be a bit black and stinky, although the fish would still feed there at times. But the nicer spots, further out, always had a covering of long, stringy silk weed. Any attempt to pull back would just cover the hook bait in the stuff, so it was normally a case of just feeling for a decent drop and leaving it there. Odd bits were slightly clearer than others and I found one little channel which I could line up with the corner of a building on the far bank.

It was a bit chilly at the start, with overcast conditions and drizzle falling every now and then, but with the slight breeze coming into me it looked good and indeed a few fish showed in front of me with some of them quite close in. I put one rod on the baited area in the middle but the other one dropped shorter where some fish had shown. Even though it was a bit choddy, it was the close in rod that went off first, only an hour or so after casting, and after a short tussle I had a 21lb common in the net to get the season underway.

There wasn't too much else happening around the lake but the fish seemed to be fairly willing to have a feed and through the first day I managed another two or three fish up to 25lb. It was nice to get the action but I'd had action virtually every time I had fished there and this time I only had one fish on my mind. Of course it was impossible, or almost impossible, to single out that one fish amongst all the others, so at least by catching fish I knew that I was doing things right. A couple of days passed and the weather improved a bit and the fish kept feeding, then I noticed the guy across on the A4 Point landing a fish one afternoon. The bloke in the swim next door went to have a look and shouted across to me that it was Warty. My heart sank. I can accept it pretty well, normally, when someone else catches the fish that I'm after, but this time I really felt that I was going to be the one to get it after things had started well. I was still busy sulking, like you do, when news filtered through that the guy was mistaken and it wasn't Warty that the bloke had caught but in fact Half Tail. I would've thought that the difference was obvious enough, but that didn't matter as my spirits were once again lifted and the plan was back on track.

For the first few days the fish had come from all different areas. I was casting to showing

The plan worked! Well almost as Warty still didn't weigh over forty.

fish and I was picking them up fairly consistently. But the baited area hadn't really kicked in until the fourth day and then, all of a sudden, for some reason the fish seemed to home in on the bait and get their heads down. I must have caught five or six fish during the day, again not big but it was all starting to happen how I had hoped it would. Then, at around 5pm the rod on the baited area was away again and as I picked the rod up I knew straight away that this was different to the other fish. It held itself out in the lake, just kiting from left to right and back again but not giving up any line. I had my thoughts but dared not say anything just in case I was wrong. Gradually I began to gain some line but it was not like playing any of the other fish I'd caught that week and, eventually, when it came within viewing range, I could see that it was definitely Warty. That made the old heart miss a beat, and the fish just plodded up and down in front of me for some time. I stayed as patient as I could and just waited for the fish to tire and, slowly but surely, I edged it up to the waiting net and Warty was mine! I dropped the rod and raised both arms to let everyone know which fish it was, although most of them had already guessed. It looked big, every bit as big as when Colin Webb had caught it the year before, and we all guessed at 42lb or 43lb. So I was a little shocked when the scales read 38lb! I re-zeroed everything but sure enough 38lb was the weight. I have to say that I was a little disappointed at the weight. I was, of course, over the moon to have caught the fish and the plan had worked perfectly but really, the reason for targeting the fish again was to try and get it at over forty.

It was the end of an era for Colnbrook West.

Some things are just not meant to happen; believe it or not Warty was captured about another eight or nine times that season and every time it was caught at over 40lb, even just a couple of weeks after I caught it. That's life and I still have very fond memories of the fish. I gave up with Colnbrook West after that as I'd done almost all I could do and I wasn't going to keep trying for the fish until it was 40lb, as there were plenty of other fish to go for. As it happens, poor old Warty was found dead some time later and it was the end of an era on that little lake. There are still other good fish in there and more recently I did go back for a couple of nights in the Bailiffs swim. First night I had two smaller mirrors, but the second night I ended up with a cracking common of 35lb 4oz, which was an English PB at the time. How strange that, after all the commons that I caught during my time there, I caught the biggest one when going back on the off chance. It was a nice moment for sure but the lake just didn't seem the same without Warty in there, so I packed up the gear for the last time and said my farewells to that great little water.

I returned sometime later to land my best Colnbrook West common.

The Colne Valley

Clusters Last Stand

I don't know how many nights I had fished in total on Colnbrook West, I never kept count, but it's probably fair to say that it was quite a few in the end. It wasn't that I was just in pursuit of the one fish – although that was of course a large part of it. But I just enjoyed my time on there, and there were a great bunch of anglers fishing the lake. Sometimes it is ever so easy to just keep fishing a lake because we enjoy it so much and after all, the very reason we go fishing is to enjoy what we do and if that enjoyment is not there, then why go at all? However, during my regular conversations with Simon Crow he often said to me, "Why are you still fishing that same lake when you've caught the fish anyway, and there are so many other good fish in the area to go for?"

I suppose, looking in from the outside it was easier to come to that conclusion and I have to say that sometimes it does take someone else to point out something that does make good sense, which you cannot really see yourself.

"You should get yourself down to Wraysbury 1 and have a go for Mary, it's only down the road from you and it's one of the country's biggest carp!" Crowy would continue.

He had a point, and the more I thought about it the better it sounded and the more excited I got. But – and this was quite a big BUT - Going back several years to the days of fishing Darenth, when Leisure Sport (now Cemex) waters were run by Jack Ashford, I had received a rather un-deserved (in my opinion) ban from their waters. I'm no angel, but I felt like I had really been stitched up at the time and no matter who I called to discuss the matter, none of them could actually say what I'd done to get this ban, only that I was banned and it wasn't open to discussion. Years later I did actually get to find out what it was all about and who was behind it, but let's just say that's another story and it only backed up my original thoughts. The problem was that I had just gone off and fished other waters and forgotten about Leisure Sport totally, and if I wanted to fish Wraysbury I would first have to get the okay to have a permit once again.

In the intervening years, Jack Ashford had retired and the post had been taken over by Ian Welch and first job would be to contact him to see what the score was. I found him to be a really nice guy and, although our paths had never crossed before, he knew enough about me and thought that whatever the circumstances were before, he couldn't see any real reason why I shouldn't be able to have a permit now. That was music to my ears and so the relative forms and bits and pieces were filled in and sent off in double-quick time, it was already mid to late summer and a strange time perhaps to be starting on a new water but it was just how things happened. There were various different permit options for Wraysbury 1; you could have a two rod, three rod or four rod version and the price obviously increased the more you used, but I figured on a water like that I needed to give myself as much chance as possible and went for the four rods. The other thing that had to be obtained was a boat permit, which was optional depending on whether you wanted to fish there with a boat or not. Well, having used a boat for much of my fishing, I couldn't imagine trying to tackle Wraysbury without one, so that was sorted out too.

Wraysbury 1 is around 120 acres in size and it held just twenty 'original' carp, which obviously meant that it was going to be a much harder task than almost anything I'd taken on before. Amongst those carp, though, were some real prizes, such well-known names as Mary's Mate, The Pug, Mallin's, Cluster, Measles, Three Scales and, of course, the magnificent Mary which was the main target for everyone who fished there. But to find those carp in that expanse of water, when I didn't really know anything about the place, was going to be a job-and-a-half at the very least. Crowy had already been down a few times himself and told me what he knew of the place so far, and I have to say it sounded lovely. It was big and wild and open but in the crystal-clear water you could often find places where the fish had fed and cleaned off and, for that matter, you could often see the fish too! They were known to be very mobile fish and that would present obvious location problems. Wraysbury 1 is an interesting water, to say the very least, with islands, bays, narrow channels and large, open expanses. Really it was split into two main areas, the South Lake and the North Lake. These are, in fact, all part of the same lake but the two bodies of water are joined by a fairly narrow channel of water. The South Lake area is probably getting on for twice the size of the North Lake in total area. "Look under the trees, that's where you'll see 'em mostly," was the main advice that came from the people I asked, and so with a little bit of knowledge and a fair bit of anticipation, I just waited for my permit to arrive.

An atmospheric dawn in Dredger Bay.

The day came and the brown envelope dropped through my letter box, but what a day of highs and lows it was about to become. I opened the envelope and sure enough there was my Wrasbury permit – but a short time later the phone rang and I can't even remember who was on the other end now, but I'll never forget the words that I heard next.

"Mary has been found dead!" I couldn't believe it.

I sat down and thought about what I had just heard. After all those years without a Leisure Sport permit, the very day mine arrives, the carp that I really joined for had died. It was a real shame, no carp lasts forever but it's always a bit sad when a fish with so much history passes on. I was in limbo – what was I to do now? The first thing I did was to get in the car and drive down for a look around. I expected the place to be empty after the news of what had just happened, but surprisingly there were a few people fishing. I bumped into Derek Rance, who I hadn't seen for years, in fact it was at Cassien where I had last seen him. He was fishing the North Lake and, of course, the conversation was very much about Mary but, as he pointed out, there were still many great carp in Wraysbury 1 and just because the biggest had gone, it didn't mean that the others shouldn't be fished for. Of course he was right and that changed my view of the whole situation. Why shouldn't I fish there and try for one of those elusive but magnificent Wraysbury carp?

So that was it! It was already early September by then and time was of the essence. I didn't fancy fishing through the winter so much, although it was always an option, but I could at least get down there and build up some experience of the lake for the following year, before it got too late. Rods were all sorted out and I already had a supply of the MC Mix boilies in the freezer, along with a variety of pellets, and my little BIC 252 boat was secured onto the roof rack in readiness for a much shorter journey than it was normally used to! The plan was to base myself in the Sailing Club car park and work from there. It was the central point on the lake and seemed the better option. The other car park, at the end of Douglas Lane, was right at the far end of the South Lake and apart from being a bit more out of the way, Wraysbury had the reputation for cars being broken into now and then, and the Sailing Club looked to be the safer of the two car parks.

I arrived at the gates early the next morning. The lock was still covered in dew which showed that I was the first that day to unlock it. The gates creaked open and I made my way in. I always have mixed feelings the first time on a new water, I was excited, of course, but also felt a little nervous to be setting out on my own onto such a famous water. The plan was that I would just load up the boat with everything I needed and literally just set off and look around until I hopefully found somewhere which looked promising. The weather was good, with clear skies and not much wind, so I had a good few hours ahead of me and I was in no rush to get set up.

No sooner had I launched the boat than Crowy was on the phone. "How you doing? Where are you? Have you seen any yet?"

"Blimey give us a chance, I've just got here – but it looks good!" It wasn't going to be easy.

"Look under the trees," they said, the trouble was that the whole lake was covered in trees, most of the bank was tree-lined and so were all the islands and it would take an eternity to check them all out properly, but I had to start somewhere, I suppose. A few

I scoured the lake all day long and ended up back where I'd started!

people were fishing the North Lake, including Derek Rance who was still there, but the South Lake was empty so that was where I would concentrate my efforts, at least to start with.

I looked long and hard, but I have to say that I didn't really find anything that stood out and screamed 'this is the place to fish'. The water was lovely and clear and it made viewing the bottom quite easy, even in depths approaching fifteen feet. There was a great deal of weed everywhere but there were also clear spots here and there but, to be honest, all of the spots had that look about them that I could have fished them for a month before any carp came across the baits. In fact I did find the occasional spots that had been baited up previously, by other anglers. I remember coming across one spot just along from the Finger Bays which looked really nice, but there were about a dozen furry little boilies that looked like they had laid there untouched for some time. Really, I had seen so much in those first few hours that I was completely lost as to what to do, but I had yet to see any sign of a carp and that was what I wanted to see most of all. If I could find a fish or two somewhere then I would have the confidence to give the nearest swim a go. But after spending most of the day afloat on the water, and stopping off in all of the swims, I found myself back at the point from where I started. That was known as the Main Dredger Bay swim, so called because out in the

middle of the bay was an old sunken dredger from the days when Wraysbury was a working gravel pit. I knew that fish had been caught from this swim in the past and so, with little else to go on, I assembled my gear in Main Dredger Bay with the idea that if nothing happened, and didn't look like happening, I could start the whole process again the next day.

The fishing at Wraysbury could hardly be called peaceful.

Although this was the main area for people arriving and leaving, it was incredibly peaceful..........well I say peaceful, that's probably not exactly right for any water in the Staines/Wraysbury area, as you always have the planes landing and taking off from Heathrow, which is just down the road. But you soon get used to that and I certainly had got used to it over the years. Apart from that it was very pleasant and quiet.

The rods were put out in hope more than anything else. There were two main islands in front of the swim and it was obviously one of the possible passing through areas which the fish could use on their way from the North Lake to the South Lake, and vice-versa, so I felt that if the fish were mobile then it was as good a place as anywhere to start. Although the main channel in between the islands was quite weedy, there were some clear, gravelly areas closer to the bank under the over-hanging branches. Down to my right was an area that perhaps looked the best as it was a cleaner strip coming away from one end of the island, which just looked more 'carpy' than the rest. With baits placed on all of those spots I sat back and relaxed, not feeling that I was really in with a chance but pleased to have the rods out on Wraysbury at last, all the same. I kept my eyes peeled for any possible sightings that might give a fish away but it was the birds and animals around me that were most willing to be seen. A rustling in the bushes next to me made me glance around sharply to see a mink that had just caught a grass snake. The noises that mink made as it crunched and chomped through its latest meal weren't for the faint-hearted, but it seemed quite oblivious to the fact that I was crouching there watching it.

I knew that the bait would work if I could find the fish.

Wraysbury 1 bait

1kg Hutchinson MC MIX

3ml Amino Blend Swan Mussel

2ml Shellfish Sense Appeal

2ml Monster Crab

Darkness came and in the end it got to the stage where I couldn't really see anything so there was nothing else for it other than to get a good nights kip. That was exactly what I had, as the next time I opened my eyes it was already light and, as expected, the indicators had stayed precisely where I had placed them the day before. It was just the first step of what I expected to be a long journey, the kettle went on and I made myself some breakfast. Soon after, I had the first visitor in the swim and it was someone I recognised from the past. It was one of the twins who I had met some years earlier on Fox Pool and it was good to see him again. I hadn't seen him since those days and I haven't seen him again since but that one meeting was to be so important to me that I look back now in amazement at the sheer chance of it all happening. He wasn't fishing, but stopped by for a chat and it was obvious straight away that he had a good knowledge of the lake and it was really interesting listening to what he had to say. A few areas were pointed out where fish were likely to be seen and one in particular was along one of the islands. The spot he was talking about was out-of-bounds to fishing but some of the famous residents could be found there at different times, knowing that they were safe, of course. The whole conversation lifted my spirits and after he departed I was full of ideas and renewed confidence to go on the search for a Wraysbury carp. The main area to check out was the island margin as it was closest to where I was set up and I could leave my gear relatively safe in the swim for awhile.

I rowed across and pulled the boat up some way down the bank and made my way through the dense trees. All along the bank there were over-hanging trees and it looked quite good under all of them, although there was nothing to really see. As I got further down the bank I stopped abruptly. It front of me was a clear area that looked different to the others I had seen, it was obvious that this one had been cleaned and well used by carp! As I glanced around I caught sight of a fish at last – and it was a carp, although it was certainly one of the more recent stock fish and not one of the most sought after originals, but it was a carp and the first one I'd seen. It just sat there, motionless, under the surface and I don't know how many minutes I crouched there for but I suddenly saw something out of the corner of my eye. I looked around just as this great big mirror glided into the area. This certainly was one of the originals and at first I thought it was Mallin's, but it was almost certainly the Pug and sure to be over 40lb. With the clear water I was worried that I would spook it quickly, but the fish seemed to know it was safe and just circled around in front of me. I had almost forgotten that I had taken a bag of baits over with me to bait up a few likely areas, should I find any. Well, I couldn't fish this spot but I couldn't help thinking that it wouldn't hurt to put a few baits in to see what would happen. I threw about ten MC Mix boilies onto the clear spot, expecting the fish to bolt off and not come back, but instead it just backed off a few feet and after about a minute it swam back over and its head went straight down onto the baits! I could see each boilie disappearing between those big, rubbery white lips and I was mesmerised. I put some more bait in and again it came over and picked them up, the smaller mirror also came over and joined in the feast. I couldn't believe what was happening, here I was at Wraysubry 1 and I had two fish, including one of the big originals, eating my bait right in front of my eyes!

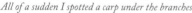
All of a sudden I spotted a carp under the branches.

I must have watched them for a couple of hours before I started to wonder how I could draw these fish out into the open water, or at least down to where I was allowed to fish to. Only yards away was the old dead tree which marked the boundary to where I could fish, but I did wonder if the carp would vacate the safe area at all to feed elsewhere. I was absolutely 'buzzing', the fish obviously liked the bait so that was a huge confidence booster and if they came across it I was sure that they would eat it, so I trotted back to the boat a lot faster than I'd left it earlier and planned my attack. The swim I was set up in didn't give the right angles really but there was another swim in Dredger Bay called Little Dredger, this was situated right next to the channel that joined the South and North Lakes but faced out to the area where I needed to be, so I quickly got all of my gear together and bundled it into the boat. Really, there was no need to rush as no one else was going to go in the swim but you know how it is in these situations, I just had to make sure.

I moved everything over to the Little Dredger swim.

With the new swim secured and all the gear set up I could set about trying to find the best spots to lay my traps. As with the other swim, there was a channel running straight into the bay between two islands and it was further up this channel where I had seen the fish, so I went out to see what was out there. There was a boundary sign on both sides of the channel marking the line which I couldn't go beyond, so I drew a sort of imaginary line between the two and slowly paddled my way across, whilst leaning over the end of the boat with my sun glasses on, which gave me a clear view of the bottom. I could see plenty of weed as usual …weed …weed …weed ….clear! Right in the middle of the channel was a big clearing in the weed, in fact not one but two. I could feel my heart beating faster as I felt that I had found just what I was looking for. I checked all around and, sure enough, it was in the water I could fish so I went back for some bait. Both clear spots received a sprinkling of pellets and a few boilies, I can remember thinking how good they looked and I glanced back up to the tree where the fish had been earlier and it wasn't all that far away. That was two rods sorted and they were the main ones as far as I was concerned. The third bait was placed on the margin of the right-hand of the two islands on a small

gravel patch, which like before looked quite good, although I wasn't particularly sure if it would be a place the carp would visit or not. That left one rod for the left. Time was getting on now and the sun was going down, I had spent so long doing the other rods and making sure that they were right, that I didn't have too long left to find somewhere for the fourth rod. I looked along the margin of the left-hand island and it didn't look quite

My baits weren't too far from where I had seen the fish.

so appealing, the bottom was more silt than gravel and there was a fair bit of weed about, although it was much thinner than in some of the other areas. Time was short so I dropped the rig. I was using a combi-rig made from a stiff section of abrasion resistant Fireline leading up to a soft section of 25lb Kryston braid (I can't quite remember which one now), this was knotless knotted to a size four Hutchinson long shank hook and on the hair was one 18mm MC boilie. As the 4oz lead hit the bottom the bait actually settled quite nicely in amongst the weed and I remember looking at it and thinking that it looked a better presentation than I'd thought it was going to be. I sprinkled about a dozen boilies around the spot before making my way back to the swim. That was it – the four rods were out and I felt really confident that I was fishing as well as I could, and that I was in with a chance even this early into the proceedings.

With everything done I could at last sit back and relax.

The kettle went on and at last I could sit back again and relax. I was quite tired, I had been on the go for quite a few hours getting everything sorted but I felt like it had been a really productive day, and I was fishing positively and not just fishing blind and playing the waiting game – although it was still very likely to be like that anyway. Darkness fell again, but I wasn't so keen to sleep this time around, there was an air of anticipation in the Little Dredger swim that evening, but as ever, as soon as I laid down to have a little rest I was knocking out the zeds in no time.

At 11pm I was awoken abruptly by a single bleep on the left-hand rod. I sat up and opened the bag in one swift movement. I could see that the indicator had pulled up tight to the rod and I jumped out quickly. As I got to the rod there was another bleep and the line pulled from the clip, but I already had the rod in my hand by then as the baitrunner started to tick. I knew how close I had dropped this bait to the branches so I didn't want to give it any line. I held on tight and as the rod arched over I heard a big eruption on the surface out in the distant darkness. Even at that distance I could feel the fish thrusting its tail, trying its best to make some purchase away from me, but after a few seconds the fish thankfully began to relent a little and I gained a few yards of line. That was the main thing that I knew I had to do, now the fish was away from the main danger area and it started to kite left into a large open bay. In the bay were a few bars and weed beds that had me more than a little worried. My heart was pounding so hard I thought it was going to burst. Huge oily ripples came out of the bay as the fish boiled on the surface, at least it was staying near to the surface but it could dive into the thick weed at any moment. Slowly, ever so slowly, I eased the fish towards me, so many times over the years I had hooked fish early on in the proceedings only to lose them. It had happened at Fox Pool during my second trip and I never had a better chance than that, afterwards. Those thoughts were racing through my head, but the fish was still on and it was getting closer to me all the time. Eventually, it was just a few yards out in front of me and I reached back for the landing net that was leaning up against the umbrella. Just as I did that, the fish shot around to my left and into the channel that led out to the North Lake. I dropped the net and held on.

I was over the moon to see what was lying in the bottom of the net.

The line cut tightly around the bushes and I felt the line starting to grate against some underwater object. I had seen some mussel-covered rocks there earlier and knew that's what the line was around – surely I wasn't going to lose the fish now, after all of that! Inch by inch I edged the fish gently back towards me until it moved slightly to the right and I felt that lovely feeling of direct contact once again. I breathed a huge sigh of relief and reached back for the net again. This time the fish stayed where it was and I dropped the net in front of where I was crouching and let it sink to the bottom. By now the fish was just circling in front and for the first time I felt like I was in charge and near to winning the battle. A short time later the fish surfaced and I new it was mine, I lifted up the mesh around the fish and just dropped the rod on the floor so that I could punch the air in victory. I don't know if I've ever been more excited to land a fish. My second night on Wraysbury 1 and I had a fish in the net – although I still didn't know what I had. It was so dark and, for some reason, I had it in my mind that if I was going to catch one, it was going to be the smaller stocky that I'd seen earlier in the day, but as soon as I flicked the head torch on I realised that I'd got something much bigger than that! My first thought was that it must be The Pug, after seeing it eating the boilies just yards from where the bait had been, but as I turned the fish over I clearly saw a little group of scales down the flank of the fish towards the back end. I didn't know this fish so well but I knew that this just had to be the one known as Cluster, one of the big originals, although just how big it was meant to be I had no idea.

To weigh the fish I figured the best way to do it was to wedge a long pole onto the branches of one of the bushes next to me and rest the other end on my shoulder to get an accurate reading. With everything ready I got the fish out onto the mat and looked at it properly for the first time. The hook was neatly embedded in the middle of the bottom lip and was never going to fall out. With the hook out I slipped the fish into the weigh sling and hoisted it up on the scales. The needle settled on 44lb 7oz, a new English best for me and what a fish to do it with! I quickly sacked the fish up and placed it in the margins in front of me. My heart was still pounding and although it was getting on for midnight I just had to call someone and tell them. I knew Joan would still have her mobile phone on and sure enough, after a couple of rings, she answered. After a few 'oohs' and 'wows' she agreed to come up at first light to do some pictures. Next was Pete Jones, I guessed he might still be up watching TV and indeed he was.

At 44lb 7oz it was a new English best and also the biggest fish in Wraysbury 1!

"Bloody hell, that was quick!" he said, "I'll be there at 7am," and, considering he would have to drive all the way from Brighton, I was more than grateful for that.

With that done all I could do was put the kettle on for a much-needed cup of tea. I knew that there was no way I would be going back to sleep that night and, literally, drank one cup of tea after another and just sat there watching the sack in front of me, until it started to gradually get light. True to form, Joan and Pete arrived at 7am and we got the great fish out for the pictures. It was the first time that I could really admire just what a wonderful carp this was, with its big, chunky shoulders and deep chestnut-coloured flanks. I knew that I'd been fortunate to get a run so quickly on such a daunting venue but it had happened for me on a few occasions before on different waters, but I had often lost those fish. If anything, it made the whole excitement even more intense and anyway, it certainly wasn't a chance capture as I'd put myself into the position where I had what I felt was a really good chance. I waded out with Cluster and the best sight was watching her charge angrily off into the depths. I always love to see them swim off like that.

"I'd better ring Crowy soon," I thought to myself, but he beat me to it and I saw his name come up as the mobile rang.

"Hello mate, how's it going? Have you seen any yet? Where are you?" Etc. etc.

"I've had one," was my reply.

"Yeah, yeah," he said, "now how's it going?"

"No, really, I'm not joking, I've had one and just put it back!" I said.

"Really, what have you had?"

"I've had Cluster."

"You what, you......!" The rest I'll have to leave to your imagination but needless to say he was more than a little surprised.

I was on cloud nine and the nicest thing after that was the reaction of the other people who were fishing, and others who had just heard about the capture. John McAllister came through with his boat loaded up and stopped for a chat. A nice guy and a great angler - as he proved just a little while later by going off and catching Mary's Mate, no less! Steve Allcott and Jim Shelley both paid a visit and it made me feel even better as I was a newcomer and I didn't know how it would go down with the regulars, but as ever they were all great about it. Last, but not least, Chris Ball came all the way over to have a cup of tea and shake my hand. Years earlier, when he had fished Wraysbury, he had a brace of carp off the top one afternoon and one was Mallin's, the other was none other than Cluster at 22lb. All these years later, and with the sad demise of Mary, it dawned on me that Cluster was now actually the biggest carp in Wraysbury 1.

The best sight of all was to see Cluster charging back off into the depths.

Apart from a pike of about 17lb that snaffled one of my baits, that was the only run of the session. I had been fortunate to get the one bite but there were more fish still in the area, so another fish was always possible and it was certainly the right time to be there. But, after catching Wraysbury's biggest carp it was very hard to really get my head around any more serious fishing for that moment. The despair of hearing about Mary had been replaced by the amazement and excitement of getting the fabulous Cluster and I could pack the rods away with a big smile on my face.....thank you, Wraysbury.

Cassien – Summer Days

Cassien – Summer Days

Back to Basics

The rules and regulations have changed constantly at Cassien since I first started fishing there in 1986. First of all, in those earlier years, night fishing was strictly forbidden and although some people did take the risk of doing a few nights here and there, those who were unlucky enough to be caught ran the risk of having all of their gear confiscated and facing heavy fines - there were even cases of anglers being held down with guns against their heads! But as strict as the rules were, the amount of visitors increased year by year and there followed a period where carp anglers were tolerated a little more and as long as you didn't do anything too blatant, you were more or less left alone to carry on and enjoy yourself. Carp fishing began to become more accepted, especially when the number of French carp anglers increased and in 1994 this led to night fishing being allowed at Cassien for the first time. As you can imagine, there was immediately a big increase in the amount of people fishing the lake. Before then many people just wouldn't bother going if they couldn't bivvy-up and fish in comfort, but with the restrictions lifted, the banks of the lake became filled with carp anglers all trying to catch the fish of their dreams. This of course brought with it more problems, especially during the summer months. The authorities have always viewed Cassien as a lake to be enjoyed by everyone and although carp anglers were included in that, it was getting to the point where they were taking over the lake and I can imagine how difficult it must have been for families arriving on a summers morning complete with lilos and cool boxes and kids, only to find every nice

little beach area filled with a carp angler who'd been there for several days and had rods splayed everywhere. Something had to give and around 2001 the decision was made to ban night fishing once more, but this time just during the period of the summer months when it was used most by the general public, Once the holiday period was over then the lake would be a lot quieter and carp anglers could carry on as before and bivvy-up etc.

The best road sign in the world!

During the first summer when the night fishing ban came into force it was more like a close season than just a restriction as most of the anglers just stayed away. In a way it was understandable, as Cassien was difficult enough when you could be there all the time and fish right through, but if you could only fish the days and then have to pack up and leave in the evening, then it was hardly worth bothering at all – or was it? Of the few people that did bother to go down that first year I seem to remember Alijn Danau being amongst them and his results surprised me a little. Although he never caught anything particularly big, he did catch a lot of fish while he was there and for that matter so did a few other people. It seemed that the night fishing ban had more of an effect on the lake than anyone thought it would and there was a different side to the Cassien that we all thought we knew so well. The fact was that with no anglers on the banks and much less bait going in, the fish not only felt under a lot less pressure, but with the lack of food they were also a lot more hungry and for the first time in ages they had to go out looking for it instead of being able to take their pick. Of course back in the early years, before boilies were even introduced, the carp had no worries when it came to food as the lake was full of crayfish to feast on and they didn't really have much in the way of competition. But now the balance had changed and the introduction of catfish, both the silure and poisson chat varieties, had quite a dramatic effect on the natural food supplies. All of them eat either the crayfish or their eggs and they were big competition for the carp – especially in the warmer months and as a result it looked as if the carp were now becoming more catchable.

Catfish have become more numerous over the years.

I found the idea of day fishing quite appealing, not so much for the amount of action that might be possible, although that was certainly part of it. But it was the lack of anglers which I really found most attractive. Throughout my time at Cassien, or any water for that matter, I've always tried to avoid the crowds. In the early 1990's it seemed like no one wanted to know about Cassien, in a way it was almost as if it was out of fashion for awhile and looking back, those few years were some of my favourites, simply because for much of the time we virtually had the place to ourselves! My only regret now is that I didn't fish harder and perhaps catch a few more of the big fish while it was almost devoid of pressure, the chances were obviously there, but the fact was, I was just really enjoying my time there. I've always tried to pick the quieter times and it's not particularly easy as you never know what people from other countries will be doing during different periods of the year. But if people were now staying away simply because they couldn't night fish, then I would definitely consider going back just to experience the peace and solitude that I'd once known.

Cassien in the summer is a much different prospect to the winter, the fish might be more active and perhaps more hungry, but there are so many other mouths to feed that they can make the fishing more than a little difficult if you are not prepared properly. I loosely refer to these as the 'nuisance species' but they are quite an important topic to cover and I suppose it means just about anything that wants to eat a boilie other than a carp. The bream, tench and roach aren't as bad as they once were, unless you are using small particles and mini boilies. They can still be a pain in the butt at times but they just aren't present in the numbers that they once were. There have been several stockings of catfish in more recent years and they have also bred successfully to the point where they are present in such numbers that several anglers do now target Cassien purely for the catfish. They are not only the largest but also one of the most successful freshwater predators and undoubtedly that has caused a reduction in the numbers of smaller fish in the lake today. The catfish have grown to incredible sizes in the past, but initially there were only a few of them, whereas now I wouldn't like to put a number on how many weigh over 100lb. There are certainly more than enough and on top of that, there are an even greater number of smaller ones that have developed a taste for boilies.

Like the smaller fish, the crayfish numbers have also declined in recent years, undoubtedly much of this is down to predation. Crayfish were the original problem when we first fished the lake, but really they were not that difficult to overcome. Very hard boilies which had been air-dried for some time or made with a hardening ingredient such as egg albumin, were normally enough to withstand the attentions of crayfish and when you reeled in to re-bait, there would invariably be evidence of claw scratches and a few chunks missing but most of the bait would still be intact meaning that you were still fishing effectively. Years ago if you were to shine a torch in the margins after dark, the bottom would almost be a moving mass as the crayfish came out of hiding for their night time foray, especially if you dropped a few baits in the edge. Nowadays it is still possible to see numbers of them in the right places but nothing compared to how it used to be. It's quite a pleasing sight now when I do see the familiar scratching on the baits just to know that there are a few crayfish around the baited area, in the knowledge that they could attract a few fish in.

Who would have thought that these things would become a nuisance?

One of the things that I never expected to be talking about as a problem are the terrapins. At one time it used to be quite a novelty to see one stick its head out in front of you while you were watching the water. Now it's more of a case of how many you will see in the summer! To think that many of my friends used to keep those things as pets and give them daft names like

Dick Terrapin, after the highway man, or Randolf Terrapin after the famous boxer (if you can remember back that far!) Well I've got a few names for them too, but unfortunately none of them are printable here! In fact unwanted pets are probably the reason they found their way into the lake in the first place. They have bred well in the lake and they are quite intelligent little things – although not always so little it has to be said. They do however, have an uncanny knack of knowing where you have just baited up and although you don't always see them at first, after a while one or two of the tell-tale heads suddenly appear for a few seconds before sinking out of sight again – normally after a stone has been aimed their way! The most that I've counted at one time over one baited area is seven, and that is more than enough to clear you out of bait before too long. They are not yet a severe problem but they can be a nuisance and they are increasing in numbers every year. It's not just in the shallows that you have to watch out for them either as I have hooked and landed quite a large one from a depth of 25 feet and I've no doubt that they will go deeper than that.

The dreaded poisson chat!

Without a doubt the worst of all the pests though, are the poisson chats. These horrendous little catfish only grow up to about a pound or two at best but they have ravenous appetites and strong jaws with serrated teeth like sand paper that soon whittle away the toughest of boilies. If you've ever played that old computer game, Pac Man then that will give you some idea of what those things are like as I'm sure that all they do all their lives is go around chomping everything in sight, in fact I'm sure that game had to be designed around poisson chats eating boilies. The worst thing about these little catfish is that they were not natural to the lake at all and were stocked sometime in the early 1990's. There are various stories that go around that they were stocked by mistake by someone thinking that they were baby silure's. Or it could have been that whoever stocked them knew what they were and just didn't care one way or the other. Perhaps a more sinister reason that's been bandied about is that it was done just to antagonise and perhaps put off carp anglers from fishing the lake. It certainly hasn't stopped carp anglers visiting Cassien, but the poisson chat have ruined many peoples trips. They are the hardest problem to get around as they always seem to be hungry and once they find your bait, they never leave it alone. Not only do they whittle away the baits incredibly quick, they also have the knack of twisting the hook link and making quite a mess of the set up, often with no more than the odd bleep or knock on the rod tip to let you know they are there.

Being able to travel so light is a huge bonus in the summer.

After reading all of that you might be left wondering what the point is of going to Cassien at all in the summer? Well besides all of that, the fishing can be very good and there are some things that you can do to get around most of the nuisance species. For me, it has been a learning process which has been going on for the last twenty years or so and you would think that in that time that I would have sorted all the problems out completely, but that's not really the case. Yes there are things you can do and baits that you can use, but they are not always the most effective way of catching the carp. It's normally the case that the baits that you most want to use and the ones that you think will be most effective for the carp, are also the ones that you will have most problems with from the pests.

It was in July 2002 that I first went back down to Cassien for a go at the day-only summer fishing. I didn't really have any new ideas on how I was going to approach the fishing, only what I'd tried and been fairly successful with before. There were two main tactics. The first one was the old, reliable tiger nuts. They were always one of the few baits which could be relied on to be ignored by many of the species other than carp, the only problem being that anglers soon twigged on to this and it had got to the stage where they had been hammered and the fish had become more wary of them. But they still represented the most hassle-free way of fishing in the shallower water. The second tactic was to fish in the deep water over forty feet.

I started up the top of the North Arm at Ollies Point.

For some reason the poisson chat don't like going down much beyond thirty-five feet, which is a blessing, whereas the carp have no problems feeding in anything down to sixty or even seventy feet which has been proved many times in the past. So I had a reasonable plan of attack, I just needed to get to the lake and put the plan into action.

We arrived early one morning in the middle of July to the pleasant sight of the water level being very high, something which I always hope to find at any time of year as it always seems beneficial to the fishing. To start with I had no real plans of where I was going to fish or for that matter where we were going to stay at night. That, of course, all had to be sorted out as staying on the bank was forbidden just as the night fishing was. First port of call was, as always, Pierre's restaurant, which was now in the capable hands of Philippe, Pierre's eldest son who had taken over after he had decided to retire. It has always been a nice feeling to pull into the car park and to be welcomed back to the lake at the start of a trip. I suppose it's a part that is missing when you go to fish many of the other public waters across France. But it was also the place where we could obtain our permits and leave the car. Over coffee we discussed where would be the best place to base ourselves as there are several campsites in the area, but Philippe said that we could sleep in the car in the grounds of the restaurant if that would help us. Now don't get me wrong, this wasn't a regular thing but he offered it to us because we had visited so many times over the years and had become good friends with all of the family. It was something I hadn't even considered on the drive down and no doubt it would make things much easier as, for one we wouldn't have to book into a campsite and, secondly, wouldn't have to pack up and drive there every evening. Instead, we could just leave everything covered over in the boat and just grab a few hours kip in the car or maybe even on the lilos.

I got off to a decent enough start.

The great thing about that style of fishing is that you don't need loads of gear. Normally it's like an expedition going off up the lake for a session with two boats loaded to the brim, but of course there were no bivvies, no bedchairs, sleeping bags etc. Just enough gear and bait for the days fishing. The only problem for me was getting up in the morning, which of course has never been my strongest point, but I hoped that the excitement of what might lie ahead would be enough to get me going. No chance! It was around 10am the next day when I finally got my act together and headed off up the lake.

The first three days were spent up the top end of the North Arm around the Ollies Point area. I don't know why as it was a long way to go, but I thought that the fish might be there in sufficient numbers to make it worthwhile, but that wasn't really the case. The aim was that, by concentrating my efforts on one area and keeping the bait going in, it would gradually build the area up. The first day was a total blank, whilst the next two days brought mirrors of 33lb 8oz, 30lb 12oz and 29lb 4oz plus an un-welcome catfish of 22lb. Now don't get me wrong, I was pleased to be off the mark and in normal circumstances I would've been more than happy with those fish to begin a trip with but although it wasn't a bad result, I just felt that I could and should be doing a little better. Not only that but the distances involved in getting to the swim every day were quite time consuming and tiring. Two of the fish had come at around 8am and that meant getting up at around 4am to be sure of getting everything in place for bite time, which of course was a bit of a struggle for someone who likes their bed as much as me! The great thing was that the lake was more or less deserted, as I'd hoped it would be, and it gave me a lot more options. I could keep baiting up one or two areas without too much fear of finding someone in there the next morning when I arrived, or for that matter I could bait up several areas, although I didn't really have enough bait with me to do that effectively. Incidentally, all of the action those first few days came from the deeper water of around forty five feet and all were on boilies. Although I had tried tigers in shallower areas, they hadn't produced as I thought they would, although that might have just been down to the swim, but my early thoughts were that the fish were more likely to be found in the deeper water during the day even when not under great pressure. The only other angler I'd seen to that point was a young French guy who'd fished for the day on the opposite side and I'd gone across to photograph an upper thirty for him in the afternoon. So it showed that the fish were fairly spread out and were willing to feed once you were on them.

The shallower water around the weed beds began to produce more fish.

Tiger nuts were the first choice for the shallower depths.

I figured that if the fish were well spread, then the best thing was to try somewhere a little closer to base and planned to fish the next few days still in the North Arm but much nearer to the central section. The next day brought one mirror of 34lb at 1pm from forty feet, whilst a move 200 yards further up the bank brought me mirrors of 23lb 12oz, 31lb 12oz and 41lb 8oz the following day. The difference this time was that those three fish all came in a short spell between 9.30am and 11am from the shallower depth of fifteen feet on the tiger nuts. So, if anything, it was all a bit confusing but there were some positive leads to follow and, as ever on Cassien, each swim seemed to be different. But each swim seemed to hold carp which was the main thing. I tried another day in the same spot but this time only had one small mirror of 15lb. It was starting to appear that there were small groups of fish everywhere and action could come fairly quickly when you dropped on them, but after a few had been hooked they would disperse and the choice I had was that I could either sit and wait for them to come back or move onto a new area.

I had figured out by then that fishing a new area every day would be the best way of keeping the action going. It was fairly obvious that the swims which had been left alone offered the best chances so I was able to monitor which areas had been left alone the longest and looked most likely to try next and in some cases I would be able to bait up the swims for the next day before heading back for the evening. Just for a change of scenery I headed right to the top end of the South Arm the next day, which meant one of those dreadful 4am starts again but even then it was still 7am before everything was in place – it was certainly some of the hardest fishing I've done but if the rewards were there to be had, then I didn't mind working for them. Even whilst setting the rods up I watched one guy on the other side land three fish in quick succession. There seemed to be more fish in that part of the lake but there were also a few more anglers which put me off a little. However, at 9.30am one of the baits in fifteen feet was picked up and after a good fight I landed my second forty of the trip at 40lb 12oz. It was a nice fish for sure and there seemed to be more about but I wanted to be away from other anglers as much as possible and so decided to head back up the North Arm for the next three days. That was probably a wise decision as it was also the weekend period and the lake was very busy in the south as is normal in July. Over the three days, by trying different spots and depths, I landed a further five fish up to 35lb 2oz and lost another one.

A move to the South Arm produced this cracker from the Island Bay.

Next, it was a move back to the South Arm but only as far as the Island Bay which was a pleasant, short trip from the base. I was getting it down to a fine art by then and from setting off, to having the baits in the water only took something like 45 minutes. Everything was always ready to go and I knew the depths I wanted to fish and it's quite surprising how quick it can all be done when time is of the essence. Rods out, breakfast eaten and sometimes even time for a bit more sleep before the sun was up, if the fish would allow it – but they rarely did. I started with two small mirrors of 12lb each which I guess were recent stockies, they both came from much shallower water of six feet. The shallower spots were starting to take over and produce virtually all of the action for me, after the deep water had worked better at the start.

Sometimes it's best to leave the echo sounder behind.

Look hard enough and you never know what you might find!

This of course meant using the tiger nut hook baits, actually the set up I was using consisted of two tiger nuts along with a small cork ball to balance the baits. But I was still using the boilies as freebies; they were just chopped up and used along with tigers and some small particles. To be honest it didn't really seem to matter too much which bait I used, the fish were just hungry and as long as the food was put in front of them they were willing enough to eat it. One more fish of 33lb 12oz came that day and it looked to be a good area but the next morning I decided to move over just a little bit to one secluded little corner where no one hardly ever fishes and, over the next two day sessions, landed fish of 18lb, 20lb 8oz, 22lb 8oz, 32lb 10oz and a lovely mirror of 42lb 4oz. The trouble was that with more people around in the South Arm, my action hadn't gone unnoticed and during the second afternoon two French guys came and baited up very close to where I was fishing, obviously intending to fish there the next day. I also wanted to come back the next day and carry on fishing there, so I made sure that I was in the swim at 4am the next morning. By now I was just getting used to the lack of sleep and if anything all of the work involved was just getting me into better shape and although it might have been tough to start with, I was getting into quite a good routine and really enjoying it. Of course, a lot of that was due to the constant action I was getting and when I'm catching fish I can put up with most things. I knew that there would be more fish in the Island Bay and I just hoped that I could get a few more of them. But even though I was in there first, the two French guys arrived soon after and set up fairly close to my right and fished where they had baited the night before, but to make matters worse another guy arrived and set up to my left! This wasn't really what I'd gone there for but I would have stuck with it if the action was still coming, but by midday nothing had happened and so it was perhaps the right time to look elsewhere. Maybe the extra pressure had pushed the fish out. Anyway, there would be more fish to catch elsewhere and more peaceful areas to fish.

The area hadn't been fished since I'd arrived.

The rods hadn't been out long but the move had paid off!

With the gear back in the boat I headed back off towards the North Arm not really knowing where I would end up, but one place that grabbed my attention was the corner, right at the start of the West Arm opposite the bridge. It was quiet enough for sure as I'd not seen anyone in there since my arrival, although it was a bit late in the day to be setting up in a new swim as it was now early afternoon. But the move paid off at 5.30pm when a bait in just twelve feet of water rattled off and one of those long, hard Cassien battles commenced. On the end was a cracking common of 41lb 6oz, my fourth forty of the trip and my first Cassien 40lb common – a good move after all! The two remaining days were both spent in that same swim and I landed a further three fish up to 29lb 4oz. It had been extremely hard work, there was no denying that, but it had also been extremely enjoyable and productive. In thirteen days of fishing I'd landed twenty seven carp from ten different swims, including four forties. It was a totally different way of fishing Cassien to what I had been used to and, although I had been expecting to catch a few fish, this was a result far beyond my expectations – it was alright, this summer fishing!

Cassien – Summer Days

July 2003 – Back for More!

Needless to say the summer fishing in 2002 had been so good I was going to be having some more of that, and the following year I was back again in the July with Joan. It was to be quite different in a few ways that year, though. I already knew from the year before what I needed to do and, so, I was prepared to travel light and keep moving around to different swims every day. Again, the water was quite high and as ever it looked lovely and blue in the warm sunshine. The first day started well enough back in the South Arm's Island Bay where I got going immediately, that first afternoon, with two mirrors of just over 30lb apiece. Two more days in the South Arm brought a further three fish up to 39lb, plus another two lost. It was just like I'd never been away and once again the fish were well spread out and well hungry! From the previous year's experience, I knew what to do and I also knew of a few areas that were well worth a try.

It was a good start in the South Arm with fish up to 39lb.

I figured that it was worth a look at the start of the West Arm where I'd caught the forty common from the previous year, and thankfully once again I found the area devoid of anglers – but it certainly wasn't devoid of fish. I never even made it to the swim I was heading for as there were fish rolling and jumping within fifty metres of the bank as I made my way up. The weed beds were quite thick in that area and I guessed it was the reason that the carp were there in numbers. I just knew I was going to catch – it was just a matter of how many! In the clear water it was easy to see the edge of the weed beds and all I had to do was to place the hook baits just over the weed, where the bottom was clear and sandy. Within minutes of putting the rods out I was into a fish and soon had a 28lb mirror on the bank. With a few early mornings already under my belt I got the rod back out and then put the lilo in the shade of a big willow tree to try and catch up on a little bit of lost sleep. I soon drifted off into the land of nod and I must have been more tired than I realised as it was around 11am when a couple of bleeps woke me up. I ambled down to the rods, as nothing really seemed to be happening, it must have just been a liner or something. But then I glanced over at one of the other rods and noticed quite a bit of line missing. Somehow I'd left the alarm switched off in the rush to get set up and, although I knew that I would be lucky if that fish was still on, I figured that I'd better get out in the boat to see what was going on. The run could've happened five minutes earlier or it could have happened two or three hours earlier. I'll never know, but I followed the line across to where it was obviously caught on something. As I pulled harder, someone's old discarded marker rose to the surface. It had obviously been there for some time and the fish had just kited around it. I pulled it all into the boat and freed my line and as soon as I did I felt a pull on the other end – the fish was still on! It wasn't going far and just circled in the depths below the boat. It felt a bit different to the rest and when it surfaced I could see why – it was a lot bigger than the rest! It went straight in the net first time, thankfully, and I made my way back to the bank with a big smile on my face. It was a cracking mirror of 55lb 4oz and my biggest Cassien carp since the Hippo way back in 1987. It was a fish known as Timotei, which would go on to be the biggest carp in the lake in years to come. I had been more than a little lucky to land that one, but sometimes that's how it goes and when it goes right you don't ask questions, you just accept it gratefully.

I'd left the alarm switched off – but the fish was still on!

It was just the start of an incredible day that saw me land a further four carp up to 34lb and lose a further two. At some stage in amongst all the action my old friend, Pete Jones, who now lived abroad, just happened to call to see how things were going. The excitement in my voice must have been obvious and when I told him what had happened, his immediate reply was,

"Save me a space I'll be there in a couple of days!"

"Blimey, he's keen!" I thought to myself.

It would be nice to see Pete again but at the same time I wasn't quite sure how it would work out with the extra lines in the swims, and just how and where we would fish. I just hoped that we could still catch a few, which in reality I was sure we would. The next two days were spent in the same area and it produced another six carp, but they were smaller, with the biggest going just 24lb 8oz. Even though there were more fish to be caught in that area, I felt as though I'd had the best out of it, and I was ready for a move anyway. We quickly went back to Pierre's, where Pete was already there waiting for us. He hadn't been fishing for ages and he was chomping at the bit. Mind you, it was just as well we had some spare gear with us as he had a bed chair and two reels – that was it! Nothing like travelling light, but when you've gotta go, you've gotta go, I suppose.

With an extra person fishing, albeit with only two rods, it would affect the swim choice. We'd need somewhere with a bit more room and it seemed like the best place to have a look at would be up on the Third Point in the North Arm. I had been watching it for a few days and it had been left alone, plus it would have more than enough room for us to spread the rods out while still being able to have a bit of a social. It must have been around five years since we'd last fished together so I was looking forward to catching up on what had been going on whilst we'd not seen each other.

Until then I'd been getting virtually all the fish in fairly shallow water again, in fact the 55 had come from just eleven feet in the middle of the day. But the Third Point is a bit different, or at least I felt that it was, and I put most of the rods out in depths of around forty to forty five feet. At that depth I could safely use boilies and at the time I was heavily into the Hutchinson MC/Addicted mix in 24mm sizes. I'd had some good results with it on various waters (Cassien included) and so I was pleased to be in an area where I felt I could use it properly. The first day on the Third Point only produced one small fish of low twenties, so it wasn't a great start by any means but, somehow, it felt right to be fishing there and we spread a fair bit of bait all around before we left later that evening. It must have done the trick, as the next day, I landed three fish including the second fifty of the trip at 50lb 12oz! Pete also got in on the act and was making up for lost time, from memory I think he had around eight fish up to mid-thirties, which was a great result with only two rods. He was like a man possessed and I'm sure he was wearing a groove in the beach where his little legs were running backwards and forwards all day long! Joan also had a couple of low twenties, so all of a sudden it looked like we had created a decent area.

The baiting up worked – another fifty of 50lb 12oz.

The more bait we put in, the more action we received and although we spent one day further up the North Arm at Ollie's Point, where we still caught four fish, it was definitely the Third Point where most of the fish were. It was the first time where I'd found a big group of fish that were staying put, rather than having to chase them all around the lake. Many of the fish were slightly below the normal Cassien average, but there were a sprinkling of good ones mixed in with them. During the next full days fishing I landed no less than ten fish and lost another three, whilst Pete also had a few and Joan had one. The days were just filled with action, which was what we wanted, but inevitably supplies ran short and the daytime is the only time to do a bit of shopping. I didn't want to leave the swim but it had to be done and the quickest way would be if me and Pete went (well you know what women are like when they go shopping!) So we left Joan in charge of the rods while we sped off down the lake. We knew it was asking for trouble – not that Joan couldn't cope, because she certainly could. But something dramatic was bound to happen while we were away, because it always did!

Our afternoon meal attracted a few 'guests'.

We were gone less than an hour and the sweat dripped off me as I rowed back up the lake in the heat of the afternoon. As we got closer it was even worse than I'd feared. There were two pedalos pulled up in the swim, which was now full of people and there were rods strewn everywhere.

"What the hells happened this time?" I thought to myself.

As expected, as soon as we were out of sight the rods started going off everywhere and whilst Joan was playing one fish, a marker from a Swedish angler further up the arm drifted down into the line and got snagged. Joan was shouting some sort of abuse at the Swede for being so careless and the two pedalos full of French holiday makers thought she was in trouble and shot over to help out. They were all now best of friends, but it looked like carnage in the swim! There's never a dull moment fishing with Joan, I can tell you. In amongst all the goings on she did, of course, land the biggest fish of the day at 35lb 8oz. The thing was that we knew it would happen, but I was still amazed at what she could get up to in just an hour. It was a strange day in many ways. When everything had died down a little and the rods were back in some sort of order, we settled down to eat something. Pete had bought one of those ready-cooked chickens that you always see turning around on a spit in the supermarkets. As he opened the bag the waft of hot food had us all drooling and it seemed like a good choice. However, the smell must have spread fast as the next thing we knew the bushes were rustling and we all looked up expecting to see some people walking through. But instead, four wild boar came trotting into the open! They seemed oblivious to us being there and went about their business, investigating the swim for whatever they could find. We sat there stunned as, normally, they would have scrambled for cover as soon as they saw us, but these seemed almost tame. Joan thought she would give them our old food, which was by now of little use to us anyway. This included some old salad stuff and ham, but also a tub of Lurpack butter that had seen better days. Well, it was the butter that got them going and they had a right tussle over that. One of them put its nose in the tub and got it stuck, so they were all charging around the swim after the one with the tub of butter stuck to its nose. It was a mad day.

Pete was certainly making up for lost time.

In between all of that we were still catching carp and it almost seemed as if the lake had more fish in it than normal. It was just crazy fishing by Cassien standards and I was catching as many fish in a day as I would normally expect to get in a whole trip. The key to the whole thing now seemed to be the depth of forty feet, and all we were doing was literally going out in the boat until the echo sounder showed the right depth, then we would bait up and fish – nothing more complicated than that. We tried fishing shallower and deeper without much success, but as soon as we put it in forty feet, off it would go! The good thing was that there were a lot of areas of that depth out in front and it didn't matter which bit we fished, as long as it was in forty feet of water we knew it would go off sooner or later. Another ten fish up to 37lb 12oz followed the next day and it just went on and on. The days just flew by and, before we knew it, Pete had to leave again, but after not fishing for at least a couple of years, and having only ever caught three Cassien carp before that week, I think he went home happy with something like twenty eight fish up to high thirties under his belt after just one weeks fishing. I ended up landing fifty five carp during the two weeks, including two lovely fifties. Strangely enough, there were no forties amongst all those fish, but it was the most amazing summer session that I've ever had down at Cassien in all my years there.

The action was just incredible.

Cassien – Summer Days

2004 – The Changes Begin

By 2004 things were starting to change. People were beginning to realise that although you couldn't night fish during the summer, good results were very much a possibility and more and more people were starting to see the potential of the day-only fishing. I suppose I was as much to blame as anyone, as one of my jobs is to write about my fishing and a few articles here and there soon get noticed. But as well as that, people were just catching lots of fish and news on the carp grapevine always travels fast. Word was getting around and as a result it looked as though it was never going to be quite the same again as those first few years. To compound the problem there were also guided trips starting up again and of course they were very keen to advertise how good the fishing could be.

In all fairness the fishing was still very good that year. The lake was indeed more busy and in particular, there were a lot more English anglers arriving every week – well really there were a lot more anglers of all nationalities. This of course changed the fishing somewhat, no longer could I just pick and choose the swims I wanted to fish and it wasn't really worth baiting up swims in advance because I couldn't be sure of those swims still being free when I arrived to fish the next day. What I did have in my favour was the experience of fishing the lake for several years and I knew of several places that could produce fish, which were still likely to be left alone for a while by the majority of anglers.

It's quite normal for anglers when they arrive at the lake, especially for the first time, to head for the obvious swims, the ones that give the most room and that generally means the places where access is easy or the big points etc. In my experience those swims are likely to be good 'session' swims. When you have plenty of time at your

I knew of some good spots which were likely to be left alone.

disposal the big points and plateaus will inevitably see fish pass through at some stage. But often they are not the most productive spots over a short period. Even before arriving it is possible to predict where anglers will be fishing and concentrating their efforts, and of course with those spots receiving more pressure, the fish do become more wary of them and although they can still be very good at the right time, as the Third Point had been the year before for me, as a rule I made a conscious decision to try and avoid those more obvious areas and concentrate on the bits which get left alone.

When you start really looking, there are lots of places on Cassien that don't receive much pressure. Even in the swims that do get hammered, there are still certain spots that don't get fished much. You see it happen all the time when different people arrive in a swim. Very often to start with, they tend to fish the same spots within reason as everyone else, so it does give you a chance to fish a little bit different to everyone else if you want. The Cassien carp really do get everywhere and often the places which get overlooked can be amongst the best.

After saying all of that I still started the 2004 trip off back at Third Point. It was empty and I couldn't do anything else really after the amount of action I'd received there the year before. It started off well enough when, during the first day alone, I landed a 39lb common and a 37lb 4oz mirror. I recognised the common as one I'd caught some time before at 44lb so it was well down in weight and it's not that unusual to find that in the summer, when the competition for food is at it's greatest. Despite the good start, the action soon

I went back to the Third Point for the first day.

tailed off and it was obvious that the fish weren't there in the numbers they were before, plus there was quite a bit of interest in the swim from other people. During the first two days, I'd only just arrived in the swim each day when other anglers were coming up, obviously intending to fish the swim before seeing me and diverting off somewhere else.

It was a familiar common but down in weight from the year before.

So I started to look elsewhere and concentrated my efforts for the next few days at the far end of the South Arm where there seemed to be little activity. I fished three different swims and caught from all of them although nothing of any note with a 28lb mirror being the pick of the bunch. But it was nice to be catching and just as nice to be fishing away from everyone else. It's strange how the pressure comes and goes at Cassien. That part of the South Arm is often one of the busiest areas especially as it is so accessible, but this time around it was being left alone and the people were heading more for the North Arm. I suspect it's one of two things, either someone's had a result and the news has spread around the lake or people are unsure where to go and if they see people fishing one area they think that must be the best place to have a go. Either way, I tend to do the opposite as I always find that the less pressure the fish are under, the easier they are to catch.

After a morning with no action at the top of the South Arm it was time for a move and the obvious choice was to head up to the Island Bay which had been a good area in the past and again it was being left alone. I tucked myself away in the corner of the bay and fished all of the rods at fairly close range. There are a lot of features close to the bank in the Island Bay and if you can do everything quietly enough the fish will come in close too. There is one little plateau, which I always like to fish, it depends on how high or low the water is at the time but generally I find that fifteen feet is about the right depth and although it doesn't produce many fish, it can come up with a good 'un every now and then.

The fish moved to the deep water – and I followed!

As is often the case, I hadn't been in the swim long when the first run occurred from the plateau spot. I got in the boat straight away and with the engine on, I made my way out to the fish. There was quite a breeze blowing which didn't help and the fish was fighting hard too, but as long as you do everything right it's normally okay. What really makes a difference is using the buoyancy balls on the line. What they do is keep the line up and away from most of the snags and then when a run occurs I don't tighten into the fish too much, but just let it swim out into the deeper water where the fish can then be played a lot more safely. It stayed down in the deep water for a long time before it finally began to give a little here and there. Eventually, in the clear water I could see the fish, but more than that I could actually tell which fish it was by the recognisable group of scales on its flank. It was clearly a fish known as 'Fleur' and one which had been on my 'most wanted' list for a long time so the knees began to tremble a bit. It was a proper old warrior and it fought like one, it must have been close to 30 minutes before I finally had it in the net. I felt well chuffed to finally catch such a lovely carp – one of the Cassien jewels.

It was Fleur at 51lb 2oz – one of the Cassien jewels.

At 51lb 2oz it was another great summer 50 from Cassien but just the first in a string of captures from the Island Bay over the next couple of days. In all, I landed a further six fish with the best of those going 39lb 4oz, it was a great result and it showed what was still possible just by doing things a little different and keeping away from the other anglers. It turned into another one of those trips where the action just got better and better and although I had to keep moving to keep catching, I did end up catching a further twenty seven carp and losing another three during the last seven days. Most of those were either doubles or twenties but they were topped by two mirrors of 38lb 12oz and 40lb 12oz. The vast majority of the fish were coming from a depth of thirty five feet. I think that the reason for that was that the water was

Back you go sunshine.

The biggest of twenty seven carp during the last seven days!

lower than it had been the year before, and I was actually catching from the same spots which had been forty feet the year before but now those same spots were only 35 feet. At that depth it was still fairly safe from the poisson chats, it seemed to be just beyond their limits, but for the silure's it was a different matter. They were getting a taste for the boilies and I think I caught something like thirteen or fourteen of them ranging from 2lb or 3lb up to 35lb. The numbers of those things were increasing every year and perhaps the most annoying thing about them was that they nearly always seemed to pick up a bait when there was about an hours fishing left before packing up time. It was really frustrating to see the sun going down and the fish start to show in front only for the alarm to go off and find that there's a catfish on the end. By the time that was all sorted out it was hardly worth putting the rod back out for the time left, but it was just one of the things that had to be accepted, and after another good trip with so many fish I could hardly complain.

Times were changing though, and 2005 was different to how the previous few years had been. The water levels certainly didn't help, as I've already stated, Cassien always seems to fish better when the water level is high, but also by the same token is a lot more difficult when the level drops. The lake was very low – possibly the lowest I've known it at that time of year. The dry summer was certainly one reason for it dropping so much, but there were other reasons. A lot more water had started to be taken from the lake for various things, Cassien is a reservoir that is used for generating electricity and water is run off regularly for that. You would normally associate the winter time with the higher use of electricity but in the warm weather many people now had air conditioners in their homes, amongst other things. Besides those things, there was also a new golf course being built close by and by all accounts a lot of the water was being used up there. Whatever the reason was, it didn't help the fishing.

Relaxing for the evening outside 'Lola'.

I had another problem too. During the previous winter I had been spending a lot of time at Gerard's restaurant further along the South Arm from Pierre's and when packing up after the winter session, I'd decided to leave my boat there for a change. For the winter it was fine but I soon realised that I'd made a mistake for the summer. I couldn't sleep on the beach as I had done at Pierre's and Martin Russell, who was in charge of the restaurant, ensured that the car park was empty of cars every night before locking the gates at 10pm. That meant we had to find somewhere to stay which in itself was no problem, as we knew Sandy and Geoff who owned a place just up the road with rooms and a gite which would be ideal. As it turned out they also had the very comfortable Lola, which is an old camper van that the pair used to go travelling around in at one time, but it was ideal for us to spend the nights in after a days fishing. Of course we had to unload the boat every night also which was extra work but then no different to what everyone else has to do so I wasn't complaining. The worst bit came in the mornings when we had to wait for Gerard or Martin to arrive to unlock the gate. Well, the first few days no one arrived until about 9am which left us stewing in the car for hours, eventually Sandy loaned us a key, which helped but it felt like I was struggling just to get fishing.

The first few days were fishless and it just didn't feel the same. We were that disappointed that we even went to look at another lake to see if it was a better option, although looking back I can't believe that we thought any other lake would be better than Cassien. The other lake didn't match up and after returning at around 3pm we decided to spend the evening right at the very top of the South Arm. We only had a few hours but then, as many people say 'A few hours in the right place is better than a few days in the wrong one. It turned out to be a good move as although there was little water in the top bays, there were quite a few carp about and they were certainly showing themselves. Once again, it was the same old story that the top bays had been left alone for some time and the carp were quick to realise that and were enjoying their peace and quiet – at least until I turned up! I managed two mirrors that evening of 32lb and 38lb and the world seemed a better place. The only sad thing was having to leave at 9.30pm when things were just getting going. Carp were crashing all around me and a big hit would've been on the cards for sure, but rules are rules and we had to go. Well it wasn't so much the rules, but the fact that certain people knew my car and knew where I was so I had no option but to leave, otherwise the temptation of staying on for a bit longer might have proved too great – not that I would ever consider breaking any rules of course (cough!)

It was worth getting the rods out for a few hours.

It soon became clear that the fish were only feeding in the afternoons and evenings, so how good was that! All of a sudden I didn't have to get up at the crack of dawn to race down for the early feeding spell. Instead, I could have a nice lie in, potter about a bit and then get to the lake just after midday for when the fish were just getting hungry. That was right up my street and although it might seem that I was losing a lot of fishing time, the important thing was that I was there at the right time and my disappointment of the first few days now turned to excitement as I wondered what was still to come.

The Third Point looked totally different from the previous year.

For a change it had been a slow start in Island Bay, but I still had faith that it would turn on sooner or later, so before looking elsewhere I had baited up quite heavily with the old MC/Addicted baits. I probably spread about 10kg of 18mm and 20mm baits all around the area and then just left it alone for awhile with a view to going back there in a few days time. Well, the baiting paid off and when I did return the fish were there. I started off with two small mirrors and then landed two larger ones of 32lb and 41lb over the next two afternoons. It was very different to the other summer sessions and I was getting far less action, but every Cassien session is different. Perhaps I had been spoilt a little bit by what had happened the previous summers, and I had to remind myself that it couldn't always be like that. The good thing was that I was at least now catching fairly regularly. The next afternoon I ventured back up the North Arm to my old favourite Third Point swim. It looked totally different up there this time around with the water right down. There were no real signs of anything for the first few hours. I thought back to how it had been 2 years earlier, when I hardly had five minutes to sit down and relax in between the action. It was amazing how different the lake could be from one trip to the next and now I was wondering if there were any carp out there at all? It was late afternoon when I received a slow drop back on one of the rods being fished out to the old forty feet marks. At first I had no idea what was on the other end, it could've been a bream or anything but it was a welcome bit of excitement when it looked like nothing was going to happen. It was only when I was out in the boat that I began to feel the weight of something a bit more substantial on the end. The longer the fight went on, the better it felt and it turned out to be a very nice common of 43lb, one that I'd seen pictures of a few times in the past and had quite fancied getting my hands on, so I was well chuffed to see it in the bottom of my net.

In fact, that was now a couple of forties in the space of a few days and really that wasn't a bad result considering when I'd caught all of those fish before, there hadn't been a single forty amongst them.

Nothing showed, but this common came from the deep water in the afternoon.

It was a shame to have to pack up again that evening as the fish were just starting to show when it was time to reel in. There was little doubt that they were feeding well through the hours of darkness and it was disappointing to think what I might be missing out on. I was even more disappointed when we were on the way back to Gerard's as there were boat loads of anglers heading out up the lake and we seemed to be the only ones heading back! They had been dropped off or were parking elsewhere but obviously intending to fish. I felt so deflated to be doing things by the book when I seemed to be very much in the minority. Nevertheless, I couldn't dwell on that and for a trip that had started off quite badly, it was turning out alright and as ever with Cassien it was a case of keeping an open mind and making the most of the opportunities when they arose. There were plus points to packing up early. There were always a few bottles of wine waiting in the bar and a few regular faces to have a social with. Sometimes band nights were organised and they were always good. Some of the party nights in Gerard's were legendary with bands such as Blah Blah or Waste blasting out their sounds into the early hours. However, on this particular evening as we neared Gerard's beach I could hear this noise coming from up the top. It was someone singing – or at least attempting to! "They must have a karaoke machine in" I thought to myself as I loaded the gear in the back of the car. As it happened it wasn't karaoke but it was the 'entertainer' for the night. "God help us, they're really scraping the barrel now" I thought. But perhaps I was a little hasty as although the guys singing never really improved he made up for it by being quite a character and his jokes were quite good, well some of them were. In the end, with the help of a fair bit of wine it should be said, he had us all laughing and it turned out to be a good night.

"Glad all you men are drinking wine as beer only turns you into women" he said.

We all looked at each other a little puzzled.

"Well think about it" he continued, "What happens if you drink too much beer? For a start you put on weight. You talk a lot more, but make less sense. You are more likely to start an argument and then blame everyone else for it and the more beer you drink the less you are able to drive a car properly!"

All around the men were in stitches while all the women gave him that icy cold stare that only a woman can give. In the end I think he was lucky to get out alive, but it was all good fun. It was all part of the charm of being in that part of the world, I might not have had the rods out but sitting there with a full glass of wine with the warm southerly breeze blowing through the trees, it was difficult to be too worried about anything – and besides, there was always the next day.

It was a fitting end to the trip.

For the final day we went back to the Island Bay. There was a mistral wind blowing in from the south making things more awkward than normal, but I spotted a couple of fish show further around to my left, in fact right on the last corner of the bay. There was only one thing to do, so I gathered all the gear together and made my way around the margins to where they were. The fish can be so localised at times and being a few yards away just isn't close enough. The waves were crashing into the bank but all I had to do was cast out around thirty or forty metres to reach the fish. It was very rocky out in front but the leads seemed to land on good bottom and it must have only been around ten minutes before the first one rattled off. To cut a long story short, over the next few hours I landed three mirrors and lost another one, the best one going 38lb. It was a fitting end to the trip, a final flurry of action to finish up with. It's always good to end on a high and it certainly felt like we'd done that. It was a different sort of trip but still good in its own way. I had to work harder to keep on the fish but I'd fished a lot less hours than I would have normally, just going out in the afternoons, so all things considered I went home happy.

There was little doubt that the best years for the summer day fishing had already gone. When I looked back to the first couple of years when the banks were virtually empty and the fishing was out of this world by Cassien standards, it was a far cry from how it was now. It was becoming more busy and more difficult year by year. But nothing lasts forever and Cassien has always continued to change in one way or another. I've always been of the same opinion, either accept the changes or stop fishing Cassien and look for somewhere else. Well I couldn't think about not fishing Cassien so I would just have to accept how things were and get on with it! The plain and simple fact is that I've lived with Cassien through the good and the bad times for over twenty years, so I know that it is almost always possible to catch fish and it often just needs a bit of hard work and the understanding of how the place 'ticks'. It's not like any other lake, the Cassien carp are a law unto themselves and it is never easy to predict how or where they will be caught. I've lost count of the amount of people I've tried to help when they've asked for advice. But many times that advice hasn't really turned out to be a great help because the fish aren't doing what I thought they would be – and it is the same situation for me on most of my trips. I start off where I think the fish will be, but invariably it's not that simple and I have to go off searching for the answer. If the lake is busy then those problems are magnified because places that you plan to fish are already taken and the fish are more cautious because they are aware of the extra pressure they are being put under. But many people still enjoy the summer trips to Cassien, myself included. There are few places in the world that can match what that lake has to offer - in fact nothing can match Cassien because it is unique, but somehow I don't think that any trips will be as good as those I've just written about – but you never know!

Tips, Tackle and Tactics

Of all the parts of this book, this is perhaps the most difficult to write. I often get asked questions on fishing waters around the globe and often those questions are quite generalised: "I'm going to France in a few weeks time and want to know how much bait to take?" or "Which type of line would you advise me to use – braid or mono?" They are typical of the questions that come my way, and there's nothing wrong with that and I'm always willing to help if I can, but the trouble is that every water in every country is different. It is very difficult to generalise about any of the tactics that I use because I tend to tailor them to suit wherever I am fishing at the time. My initial idea was to try and cover the tactics as much as possible when writing about the sessions but, however much I tried, it just didn't seem to work out that way and I couldn't put down everything that I did or what I used without going off track a bit, so in the end the only way to do it was to give the whole subject a chapter of its own. So, needless to say, what follows is the methods and bits and pieces that I've used successfully at different times on different waters and, hopefully, you can pick the bones out of it and find something that's useful to your fishing. One thing I most definitely would say is that after fishing so many different places over the years, I do get a feeling of the right approach and the right methods to use. Sometimes I slip up, but experience in a variety of situations does help out a great deal in the long run. I admire people that can fish on one water for several years and get it down to a fine art and end up catching all, or nearly all of the good fish that the water holds, but my life simply doesn't work that way. I need variety in my fishing and in a way it's the best and worst thing about what I do. It's great in one way because I've been able to travel far and wide to several different countries that I certainly wouldn't have been to if it wasn't for carp fishing. But the downside is the amount of different tackle that I need and the amount of times that I have to change it all around before going away. I sometimes look back at the old days when all I needed was two rods, a small bag of tackle and a few bits and pieces and that did me for the year - how times have changed!

Having fished so many different waters over the years I normally have some sort of idea of what I need to do.

Bait

Where shall I start? Well, I suppose bait is the best place to kick off and probably the area that most people seem to have problems with. There have been some huge changes in the bait industry since I first started travelling around. Anyone who has problems with bait these days just doesn't realise what it was like years ago when we had to make it all ourselves with our own ingredients, then we could have some real nightmares! For me, bait is the first thing to consider when planning any trip. A lot of things can be adapted, other things you can do without, but if your bait is no good for the job in hand then you really are going to struggle. Some of my views have changed over the years and I don't think that's a bad thing, times change and sometimes people will come along with new ideas that open my eyes and change my thoughts on how things work. Above all, my view is that there is no substitute for quality. The better the quality of the bait that you use, the better your chances of a good result will be. That comes as a result of getting to know people such as Rod Hutchinson, Tim Paisley and Martin Locke and listening to what they say. I don't agree with everything they say, but when it comes to bait there's little doubt that they know their stuff. Bait making is something of a dying art amongst most of us. Back when we had to make our own baits, our results depended purely on how good our knowledge was, okay there were base mixes on the market but many people made their own. Now we don't have to know anything about bait, as such, as the bait companies take all of the hard work out of it for us, but that doesn't stop people worrying about what to use. The great thing is that, with so many carp anglers around these days, it is easy to pick up on what is doing the business and what isn't. Bait companies are keen to let everyone know about it when someone's had a good result using their stuff so I always keep an eye on who's catching what and what they are using.

It was when I first joined Rod Hutchinson Products that it really began to hit home just what a difference a good bait could make – don't get me wrong, I'd used plenty of decent baits before that from companies such as Richworth, Geoff Kemp and Carp Company but switching over to Rod's products was the first time that I had access to more bait and also to a bait rolling company that could deliver baits to my doorstep already rolled to my own specifications. Of course, this is something that all of us have at our disposal now and it does make life easier. My first real success came with the MC Mix, which is one of Rod's fishmeal based baits, using that with the incredible Monster Crab and Shellfish Sense Appeal flavours. I caught no end of good fish on that bait and it was also the bait I used when winning the 2000 World Carp Cup with Tim Paisley. If tackle and tactics vary from lake to lake, then bait is a lot more reliable and a good bait is generally that – a good bait, and I used to take the MC Mix with me everywhere. Things only changed when one time I was off to Lake Raduta with Simon Crow and he'd ordered some bait from The Bait and Feed Company but, due to lack of stock, they had to make up the base mix from 50% MC Mix and 50% Addicted Mix. Well it turned out to be such a good bait that it became their

Good quality bait is always at the top of my list – there is no substitute.   *It always helps to know what problems you might be faced with.*

best seller and the MC/Addicted was born; I would still back that bait to work on just about any water.

Since then I've moved on to using Solar Baits for most of my fishing and results have been just as good, maybe even better! The first time I used the famous Club Mix I caught several fish up to 57lb on it and I just knew it was going to be a good one for me, and so it has proved to be, along with the BYT Mix which is a little different to most other baits but the carp just love it.

So, I think that quality is definitely the way forward, but what about amounts and the sizes of baits? The best advice that I can give anyone is to do their homework on a venue before going. There are all sorts of things that you would need to know beforehand, such as will there be freezer facilities where you are going? How many carp are in the venue? Are there any nuisance species such as crayfish or poisson chats? And another question that could be important is what the carp feed on naturally, but I'll come to that in a minute.

If freezers aren't available air-drying is the best way to keep bait in good condition.

If you are going for top quality bait then that will generally mean frozen bait. A great many venues, of all descriptions, do have freezers available for use now, but it's worth checking first. Some people do rely on drying their bait out in the swim when they are fishing but the problem with that comes when conditions are damp or wet. In my experience, baits don't really dry out well in those conditions and it's normally a matter of time before the baits start going off. I have found it better in those cases to leave the bait in the car in a cardboard box or something as the air inside tends to stay drier, although it does stink the car out a little. Personally, I prefer to take baits away that have already been air-dried in advance. Air-drying simply removes all or most of the moisture from the baits and therefore keeps them in good condition for a much longer period. Drying the baits this way doesn't affect the baits nutritionally – or at least the effect is fairly minimal, but it does make the storage and general use a lot easier, especially if there is no freezer to use. Air-drying is simple enough to do yourself, although The Bait and Feed Company, who I use for rolling my bait, also provide a drying service where the baits are literally delivered already dried in large paper sacks, which help to stop the baits from sweating. I have air-dried plenty of baits myself in the past and the best way is to lay the baits on mesh trays, or hang them in an air-dry bag, and leave them in a place that you know is dry and preferably warm. I would then turn or shake the baits around at least a couple of times a day. The time this process takes all depends on the type of bait you have and how hard you want the baits to be. There's certainly no need to worry that the baits will be too hard for the fish as I've never found them to be put off by even the hardest of baits and, anyway, the baits soon take on water once immersed in the lake and will soften up by the hour. Baits can also be re-hydrated just prior to use, which is something that has become a lot more popular in recent years. You can use any liquid for this process from plain and simple lake water up to any of the multitude of food liquids and enhancers widely available. I wouldn't advise that you use any neat flavours unless they are just to be used for boosted hook baits. Lake water, from the lake you are fishing, is obviously the safest way and it is a very good but basic method. By leaving them long enough soaked in water you end up with what is termed as 'washed out' baits which mimic baits that have already been on the lakebed for some time. It's a particularly good method when you feel that the fish are wary of bait that has only just been introduced. It's well worth considering on some of the commercial venues, where the turn over of anglers every week means that fresh bait is nearly always being used. I know that when Rob Hughes caught his massive Rainbow mirror of 75lb 12oz in 2007, he was fishing over washed-out baits during a period when the fish were playing very hard to get. Apart from just using lake water, another popular method is to use the water that particles have been soaked in. Hemp water is a popular one but the liquid from any soaked particles is worth a try as it adds flavour to the boilies as they get re-hydrated. The one thing I would definitely advise against is the use of tap water to hydrate the baits as there are too many chemicals in everyday tap water and it is likely to do the baits more harm than good. My own personal favourite, and one that I've used a lot, is the Liquid Belachan from Solar. It is slightly different to other belachan products that I've used and it's not the most pleasant stuff to use as it tends to make the baits go very sticky, and I normally have to wet the baits before they can be thrown or catapulted out, but the fish seem to really like the stuff so I'm more than happy to persevere with it for that reason.

There are all sorts of additives that can be used.
Liquid Belachan is one of my favourites.

Washed-out baits using lake water
have worked for many people.

When it comes to the sizes of baits it can very much depend on the venue which you are fishing. I mentioned earlier about finding what the fish feed on naturally and it does seem to have a bearing on what size of baits the fish will accept. For instance, the carp at Cassien eat mainly large food items naturally such as crayfish and swan mussels and, because of this, they seem to readily accept and for much of the time actually prefer larger baits. By large baits I am talking about single or double 24mm hook baits, but they will take much larger baits; this is often a blessing anyway with the nuisance species that are in the lake. But when you take Rainbow Lake the situation is quite different. I have to admit that, like many people, I don't really know what the natural food is at Rainbow. There are certainly little or no crayfish and mussels present and whatever they do eat I'm sure is on the small side, so when it comes to baits they don't seem too keen on the large baits. I have tried them there on occasions and although I did catch on them, they have been nowhere near as effective as smaller baits, such as anything between 12mm and 18mm. At Lac Serreire it is a similar situation where the carp grow big and have large mouths but they definitely prefer smaller baits. Perhaps the exception to the rule, and there are always exceptions, was Lake Raduta where most of my real success came after changing over to the larger baits. Having said that, although it did bring me more big fish, there was not

quite as much action as when using small baits. But the aim for me and most other people was to catch the better fish and not bag up with loads of the 'sprats', which would hoover up most baits they could find. It did surprise me a little, though, as their natural food seemed to consist mainly of the zebra mussels which are fairly small, but as I say there are always exceptions to any rule in carp fishing.

Bait size is often best matched to that of the carps natural food.

Plastic or imitation baits are something that most anglers have used or at least know about, now. Most people seem to be of the opinion that they would rather use a 'real' bait and I know what they mean, but imitation baits really do have a use in today's carp fishing. It was a long time before I plucked up the courage to use imitation baits and then, when I did, I was quite surprised as I caught almost straight away on them. It was out of frustration when fishing Cassien in the summer and getting pestered by nuisance fish that I thought I'd try something different and put on a plastic maize and peanut combination, popped up about three inches off the bottom. That day I caught two mirrors of 32lb and 41lb and my opinion changed a little. Since that day I've used all sorts of plastic baits with success, from the much-used maize up to the various 'boilies'. They've all worked pretty well, actually some of the best that I found were the plastic pellets, which are a bit larger in size although they are available in a variety of sizes, but I used the biggest ones I could find. The thing was that they actually smelled like real pellets too, which boosted my confidence in them. The biggest confidence booster, though, was when the alarm kept going off and there was another carp on the end – some of them were big, too!

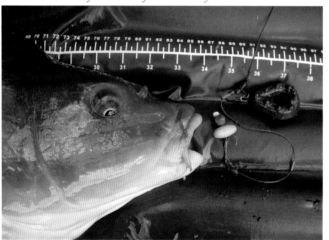

Plastic baits are a bit of a 'last resort' for me – but they do work!

The amount of bait to use during a session is another great stumbling block for anglers. I would say that, as a rule, I don't use quite so much as many people, but as ever it depends on the venue, the situation and even the swim in question. It can also depend on the way an angler wants to fish. There are always different ways to fish a venue and how you go about it can depend on how you have fished before or what you have been told. Take Cassien again. After fishing it for many years I have been convinced that the best way forward is not to use too much bait, if anything, keep it on the low side by perhaps just using fifteen or so boilies around each hook bait. That has worked time and time again for me and putting in loads of bait seemed to always be the kiss of death. But, in recent years I've now seen it many times where people have used large beds of baits and have had good results. A great example of that was when I fished with Tim Paisley back in 2000. Tim concentrated on the Bridge Swim and used his 'area baiting' approach, which has been described many times but means covering the whole area in front of you with bait. It might only be one boilie every metre or so but, over several acres, it adds up to a fair bit of bait but any carp moving through are sure to notice it. During that session I moved around various swims using the minimal baiting and, at the end of the day, we both caught well. In fact Tim had a fantastic session taking several good fish, including the famous Half Moon at 64lb, while I took fish up to 51lb 12oz. So we were both fishing the same lake at the same time but using totally different tactics, and had both had a trip to remember. I could reel off several other similar stories from a variety of waters but it just shows how difficult it can be to give advice on how to fish a water. In a way, by doing that you are lining yourself up to be shot down as, if you tell someone to fish one way and they then see someone else catch a load of fish using totally different tactics then there's only one person who will get the blame! But that is all part of the job, I suppose, and all I can do is say how I do it.

I have used area baiting myself on occasions and with some success. But the way I did it, which incidentally was down at Cassien again, was to just bait areas within a certain depth range. At Cassien I've always found that carp will feed within a certain depth range and are often unwilling to move out of those depths. In the winter time this often meant fishing between ten feet and twenty feet. To my way of thinking, baiting up in deeper or shallower water was just a waste of bait as I was sure that the carp wouldn't eat there, so the baiting was done right through the swim but only in the depths between ten and twenty feet. To me that is just common sense, it saves wasting bait unnecessarily and avoids having uneaten bait in the swim.

If ever there was a place where I thought it would be best to put a shed load of bait out, it would have to be the St. Lawrence River. There are just so many carp in that river, and they are so naïve, that I thought the best thing would be to give them a load of food that they wouldn't be able to resist. But when I fished with river guide, Paul Hunt, he surprised me by saying that it was best not to use so much bait and he only baited very lightly at the start of each day. But the action always came thick and fast. His view was that the fish would be there anyway and on the lookout for food, so putting out more bait would only prolong the time before the fish got to the hook bait. After a week of intense action I have to say that he was totally right and, once again, it shows that it does pay to listen to someone who has local knowledge.

The difference in that situation was that Paul Hunt knew more or less exactly where the fish were likely to be and on an un-pressured river it was easy enough to drop in on groups of hungry fish. For the World Carp Cup in 2005 it was a different situation. All of a sudden that section of the river had more pressure heaped on it than ever before and all the anglers fishing had to settle for the swim that they picked out of a hat. That creates a totally different situation, and Tim and I baited heavily during the first few days in an attempt to draw the fish in over the period of the five days that we had to fish. We already had some fish in front of us and caught fairly steadily, but it was on the third day when a very large group of fish moved out of the bay where they had been spawning that our baiting was to pay off. I'm sure we would have caught well anyway, but the large bed of bait that we had in front of us was enough to hold the fish there for most of the day and by the end we had doubled the weight of the team in second place!

Pellets are always a cheaper option whilst maintaining quality – and they last longer than you might imagine.

The bait used on that occasion was a mixture of maize, pineapple boilies and pellets. Pellets are a great bait for keeping the fish in an area for longer simply because they are more difficult for the fish to feed on once they break down. Most pellets break down fairly quickly and give off a good food signal without necessarily providing an easy meal, in the same way that a similar weight in boilies would. But even when the pellets have broken down the fish will still feed on them for some time afterwards. I can remember fishing Lac Serreire when it was a bit out-of-sorts, and I retrieved one of my baits to find it covered in some rather unpleasant-smelling slimy material. James Davis said straight away, "don't worry, that's the pellet that I put in for the fish over a week ago, they'll eat it when they want to." That surprised me a bit but that is exactly what happens, we often try to use the freshest bait that we possibly can, but the fish will eat some stuff that would almost turn our stomachs at times. In fact, going back to the St. Lawrence, I know that Paul Hunt uses maize that has just been left to soak for very long lengths of time. When you open the drums that it's kept in, it doesn't really smell much like maize and there is a thick crust on top of the whole lot – but most importantly, the fish love it!

I don't know if there is a limit to how long particles will stay effective for once they have been prepared properly. I know, without doubt, that I've thrown a lot away when they've started to smell a bit 'iffy' that would have probably caught me loads of fish but 'if in doubt, chuck it out' as the saying goes and I would much rather use a nice bucket of freshly-prepared particles any day – or for that matter a freshly-opened jar or tin of particles, as many of us seem to be switching over to ready-prepared particles now. Once again, it takes all the hassle out of preparing the stuff yourself and I have to say that most of the stuff that I've used has been prepared to a very high standard and you know it's perfectly safe to use. The hemp in particular always looks good and so do the tigers, which are normally contained in a sweet and nice-smelling liquid.

I don't generally use a great deal of particles for my fishing but there are times and situations when they have been essential. Tiger nuts are just a great bait, the carp love them and they are often ignored by other species, which almost makes them the perfect bait. The only trouble is that there are so many carp anglers thinking that way that they have been over-used on many venues and virtually fished-out. I've caught several good fish at Cassien and Rainbow on the tigers by using them sensibly. If they have been well-used in the past I find it best to go in with very small amounts and perhaps blend them in with either pellets or small particle mixtures, such as the Supa-Combi and Aniseed mix

I use groundbaits and seed mixes quite often but only in the right situations.

from The Bait and Feed Company, which I've found to be really good. That seems to lower the guard of the fish somewhat and prolongs the life of the tigers.

The small particle mixes have been particularly successful on Rainbow Lake in recent years and lots of people have had good results using them. Paul Hunt, who runs Rainbow Carp Tours (not to be confused with Paul Hunt from Canadian Carpin Holidays), has used the small particle mixtures for most of his fishing and his results have been exceptional, to say the least. The difference with Rainbow Lake is that, apart from a small number of tench and a few rudd and bream, the carp have virtually no competition for the food and fishing with that type of bait is very safe, whereas using the same method on Cassien is totally different. I've swum out before, with bags of small particles, and watched in amazement as hoards of small fish arrive and most of the bait has been eaten before it's even reached the bottom! I know that Alex Perrin persisted with small particles during the summer at Cassien and he had to work really hard, and bait constantly to feed off the small fish, but it did end up paying off for him with a few decent results.

Rigs 'n' bits

Where do I start with this part? Well, hooks are as good a place as any, I suppose. Hooks are definitely better now than they ever have been before; there are more patterns available and they are sharper than ever. I have my own favourites but if there was one hook that was better than anything else then we wouldn't need such a variety in the first place. Hooks are very much a personal choice and it is also true to say that certain hooks suit certain types of rig better.

For most of my fishing I've generally preferred the long shank patterns – apart from when using the hinged stiff rig or chod rigs, but other than that I've stuck with long shank hooks, going right back to the mid-1980's when I used the Drennan O'Shaugnessy's for much of my fishing. They were good hooks, but nowhere near as good as the ones I use now. At one time Hutchinson were selling a hook which they called the 'Stealth', although I think that the name changed after awhile, but they were very sharp and I did very well with them. It was the hook that accounted for my English PB, the lovely Cluster from Wraysbury 1. Then came the Long Shank Nailer from Carp R Us. I was drawn towards these hooks by the success that Tim Paisley was having with them, although they weren't liked by all anglers or all fisheries due to being linked somehow with bent hooks, I could never see the comparison really, and they were an extremely effective pattern of hook which I never found to cause any damage. There were two different styles of these hooks, the green ones and the grey ones. The grey ones I found to be by far the best and much stronger, and apart from one batch that seemed to be under par, they caught me fish from wherever I used them, including hit-and-hold situations at Rainbow Lake. I stopped using them when the grey versions stopped being produced and the green ones were the only ones I could get hold of, which I didn't feel were up to the job.

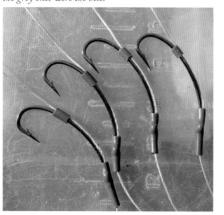

I had great success with the Long Shank Nailers, the grey ones were the best.

The Solar Stronghold's have become my firm favourite for most situations.

Thankfully, around that time, Martin Locke of Solar had just started to produce a long shank hook of his own. As soon as I took one look at the Solar hooks I knew that I had found the ones I wanted to use. I've used them for the best part of a couple of years now and they are everything that I want from a hook; a simple enough pattern but very strong and very sharp. In fact, they have become the number one choice for most of the Rainbow Lake anglers and on a venue where every item of tackle is tested to the limit that is about the best compliment they can have.

However good any type of hook is, they still need to be checked regularly when being used and, most importantly, before they are used as there will always be the odd hook that isn't up to scratch and just because a packet of hooks is new doesn't mean that they don't need to be checked. The hook is the only point of contact between you and the fish and should be treated as the most important part of all your tackle. I cannot emphasise that enough, more good fish are lost through people not checking hooks than probably most other reasons, and they are losses that needn't necessarily happen. The best way to test the sharpness of any hook is to pull the point over your thumb nail. If the hook is sharp it will scratch and dig in. If it slides too easily over the nail then don't mess around, just change it. Some hooks can last well and I don't advocate, as some people do, that you need to change the hook after every fish. I've had some hooks that have stayed sharp after landing three or four fish, the important thing is that you check the hook and are totally happy with the one that you are using.

The thumbnail test is the best way of finding out how sharp your hooks are.

Hooklength materials are like hooks in that there are a multitude of options, and one to suit every occasion. Kryston seem to dominate the scene where hook length materials are concerned and they do produce some really excellent products. The majority of anglers tend to go for the coated versions now and they always have a place in my tackle box. Which one I use depends on the type of fishing I'm doing at the time. Kryston Mantis or Mantis Gold is brilliant for general carp fishing situations, its thin but tough coating helps to make tidy and less 'obvious' rigs. Korda Hybrid, Kik-Bak from Armaled and Chakchiuma from Indyline have a thicker coating but that can come in handy when slightly stiffer rigs are needed. Both can be straightened out over steam to leave a straight hook link. They are both around 20lb and 25lb respectively and are perfectly good for most situations, I did actually catch my first Rainbow 30kg carp on the 25lb Kik-Bak and it coped well, but it seems like far more of my fishing is done these days in situations where the tackle is tested to the limit and there is no choice but to go for something more robust.

In the right situation the hinged stiff-link can be a brilliant rig.

When you need something really tough, there are few materials which can match up to Quicksilver.

I've learned the hard way that it is simply not worth taking the risk when it comes to which material to use. Strong gear is definitely safer to use – if used correctly, of that I have no doubt. It may be tempting to scale down the breaking strains and diameters to try and get a few more runs but I don't think that it really pays any dividends. I would much rather have a few less runs, but land the fish that I do hook. In reality, I'm not sure that it does make that much difference anyway and, if anything, we do give the fish too much credit at times. I've looked at some successful anglers rigs and sometimes wondered how they work, but the point is that they do work and strength is now the last thing that I sacrifice. Some of the strongest gear is not that much thicker or more obvious. We all know about Kryston's Quicksilver and Quicksilver Gold and they are simply superb, especially the latter in 35lb and 45lb which is one of my main choices for Rainbow, Cassien and the St. Lawrence, or for that matter any situation that might demand that little bit more. Spools of that gear are permanently in my tackle box and have been for some years, I don't know where I would have been without it. Something else that is worth mentioning here is a line called Corastrong Zoom. It's sold as a mainline and I bought myself a couple of spools in 79lb breaking strain to use as leaders on the St. Lawrence River, where the zebra mussels slice through normal lines like a hot knife through butter. It was great for the leaders, but looking at it I thought that it didn't look any thicker than 45lb Quicksilver, but it is quite soft to the touch and I've had some good success using it for hook lengths. I think that carp will find it difficult to break any material over 25lb b.s. so, no matter where you are fishing when using such heavy material, you should be sure that you are capable of handling the situation, and not putting the carp at risk.

I've learned the hard way that it's best to be prepared for everything.

I've used combi-rigs a lot. I'd just landed a 56lb mirror on this one.

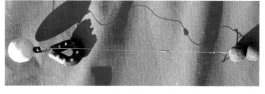

I don't use nylon hooklengths as much as I used to, the only exceptions to that are when I'm using the stiff rigs of one sort or another. I have to admit that, as much as people go on about the success of chod rigs, I just cannot get on with them. I've tried them on all sorts of waters and they just haven't performed when put up against other rigs. Maybe it's just me, in fact I'm sure it is, but for me the hinged stiff rig is a far superior rig and one that does the business on many types of water. I've used it more for my English fishing, it has to be said, but on waters where things have been tough, it has brought me some very nice fish. The 15lb or 20lb stiff link materials are ideal for the hinged stiff rig, anything more than that seems very difficult to actually tie up. This is also one of the few rigs were I use short shank hooks, such as those from Solar, or the ESP Stiff Riggers.

I have used a great variety of rigs over the years, some have been very simple, some a lot more complicated. I've been through different stages and moods and the rig I've used depended very much on how I felt at the time and which was the best in terms of putting fish on the bank for me. I try to think as clearly as possible about what will work and what won't, rather than getting caught up in trying out all sorts of weird and wonderful inventions.

Many of my rigs have been based around some type of combi-rig set up, it probably all started when the stiff booms came onto the scene. Right from the start I liked the idea of the stiff rigs but preferred to have a softer section closer to the hook. For me, this gave the rig more movement and also helped with the hooking capabilities. At the start, the combi-rig was mainly for pop ups but it worked so well that I started using it for nearly all my rigs, with great success. The materials used very much depended on the water that I was fishing at the time. At Farlows Lake, for instance, the stiff boom would have been made from 20lb Amnesia, with the softer part being 15lb Kryston Super-Nova or Silkworm. Whereas for Lake Raduta, the stiff boom would've been made from 80lb Fireline with the end section consisting of 45lb Quicksilver. So it was a very versatile rig and one which worked in a variety of situations and was my number one choice when tackling waters from Wraysbury to Cassien, it just seemed to suit them all. The rig always had to be made of two different materials, though, the coated braids, as good as they were, just never had the stiffness required to make the rig perform how I wanted it to.

Rigs don't have to be complicated to be effective.

The length of a rig is one thing that crops up every now and then. I don't place quite so much importance on this as some other people do but, within reason, it still has to be right. I suppose if anything I tend to err on the longer side. Many people go the other way and believe that shorter rigs give them a better chance of hooking the fish, but when I have used them I've had too many missed takes or fish just nicked in the edge of the lips. For the most part I would say that the length of the rig doesn't vary too much from around 25cm to 30cm. I'm never worried about going slightly longer and if anything I think it often helps to present the bait better. I have recently used hook lengths that were 65cm (25inches) long and they worked okay for me, with some really good hook holds. It all depends on the situation, I've used the long rigs on very silty lakes and also where the fish were very pressured and I've caught enough fish on them to know that it was no fluke. Perhaps the only time I will go much shorter is with the hinged stiff rig, where I'll perhaps cut the main section down to 10cm and the hook section to 4cm. As I say, I use a fair amount of different rigs at different times but I try to tailor it to suit the situation at the time and the water I am on.

Snag Fishing

Fishing close to, or over snags is always a tricky subject, but it's something that most of us have to do sooner or later. It is something that I've had to deal with for years and small improvements have been made along the way. Looking back to the first trip I had to Cassien, in 1986, the snags then consisted mainly of tree stumps and seemed absolutely horrendous, and I lost quite a bit of gear, but I have fished that same area several more times in the intervening years and now those same snags seem fairly tame by comparison. The big improvements in the tackle available now, and the tackle I own now, has made a big difference, but it goes further than that, it is also the methods of fishing around the snags that have improved over the years.

Most snags on the big reservoirs are made up of tree stumps.

As ever, it very much depends on the water in question. If it's a matter of fishing over snags, then it's normally a question of raising the line up off the bottom as that is where most of the snags are. Most of the big reservoirs around Europe and beyond were created by damming up small rivers, then flooding the surrounding countryside. Any trees that were in the area to be flooded were simply cut down, leaving the stumps in place. The stumps themselves don't actually cause too much of a problem, but it is when the surrounding area has been underwater for a while and the ground becomes softer and starts to wear away, which exposes the roots. It's the roots which are mainly responsible for catching the line, although what I have noticed too is that after some years the stumps become more waterlogged and some lines cut into the soft wood far easier. This is certainly true of some of the thinner braids that are popular now. Once they have cut into the stump it can feel like you are snagged solid. The best way around this seems to be to use a thick mono leader, which tends to slide over the rotten wood rather than cut in. That is okay for the last section of the line but often the snags are closer in. At Cassien, many of the problems come from fishing over the shallower margins into the deeper water. These shallower ledges are often strewn with sharp rocks and stumps that the line can catch on, especially if the fish kites on a tight line. The first and most major improvement where this is concerned is the addition of a buoyancy aid on the line. This buoyancy aid can be made from anything that floats and can be attached to the line. It all depends how much you want the line to float. Poly balls and similar floats of around 20cm to 40cm are what I've used most and they do the job really well. It's not until you've used these things that you realise just what a difference they make. Just last summer I watched a group of guys fishing on Cassien and when one of them got a run it was sheer panic to get to the rod as quick as possible, but as soon as they did it was already around a snag and the fish was eventually lost. They weren't using a buoyancy aid, but if they had have been I'm sure that the fish could have been landed. It takes all of the panic out of hooking a fish (well almost), but once a fish is hooked all you need to do is avoid pulling into it too tight, then just get in the boat and follow the fish out as they invariably head for deeper water, where it is much safer to play them. Once above the fish you can then tighten up more and play them as normal. Doing it this way will never ensure 100% success but I do feel like I'm going to land every one whereas the odds used to be much more in the carps favour.

A buoyancy ball in action at Cassien. You can see how well it keeps the line off the bottom.

You have to adapt your tactics depending on what you are faced with.

At Rainbow, people have taken the buoyancy aid thing a step further and actually float the line on the surface. This is only done in certain swims that demand it, the problem being that there are several bars and snags that rise up very close to the surface and it is very difficult to keep a tight line direct to the fish if it is catching on some of the obstacles in between. The floats used are simply either larger poly balls or small drinks bottles. In the right situations they do help a great deal and if there is one thing that people say they don't like about fishing this way it's the angle that the line comes down from the float to the rig. I can understand what they are saying but after using the floats and catching plenty of fish using them, I can say that the effect the angle of the line has is minimal, if anything it might actually help the situation by keeping the majority of the line out of the way of the carp. The Rainbow carp, in particular, know when there are lines in a swim and they know how to deal with them. I know of one pair of anglers who were having a tough time but when they added floats to their lines, they started catching some good fish.

Bottle rigs enable you to keep the line right up near the surface.

If used sensibly, poles to guide the line around obstacles are perfectly safe.

Actually, the anglers at Rainbow have also taken snag fishing to another level with the use of poles, as well as the buoyancy aids. For anyone who doesn't know, Rainbow contains a mass of islands of all sizes but in particular many small ones. Although they are not in every swim, most swims do have some and, needless to say, after being fished for consistently in recent years the carp tend to look for the more out of the way places, and it's often necessary to find a way of fishing in the more awkward spots in a swim. I have seen some articles written on the methods used at Rainbow which were just ridiculous and they have little to do with how the vast majority of people fish there normally. It may seem over the top to fish this way but in practice it is safer than it may appear – if it's done correctly. Again, the emphasis has to be on doing things sensibly, if the fish are in a spot where there is little chance of landing them, then it is madness to even try it. But you only have to look at the condition of most of the Rainbow carp to know that the methods not only help to land the carp, but they don't damage them either.

Most of the fishing I've done at Rainbow hasn't been around poles, but it has required that I've fished locked-up when the baits have been placed fairly close to snags. Now, when I say fishing locked-up, I do mean totally locked-up! The bait runners are switched off and the clutch screwed down tight with the anti-reverse on. This is also done with braided mainline, although I do usually have a mono leader of around twenty or thirty metres that acts as a shock absorber, as well as being good around the tree stumps as I was talking about earlier. It is certainly not a method for the faint-hearted and it does require you to be close to the rods at all times, but as savage as it sounds, it is a very effective method of stopping any fish in its tracks. The point is that you have fish of possibly 70lb or even 80lb (if you are lucky enough) looking to head for their safe areas as soon as they are hooked and if they get a chance to build up speed then they are going to take some stopping. But, if they have no slack line at all then what happens is that they cannot get their head around and get moving in the first place, and if you are on the rod quickly (which I always am) then it's much easier to get any fish moving towards you. I always aim at picking the rod up within four seconds of the alarm sounding – and that means at night, too – and by getting to it so quickly it's almost as if you gain control of the fish before it really knows what is going on. It may seem like very intense fishing, and it is, but it means that probably 95% of the fish I hook at Rainbow are landed, and that's the important thing.

I've found that a good mono leader tends to perform better than a braided version.

These aren't just for show. Good indication can make all the difference.

I've had a bit of a love/hate relationship with braid over the years. At the present time I use it for far more of my fishing on the continental waters as, once you get used to braid, it seems a superior material to mono. Having said that, there are some very good nylon mono lines on the market now, in particular the Power Carp by Ultima which is fluorocarbon coated and has much less stretch than most other mono's and, therefore, almost makes it a good in-between sort of line. Rainbow certainly requires the use of braid and I found out the hard way that there is simply too much stretch in mono and, under pressure, with a big weight on the other end, I found that the fish could still get to the snags, which they shouldn't really have reached, and wouldn't have done with braid.

Like everything else, braids have improved a lot and some of the ones that I thought were good a few years back were pretty rubbish really. The Bullet Braid by Nash is one that has definitely stood up to all the tests and has shown to definitely have longevity, too. My main requirements from a braid are that they are strong and very reliable, and also sink. I'm sure that there are many uses for floating braids, one of my friends who fishes the Orient says that floating braids really help when fishing at long range over areas of tree stumps and I can see that point but I've yet to fish anywhere where sinking braid wasn't better. I would rather raise the line up myself with poly balls if need be, but otherwise braid that floats only seems to cause problems such as bowing in windy conditions, catching any surface debris going by and, of course, if you have any boats going through the swim, including your own, it is just asking for trouble.

It's fair to say that I would use braid for the majority of my fishing, the only problem with that is that there are a lot of waters around now that don't allow the use of braided mainlines. This is certainly true for a lot of English waters but also for more and more on the continent, especially the commercial waters. Whenever rules are brought in like that I don't question why, as the people who run the commercial waters know how valuable the fish are and they want to protect them as much as possible and feel that some materials are less safe than others – or to put it another way, those materials are safer in the hands of some people than they are in others. Leadcore is a prime example of that, for many years I didn't use it at all but more recently I have used it whenever possible. I particularly like the really heavy Score Gold from Kryston, which is a heavier gauge than anything else that I've come across. I do like to pin down the line as much as possible or at least make it less visible and the Score Gold sinks very quickly if the line is just slightly slackened off. If I am using lower gauge leadcore, which might be the case with slightly down graded tackle such as for English fishing or smaller commercial waters, then I still add either some rig putty or a flying back lead to help it sink better. Of course, if I am fishing locked up with tight lines then even the leadcore will be raised off the bottom within a certain range, but I don't mind that too much as I feel that the leadcore is less likely to put fish off if they bump into it, and it is a little softer to the touch and less likely to lift any scales when playing the fish. If leadcore is not allowed where I'm fishing then I always use some sort of fish friendly tubing.

A good lead-release system is essential when fishing close to snags.

Two versions of the Gripper-type leads which are many peoples favourites.

Lead safety clips were a great invention and although I wasn't quite so keen on them to start with, most of the rigs I use carry one now. There are so many different ones on the market that perform in different ways and it's important to find one that suits the way you fish. What I require from a lead clip is that it releases the lead every time that a fish is hooked and believe me not all lead clips do that by any means. I must admit that as a great deal of my fishing is done with a boat it makes things a little easier as I'm not trying to cast heavy leads all that often. The trend is very much for heavier leads these days, the mere mention of an 8oz or even 10oz lead a few years ago would have made some people faint, but on lots of waters they are very much the norm. It's not until you've done the type of fishing where you need leads like that, when you realise just how much better they are. Fishing at range with braid, in the wind, can cause lesser weights to be moved easily and the same can be said of fishing on the side of ledges or in flowing water. But it's not just that, it's also the hooking of the fish. In most situations the hook needs to be set immediately, and properly, as soon as the fish moves off and my experience has shown that you get a far neater and deeper hook hold with a bigger lead, but the problem with those bigger leads is that you need to lose them as soon as possible after the fish is hooked and an efficient lead clip is the best way. Of all the ones I've tried, the Solar ones come out on top. The swivel locks into the clip and the clip is designed as such that the heavy lead comes away every time.

Rods and reels

With rods and reels the choice is very much a personal one, especially when it comes to rods. The first thing you need to decide is what you actually want your rods to do. As time has gone on, rods have gradually become stronger and lighter and whereas a few years ago a 2¾ lb test curve was the average, I would say that the average now is more likely around 3¼ lb. That has really followed the general trend in tackle, which has become better and stronger, but also we require more of our rods now. I can still remember when, if you could cast 100 yards you were the business, but now with today's improved tackle and technology, we are looking more towards the 200 metre mark and guys such as Mark Hutchinson can regularly achieve those sorts of distances.

Rod choice can be a very personal thing.

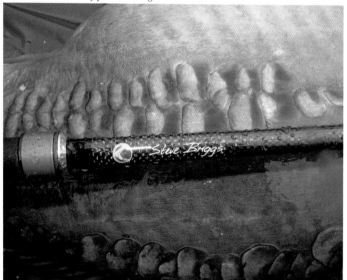

That's all very well, and I do admire people who can cast such distances but I have to say that, in my own fishing, long range casting is something that I only rarely have to do. But in those cases, power does seem to equate to distance. The Venturis range from Venture are my main choice should I need to do any heavy casting. The V1 is the 12ft 3lbs version and although very slim and light, it is very powerful and it is the main tool for my fishing on home waters. But for the really big chucks the V2 is really the kiddy. The extra length and power that this version has can launch a lead a hell of a long way, as well as being able to cope with heavy PVA bags, which is more or less a necessity for a rod nowadays. For much of my fishing I am still a bit of an 'old school' angler, though, and I like my rods to be playing tools rather than casting tools. I suspect that comes from the influence of Rod Hutchinson as his rods were always built that way and I loved his IMX's and Dream Maker range when they were about, but I have to say that the VXR-1 from Venture is without a doubt the most pleasant rod I've ever used for playing fish on. They have such an advanced quality of blank that they can really bend into a fish but still have that feeling of power. For my fishing they are the perfect tool as much of it is done with the use of a boat anyway, so I don't need them for casting, but they do act as a very good shock absorber when fishing on a very tight set up with braided line and it makes the whole experience a little less nerve wracking. But, also for playing fish from boats they are very nice. For that type of fishing a stiff, powerful rod isn't necessary. But each to their own, if that's what you like then that's your choice to make.

When it comes to reels I do have a firm favourite and that is the Big Pit Baitrunner from Shimano. The trend has definitely gone more towards large-spooled reels, as they cover all situations, particularly long range fishing where you need that extra bulk of line, but they are just as effective when fishing at close range on small waters. I've tried

Call me old-fashioned but I still prefer rods that are meant for playing fish.

smaller reels, and still own many, and some are good while others are not so good. The biggest problem I have with any reel, but especially the smaller ones, is line twist. Line twist is something that drives me mad and certain reels seem much worse than others. I don't really know what causes it but all I do know is that it's something that I have never encountered with the Big Pits. I'm sure that big-spooled reels, in general, are better in this respect, although that's only my findings and it might well have something to do with the way I reel in. It's not just the line twist – or lack of it - that keeps me using the Big Pits, but also their reliability.

My old Big Baitrunners, they've been used and abused but are still going strong.

I must have bought my first set of them around ten years ago and they are still going strong – and considering the amount of fishing that I have done with them, coupled with the lack of care that I've shown them in general, I can only say that they are right out of the top drawer, quality wise. If they have one minor fault, it is in the very cold weather where I have noticed that the baitrunner can freeze and won't switch off until it's thawed out a bit by either dipping it in the lake or just clamping a hand around it. It's caused me a few panics on Cassien, where I've gone out in the boat on frosty mornings and not been able to gain any line, but thankfully it has never cost me a fish to date.

Echo sounders

Echo sounders have to be one of the best inventions ever for carp anglers. If you can use a boat then a sounder, or 'fish finder' as they are often called, is always a big help. Perhaps what they do more than anything else is save you a great deal of time when it comes to feature finding, and they also do it a lot more thoroughly.

Most of what you do with an echo sounder could also be done with a marker rod or by 'donking' the lead on the bottom as you go along. But you can imagine the dilemma when you arrive at a big water something like 3000 or 4000 acres in size, and you've been told to look for the old riverbed as that's where the fish will be. With a sounder you simply get in the boat, switch it on and keep going out until you find the spot. Of course, it's not as easy as that most times but on the big waters it's the only reasonable way that you're going to find out what's really out there in the time you have. I wouldn't be lying if I said that I thought it was one of the most important bits of kit you can have, and I would feel a little bit lost to go off for a session without one.

Echo sounders are almost essential on some waters and they are simple enough to use.

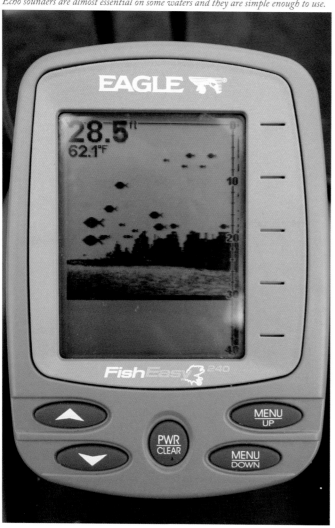

There's all sorts you can buy now that have colour screens, 3D images and a stack of settings that we'd probably never use, if you are going to get one then I would recommend just a decent but basic portable model. There are various makes that are all good, but I've normally stuck with the Eagle or Lowrance versions, which do everything that I require from them. Most echo sounders are actually designed for sea-going vessels and they do far more than is needed by us. I know I'm not wrong in saying that all you need to do is switch the echo sounder on which puts it straight into automatic mode, and away you go – it's as simple as that! You might want a backlight on at night or change from feet to metres and vice versa, but they are certainly not difficult to use.

What the screen will show you is a cross-section of the water beneath the boat. The sounding does spread out in a cone shape from the transducer downwards but it doesn't cover a big area, I imagine that if you are over about twenty feet then the area covered will be about ten feet across. It is very important that the transducer is horizontal to the water surface, but at least 10cm below the surface, this ensures a more accurate reading. Don't do as one of my friends did and have the transducer upright as he thought he had found a swim full of fish when the screen was almost black with them but in reality he was seeing most of the fish between him and the other bank 800 metres away!

I've often heard it said that you shouldn't use an echo sounder for fish location and the term 'fish finder' is misleading, well I wouldn't particularly agree with that. What I would say is that they are not so reliable for fish finding as they are for seeing what's on the bottom. Sounders are not as intelligent as some people imagine. They are only basic things that show what the soundings tell it. A mid water object shows up on the screen as a fish symbol as that's all they can do, it doesn't mean that object is a fish, even though it is highly likely, but there are times in strong winds when clumps of weed in mid water have shown up as fish on the screen. The other thing is that it cannot tell

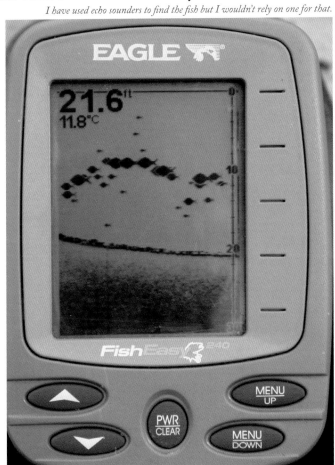

I have used echo sounders to find the fish but I wouldn't rely on one for that.

you what type of fish you are seeing. Normally the fish symbols are in three or four different sizes and the biggest size could be any fish over 5kg or 8kg, so the fish could be a carp, but it could also be a pike, zander, catfish or even a group of small fish that can show up as one bigger fish. So, you can see the problems you have and the best thing is to use the sounder as much as possible until you get a feel for what it is showing you. There are times when I have found good swims with lots of fish purely by what I have seen on the screen. I found one swim on Cassien, in the winter, where big shapes kept showing up at the same depth around the area. I thought that they had to be carp so I moved in there and had a really good session. It worked that time but, of course, even if you see fish it doesn't mean they will stop there and feed; they could be just passing through. Actually, that has just reminded me about a guy I met on one lake in France a few years back. He was a nice enough guy but must have been using a sounder for the first time as he came out with these two different statements. First time he said to me, "I've seen some fish but I think that they're all heading for the spawning bay as they're all facing the same way on the screen!"

Then, a day or so later, he came up with a better one than that, "There are still fish in the swim but they're not feeding because I haven't seen any of the symbols with their heads down on the bottom!" Bless him.

Dropping a lead down can help you to find out just what is down there.

What sounders really do best is give you a detailed view of the bottom and that is really valuable. What you see is straightforward enough and easy to work out. The greyline feature is what shows you how firm or soft the bottom is (firm bottoms eh! Ooh missus!) Sorry about that, but in laymans terms, the thinner the black line is on the picture of the lake bed, the firmer the bottom will be and of course the thicker the black line the softer the bottom is. If there is weed about it can mislead you a bit and show up as a soft-type bottom, but again plenty of practice will get you used to what you are seeing. Actually, a good idea if you are just starting to use an echo sounder is to take a rod with you with just a lead on the end of the line for 'donking'. As the name suggests, if you drop the lead to the bottom and keep thumping it up and down you will feel what's down there and get a better understanding of what the screen is showing.

Besides the obvious features, sounders will also show snags – at least those of a reasonable size. Snags can, of course, be fish holding areas, but it can also be useful to know if there are any in between your swim and where you are fishing. If there is a bad one about, I quite often drop a marker on it just for reference when I go out to play a fish or bait up. Markers of one sort or another are always a good thing to have with you in the boat, anyway. One of the frustrating things is when you find a good spot and then lose where it is. From the bank it is not so difficult, as you can line up with things on the horizon, but when you are on the water it becomes a lot more difficult, plus it is not always easy to keep still. So, the best thing to do is, once you spot something of interest, drop a marker on it straight away. H-Block markers are ideal for this as you can drop them quickly and they unravel themselves. Then it gives you a chance to have a good look around the feature and you have a point of reference to work from. If you find a slightly better spot then drop another marker rather than moving the original one as, again, you can drift quickly and lose your spot.

H-Blocks are the most popular type of marker. I normally have a couple with me in the boat at all times.

H-Block markers are the most popular it would seem, and they are very easy to use but they are not the best in all situations. For instance, if you are playing a fish that goes around the marker it can be a bit of a nightmare. If that is likely to happen then I prefer to use one of the pole-type markers, such as the one made by Atrotube, which are great as, when the line goes around them they bend over until the line flicks off them and then you just play the fish as normal. I don't normally feel that markers spook the fish at all, although I know plenty of people who have reservations about them. If in doubt, I just place the marker ten yards or so behind the feature and, again, just use it as a point of reference. Sometimes it can be a good idea to put the marker away from where you are actually fishing – especially if a 'Wolfgang' is about (sorry Si) as otherwise, if you are catching a few, it won't be long before there are two hook baits on the spot!

Anyway, I haven't covered half of the things that I was going to write here, but I'm running out of space on this part so I'll have to halt it there. But it covers my thoughts on most of the basics. So there we go – just get out there and catch 'em!

Pole markers such as this one from Atrotube are easy to see and safe enough to fish close to.

Carping in a Cooler Climate

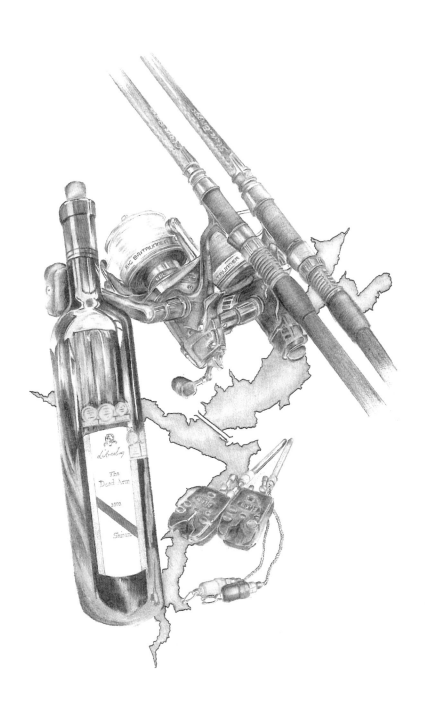

Carping in a Cooler Climate

Heading South for the Winter

Apart from the odd few days here and there, virtually all of the winter sessions down at Cassien had taken place in the North Arm. It had always been our favourite part of the lake – and also the most peaceful, but our usual session in the winter of 2001 had been particularly difficult. Again we had spent a short time in the South Arm and in the West Arm, but that had produced only a couple of fish and as-ever we relied on the North Arm for a bit of action. But that year was tough, probably the toughest trip I'd known up to that point. I still caught a few decent fish, but with low water levels and very low temperatures it felt like the whole trip was a bit of a struggle.

One year later and it was time to head off south once again but I'd thought long and hard about it and I felt as though it was time for a change. The North Arm had been great and I had plenty of good memories from our times there, but I had fished it almost exclusively for years and I couldn't help feeling that there was much more of the lake to see. I'd never given the South Arm my full attention at any stage in the past, so a proper go at it was well overdue. One thing that was very noticeable, looking back through my results, was that the big fish had been fairly elusive. I'd always caught fish and don't get me wrong, I'd had my fair share of good ones, but the really big fish nearly always seemed to come from the South Arm and I was in that frame of mind that I wouldn't mind sitting it out for awhile if the chance of something large might be at the end of it. So that was enough to make my mind up – a full session in the South Arm it would be.

The water can rise very quickly at times!

One of the big mistakes that I'd made the year before was that I'd decided to make all my bait up on the bank. This might sound like an unusual thing to do, but I wanted to have the freshest bait possible. Having good quality, fresh bait was essential in my own mind and over the long period that I was at the lake I felt that if I made the bait up as I needed it then it would be better than anyone else's, and better bait equals more fish. Well in theory it sounded good but in practice it was a bit of a non-starter. Regular trips to the shops for eggs, carrying all the bait making equipment around with us and the time spent making the stuff – not to mention trying to dry the baits out when it was wet! All this meant that I never had the amount of bait that I needed, when I needed it, so I knew I would do things different next time around.

This time I had 100% confidence in the bait.

The answer came from my old mate Simon Crow, I'd fished with him at Lake Raduta in the October and he had with him some MC/Addicted baits in 24mm that had been rolled and air-dried for him by The Bait and Feed Company. Those baits were spot on and they looked as fresh on the final day as they did on the first. I could see straight away that it was a far better way of taking bait away for a session as all of the hard work had been taken out on the bait preparation front. Thankfully, he had enough for me to 'borrow' a few kilos from him and the results we both had over the two weeks made me realise that this was the way forward. After that trip with Crowy, I just knew that those same baits would be just what was needed down at Cassien and as soon as I was home I got straight on the phone to Dave Coakley to get my order in. I've never believed in using vast amounts of bait at Cassien, especially in the winter, and I felt 40kg of boilies would be more than enough for a session of around four weeks. That would be split into 20kg of 20mm and 20kg of 24mm baits. Confidence in bait is so important and I was brimming with confidence with these, I was just sure that if the fish were looking for food then they would find these irresistible!

It was late November when we finally arrived at Pierre's restaurant. It was mild in the sunshine but there were plenty of clouds around too and it looked as though we could be in for a bit of rain before too long. The lake looked good; the water was around five or six feet down from its full level and there were surprisingly few people fishing. On the few days leading up to the trip I'd heard that it had been very busy just recently and couldn't quite work that one out, but as we soon found out, the vast majority of the anglers had only just left over the previous weekend and no more had arrived – a rare but very pleasant situation! This gave us virtually all of the lake to choose from, there was only one angler fishing near the top end of the South Arm, a young German guy fishing near the Banana swim on the road side of the lake, so I thought over on the opposite side somewhere would be an ideal starting point.

We pulled into what we call the 'Bunker swim', it was a swim that had produced a couple of 40's for me in the past and one that always seemed to hold a fish or two. The water in front drops fairly quickly off into the river bed and most of the features are at close range, also there are some interesting bays both left and right of the swim and knowing the Cassien fish as I do, I knew that there was every chance that they would be in and out of those bays searching for food. I always like to fish swims that give plenty of options rather than putting all my eggs in one basket. Here I could fish out into the river bed as well as the bays and various other features, so it was the perfect starting place.

As ever, it's always a job and a half getting all the gear sorted out on that first day, you always need more gear for a winter trip and after the long drive it seems to take even more of an effort, but once everything has been done and you can sit back with that first cup of tea, it is one of the best feelings in the world. The first nights sleep is always a good one and the thought of having to do little else but concentrate on fishing for the weeks ahead is a great feeling to say the least – the real world is put on hold for awhile.

Instant action is never a priority at Cassien and I never expect it really, but at 11pm that night the first run had me scrambling out of the bag. It was from a spot that I'd felt confident in when I was putting the baits out earlier that day, a sloping bar that shelved off into the depths, but at around 15 feet levelled off slightly forming a perfect little dinner table. However, what happened next was totally unexpected. As I picked up the rod there was no resistance at all and on retrieving the bait I found that the hook length had just parted in the middle under no pressure. I have no idea whether there was a fault in the hook length material or it had just cut on something sharp. Either way it was a disappointment and any thoughts of getting the session off to a quick start had to be put on hold. But thankfully I didn't have to wait too long before I was in again. Although it was very close in, I had found one nice-looking feature literally just a few yards out in front of the rods and in the daytime it didn't look much but I knew that under the cover of darkness the fish will come out and investigate anywhere. This time everything went as planned and a common of 15lb was soon being admired on the unhooking mat. Hardly a monster but the first one of every trip is always very welcome and after all it was still only the first night.

The following morning the young German guy came across to us, he introduced himself as Sven and enquired how the night had gone. I proudly told him that I'd got off the mark with a small common and he replied that he'd also caught a common, but his weighed 44lb and would I go across and take the pictures for him? I immediately felt a bit silly sounding so happy about my 15 pounder but went across to do the honours, and of course have a quick glance at how he was fishing too – like you do! Sven had already had a couple of other fish and was getting his action in fairly shallow water, nothing unusual there I thought and it was good to know that there were obviously a few fish in the area. We chatted for awhile and he told me that he was down for about the same length of time as me, but would have to fly back to Germany for a job interview in a few days time and then on his return he would spend the rest of his trip in the North Arm with my good friend Marcus Lamprecht. He was a nice enough guy even though he had caught a bigger one than me, and I said that I'd go over and photograph any other fish that he caught – as long as it wasn't too many. It looked like we might be in for some rain so I made my way back across to where Joan was preparing something to eat. Before long the heavens opened and it looked like it was going to be in for some time – as can happen in that part of the world. Months can pass by with no rain at all, but when it does arrive it can make up for lost time! It rained all afternoon and evening and I must have drifted off to sleep. I was awoken by Joan, who I could see was wandering about outside with the head torch. "You'd better come out here" she said. The rain was still falling very heavily and as I looked outside I could see that the water was rising rapidly, the tent was set up well back in the trees, but the level had risen so quickly that the rods, which had been on dry land were now out in the lake with water up to the reels! All the rods were all on single bank sticks so I set about moving them back one by one, but the water was literally rising that fast that by the time I had moved them all, the water was fast approaching the first one again! If you stood watching you could actually see the water creeping up and on a place the size of Cassien that's a lot of water, I can tell you! Eventually, the water was approaching the bivvy and we had to move everything back again and again until we were up against the trees at the back of the swim and we couldn't go back any further. With just inches between the bivvy door and the rising water, it finally eased up. After scrambling around in the dark, moving all the stuff and trying to keep it dry, we were both tired and were grateful for the chance to be able to grab a few hours sleep.

By daylight the lake looked totally different. The level had risen by at least five or six feet and the water was now a dark brown colour. There were boats, logs and all sorts of debris

Thankfully the water stopped at the doorway as we couldn't move back any more.

drifting about all over the lake, but somehow through all of that we had managed to keep most things dry. We were both tired but the kettle went on and we sat back in what little room we had left and thought about having some breakfast. Just as we'd done that, one of the rods fishing into the bay to our left burst into life or really I should say gurgled and spluttered into life. I was pleased that I'd made the effort to bale out the boat as it would've been unusable otherwise. This felt like a better fish and it fought hard in the murky depths. Normally it was possible to see the fish way down during the fight, but unusually I couldn't see it at all until it was almost in the net, due to the colour of the water. It was a clean-looking mirror of 36lb, which made all the efforts of the night before a little more worthwhile. Just as I returned the fish, Sven arrived in the swim and I told him about the mirror I'd just caught. This time his reply was – "I've caught a mirror too, it weighed 54lb can you take the pictures for me?" This bloke was really starting to get on my nerves now! I agreed, of course, but it was starting to grate on me a bit that every time I caught a fish it was bettered by this German bloke and the sooner he had to clear off for his job interview the better! Of course it wasn't his fault and he was just enjoying himself and catching a few fish, but you know how it is.

The rain had eased off by then but the water continued to rise as it was still cascading down from the hills around us. I went across and took the pictures as promised. It was a cracking fish, which I hadn't seen before although he knew it from a past capture by a friend of his. I didn't stop long as I knew that there was work to do back at our rather wet base. We had no alternative other than to move swims as we'd simply run out of room where we were. To our right was another swim which was normally more difficult to fish as it has several bushes growing out from the margins, but the high water actually made it an easier prospect as now we could only just see the tops of the bushes and really it looked far better than where we had started off. It also had a nice flat area where it would be safe to set the bivvy up. This was a swim that was largely ignored through most of the year as it has little going for it, but the high water opened up a lot more possibilities which looked quite enticing. Previous experience told me that the fish like to get right into the margins when the water had risen quickly – as they do on many waters I suppose. Being naturally inquisitive they can't help checking the new areas out for any food items that might now be submerged and there were plenty of such areas at close range. Although we had no choice other than to move, I felt that we'd actually moved to a better area and my only hope was that the fish would hang around for awhile. I was sure that they would keep coming back for the bait once they'd had a taste of it. I wasn't putting lots out but I was spreading it all around the area and the hope was that after time it would draw the fish in from other parts. That might sound a bit optimistic, but it was something which I'd seen happen before so I knew that the carp would

We had little choice other than to move but it was the right thing to do.

respond to good bait and actively look for it if they liked it enough. I was confident that the bait I was using was as good, if not better than anything else being used around me so it was just a matter of being a little patient and letting things take their natural course.

The first forty of the trip fed as the thunder crashed overhead.

A very pretty mirror that I caught twice in a matter of days.

The rain returned and thunder rumbled through the hills around us. When a low pressure system descends on Cassien the clouds are often so low in the area that the thunder literally shakes the ground, it feels as if everything is taking place just above your head. More rain would be coming for certain, but at least we were now safe in the knowledge that the lake was full to capacity so we wouldn't have to worry about being flooded out again, water was still coming into the lake, but the excess would now just run off over the dam. At first light I was away with a mirror of 32lb 4oz and three hours later, just after a loud clap of thunder had frightened the life out of us, another run had me out in the boat again. Both runs had come from an area just 20 yards from the bank in 15ft of water, just past the submerged bushes. This fish felt a little better than the first one and indeed turned out to be the first 40 of the trip at 40lb 12oz.

Sven continued catching too, but he would have to leave the following day and with no one else in the whole area, I felt that it would play right into my hands as the fish were obviously on the lookout for food and would be more likely to end up in front of us. I could hardly complain at the start I'd made, but the times when you have the fish in front of you and no other anglers around are few and far between and making the most of a good chance is so important. I'm sure that we can all look back and think of sessions when we could have done things differently and done a lot better, the problem is that you can never get those times back and a missed chance is just that – missed! However, I felt I was in the right place at the right time and doing the right thing so I was confident of more fish. That confidence was repaid over the next 24 hours with mirrors of 21lb 8oz, 30lb 10oz and 33lb 10oz.

One rod that had bothered me was the right-hand rod. On the right-hand side of the swim there was a small point which jutted out from the bank. It was now submerged and only the trees were visible. Beneath the surface the point gradually dropped off but also turned sharp left towards our swim. I had placed the bait on the slope in ten feet of water. It looked really good, probably the best out of all the spots I was fishing, but had produced nothing so far, which puzzled me a bit as I was sure that fish would be moving around the point. Sometimes, little things can make a difference so I decided to move it just a few yards further out around the submerged point. It was more on the side of the point than on top and it wasn't flat like before but more on the slope.

I only moved the bait a few yards but it did the trick.

The angle of the line going over the point meant that everything was quite well concealed and the hope was that it could now be in a more direct route of the fish. It always amazes me how little things can make such a difference. Moving the bait those few yards worked and by daylight the repositioned rod had produced two fish of 31lb 8oz and 39lb 12oz. The bait was put back in position but at 8.30am I had to go and meet up with Pierre's son, Philippe at the restaurant. Our solar panel, which we use for charging phones and various batteries had broken and he was going to see if he could find a replacement. I rowed off across the lake and bumped into Lee Picknell on the way down. We chatted for awhile and in the end I actually missed Philippe, who I saw driving off down the road when I was almost there. I trudged back to the boat after my wasted journey and made my way back across the lake. As ever, I looked over my shoulder as soon as I was getting close to see if any of the rods weren't where they should be – and sure enough the rod which had produced the two fish earlier was missing from the set up. I could see the landing net lying over the side of our other boat, so I knew that Joan had been in action during the short time I'd been away.

"You've had one then?" I said as I got back to shore.

"Yes" Joan replied. "I left it in the landing net until you came back. I'm not sure how big it is."

I walked down to where the net was and I could just see this big, wide back lurking under the surface. "That looks big" I thought to myself but then I turned the fish on its side to get a better look and realised that it wasn't big – it was massive! What had she done this time? I struggled up the bank with the fish and placed it on the mat. It was a lovely mirror, certainly bigger than Joan had ever caught before and without a doubt one of the biggest

I couldn't believe what I saw in the net! Joan returns her massive mirror of 60lb 4oz.

fish I'd seen in a long time. I tied the scales to the branch of a nearby tree as I knew that it would be difficult to lift and it would be the best way to weigh the fish accurately. Placing the bulging weigh sling on the hook, we watched the needle swing round to settle on 60lb 4oz! A big smile lit up Joan's face while my mouth just dropped open. I have to say that I was so pleased for her, I know how much she enjoys fishing herself and for most of the time she has to sit and watch me doing my thing, so this was her moment – what a fish! She had somehow played the fish in entirely from the bank, which was no easy job. It had got snagged over the point but she took her time and it somehow freed itself and then she had the job of guiding it through the submerged bushes and into the net. It was a job well done. What a difference it made moving that bait!

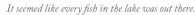

It seemed like every fish in the lake was out there.

Unfortunately, our action hadn't gone unnoticed. Two French anglers had been watching from the far bank and they arrived in fully-loaded boats the next morning intent on getting as close to us as possible. I was playing another fish as one tried to get into the swim that we'd moved out of. He was determined enough but there simply wasn't anywhere to set up and he had to go further down to the left. The other angler however, went to the point on our right which I was fishing to. He was very close and was in fact right on top of the spot which had just produced the big fish. He knew exactly what he was doing and we weren't best pleased. There was little I could do, though, other than make it obvious that I thought he was taking a liberty and thankfully after awhile he got the hint and loaded his boat back up and headed north. Why do people have to do things like that?

I lost a fish in the early afternoon, which wasn't good, but it seemed that the plan was working and that the fish had indeed moved over to our side after Sven's departure. That made it five runs for that day which was a great result for any time of the year, but especially for the winter. But I was concerned about people moving in around us. Word was bound to be getting around by now and others were sure to come. The swim we were in was perfect for intercepting the fish but it was also a swim where we could easily be cut off if people moved in either side of us. The best option seemed to be that we move on to the point to our right, where it would then make the main producing area ours for sure, plus I could still fish back to some of the other spots which I'd been catching from.

We moved up to the next point and it felt a bit safer, but the next three days only produced one fish, and that was a mirror of 33lb which I'd already caught less than a week earlier from the previous swim! It seemed as if the action was starting to slow up and the fish were on the move. It is something that can happen at Cassien. It's not often that the fish will stay in one area for long periods of time, especially when they are being put under a bit of pressure. We'd already had 13 fish and lost 2 in just over a week and Sven had also had his share as well. It had been a good start but sessions can be won or lost by the decisions you make. One thing I'd often done in the past was to stay in a swim too long after the fish had gone in the hope that they would return – which they rarely did! It had been a great start and I wanted to keep it going if at all possible. A French guy, who I didn't know at the time, had been set up in the Banana swim on the opposite side, but I'd been keeping an eye on him and over the couple of days I hadn't seen him have any action, so it seemed like it was time for a change of swim and rightly or wrongly we headed for the other end of the South Arm.

The echo sounder told me where I needed to be.

The weed beds were like underwater jungles – perfect!

Bivvy Point, which is situated in between Pierre's and Arbousiers restaurants was my first choice. It is a known big-fish swim in that part of the lake and had produced the goods in the winter time on a number of occasions, although I must admit that it's not one of my real favourites. We got everything set up and I got the rods out onto what looked like reasonable areas. As ever, with moving swims in the winter, it is always a scramble to get everything done before dark. I must have done something right as sometime in the night one of the rods went off, but I made a complete mess of it and lost the fish. It wasn't the best of starts but at least there were fish around and maybe it was where they had moved to from the top end. The next day I took the chance to have a good look around. There was hardly anyone in that whole half of the South Arm, and besides, it was a flat calm, sunny day, which is always the best time for a row about in the boat. I switched the echo sounder on, as you do, and set about covering the areas I was fishing first. Everyone tells you not to take too much notice of the fish symbols that you see on the screen as they can be misleading, but I always take an interest in them and this was one time when watching the screen would pay dividends. Very little seemed to show up around the Bivvy Point area, there was the odd big-fish symbol here and there but that was about it. I drifted across to the other side of the arm to an area that I'd fished before but I hadn't done all that well there. But with the warm December sun shining down it seemed very different this time around. The more I looked, the better it became. There were undoubtedly a lot more big-fish symbols showing up here than where I was set up and it didn't take long to realise that this was where I should be. So even though we'd only been in the new swim one night and I'd lost one fish, we quickly gathered everything together and moved over to the other side of the lake.

It didn't need lots of bait but it needed to be in the right places.

Straight away it felt right, it also felt very peaceful. I had to smile to myself as word had indeed got around and anglers were starting to arrive, but everyone was heading for the other end of the arm after the previous weeks action. I felt like I was one step ahead of them all – at least I hoped I was. Out in front of the swim there wasn't much in the way of features to fish to, if anything it dropped off quite steeply into the river bed. Most of the obvious features were on the far side of the arm and it was easy to see why most people normally left this bit alone. The one advantage that this area had were some rather dense potamageton beds along the margins both sides. I knew how much the carp loved those weed beds so that was good enough for me. All rods would have to be fished at close range, the depths dictated that, but that is the way I love fishing Cassien anyway and nothing gives me more of a buzz than the thought that a few lumps could be wandering through the weed beds just beyond the rod tips! As ever, the right depths make all the difference and although I didn't plan on putting too much bait out, I did want to sprinkle a few boilies here and there so that any fish passing through might just stay a bit longer if they knew there was some good food about. I drifted through the swim in the boat and dropped single baits every couple of yards in the 10ft to 25ft range. I didn't want to bait up any deeper than that for two reasons; one, that I've rarely caught fish at that time of year much deeper than 25ft and secondly, I wanted to concentrate my efforts around that one strip of water and keep the fish hopefully feeding in the vicinity of the hook baits. I suppose in total I didn't use much more than 100 or 150 boilies over the whole area but I was confident that any fish present would be able to locate some bait easy enough, but would still have to search around to find more. Fishing around the weed made everything so much easier. For a start, the edge of the weed was always easy to find and just beyond that it was clear and sandy, perfect for presenting baits on. But the weed also helps to disguise the lines and the way I like to do it is to fish just over the weed so that the lines are hidden but the rig and the bait are just poking out in the open for the fish to find. I couldn't believe that I hadn't found this swim before as it looked fantastic and I was brimming with confidence.

A dropped take meant that it was time for a change of rig.

As before, I didn't have to wait too long and the following morning brought the first run but after a few seconds the fish just fell off. With the fish I'd lost on the other side, that made it two fish on the trot that I'd lost and that was quite unusual for Cassien where the fish tend to have mouths like old boots and rarely fall off. I'd been using some long-shank hooks and although they'd worked well in the past, the two losses prompted me to change over to my old favourite Hutchinson size 4 Precision's. I hate losing any fish and although sometimes it is just unavoidable, I felt that I should have really landed both of those fish and I didn't want it to happen again if possible. The Precision hooks are a short shank pattern and very strong, while still very sharp. Sadly, they are no longer available. Hooks can be funny things and what works for one person doesn't always work for another – or for that matter it can also vary from lake to lake. At Lake Raduta I'd suffered with the Precisions on one occasion and had to change to the long shanks to be more consistent, this time around it looked as if I was going to have to do the opposite. The important thing is that you work at it and find a solution to the problems, rather than just losing more fish.

Just when I thought it wasn't possible to have any more rain, it started to fall again in the afternoon. We'd had a few days rest from it and I thought that we'd finally seen the last of it, but it was back with a vengeance. I pulled the bivvy door down as it was getting heavier all the time. It was quite demoralising to be stuck inside the bivvy again and I just sat there peering out through the plastic window. The sound was quite deafening as large drops landed on the outer cover of the dome. I heard nothing else but all of a sudden I noticed a blue LED light up outside. I unzipped the door to get a better look and I could see that the line had pulled out of the clip and the tip was bent right over. I didn't have time for the waterproofs, I just ran straight down to the rod. I quickly got into the boat and put the engine on to get above the fish as fast as possible, I'd lost the last two fish and wasn't going to lose this one. I was only fishing close, so I was soon over the top of the fish. I was a little disappointed not to feel more resistance. It wasn't taking much line and was moving quite erratically from side to side – the typical fight from a small fish, so I wasn't getting too excited. Thinking that it was only small made me relax and I sat there quite enjoying the whole thing until suddenly the large flank of a big mirror came into view! It took me by complete surprise and it all got a bit more serious. By then it was nearly all over anyway and I managed to net it without too much trouble. I think the fish had been taken by surprise too. It was a real chunk of a mirror, weighing 51lb 12oz. The hook hold this time was perfect, which justified the change in hooks and this one fish also the move in swims. We had done a fair bit of moving around since we'd first arrived, this was now swim number five, but each swim had brought some sort of action and this one looked like it could be the best of the lot so the effort was more than worthwhile.

The best place in the world!

A Birthday mirror for me – but there was a much bigger one caught further up the lake.

The next couple of days brought two mid-20 mirrors, I'd seen the odd fish showing out in front too. At some stage during the next night the rain had eased once more for awhile I got up and unzipped the door, it was a lovely fresh morning and very still and quiet. At around 8am I can remember looking out over the lake and saying to myself "Big fish day!" A slight mist hung over the lake, it felt as good as it ever could for a real lump to slip up. Just then my mobile phone rang bringing me back to my senses. It was Martin Russell from Gerard's restaurant and he gave me the news that a huge fish of 71lb 10oz had just been landed by the French guy up on the Banana swim. Until that time a fish known as Lucy was generally thought to have been the biggest in the lake, but this fish wasn't Lucy and there was some deliberation about just which fish this was? There was some searching done through various photo albums and it turned out to be a fish that had been caught just a few weeks earlier a little over 60lb! As you can imagine, there were some doubters at the time, but it was definitely weighed properly in front of several witnesses. The fish was immediately named 'The Banana' after the swim from where it came by its captor Michel Blondeau. In the back of my mind I did wonder if our move down to our new area was a little hasty. After all, Michel was only fishing just across the lake from where we had been, but I could hardly complain at the way it was going and later that afternoon I did catch one myself and it just happened to be a Birthday carp of 35lb 4oz.

I always say that the ideal situation at Cassien is to catch around one or two fish per day, any more than that and they either tend to be the smaller stamp of fish or they also don't stick around so long. But one fish per day is enough to keep the enthusiasm right up there without over-pressuring the fish – and of course with that situation the next one could be any size. Over the next three days I landed two fish of 37lb 10oz and 41lb 4oz, then after two bite-less days I managed four fish up to 36lb 8oz over a 24-hour period. It seemed that the fish were passing through the area at regular intervals and were willing to feed when they came across the bait. If I watched closely enough I could actually tell which way the fish were moving. I had to be on the ball to spot them as they were only just poking their heads out and hardly leaving a ripple, but as each one showed they would then leave a trail of bubbles going off either left or right. Some days I'd see half a dozen all going in one direction, while a few days later they would all be going back the other way. It was really interesting stuff and it also made a difference to which side of the swim the action would come. If the fish were coming from the left, then the action would come to the rods on the left and vise-versa.

Obviously the bait was working really well, but as a little experiment I had placed tiger nuts on one rod to see if the fish were just throwing caution to the wind, or if the bait was really that good. Tiger nuts have been a great bait at Cassien in the past but this time around the test was showing, so far, that if I'd gone armed with just tigers I would have been struggling somewhat, as that rod was out for days on end and only fooled one small mirror, while the boilies kept doing the business. There are so many pieces of the overall jigsaw puzzle that you have to get right, but undoubtedly having the right bait is a major factor and I felt that I had the best bait I'd ever used on Cassien – which was probably not far from the truth.

'Dent Back' at 45lb in the warm afternoon sunshine.

Early morning battles were a regular thing.

After landing a 37lb 8oz mirror one evening, the following morning at 11am I was out in the boat again to do battle. This was more like the old arm-aching fights I had become used to over the years. Some of the fish can put up immense struggles in the deep water, on many occasions lasting well over 30 minutes. As long as it isn't windy it's best to just relax and let the battle take its course. All the time you are directly above the fish it is almost impossible for them to find any snags and invariably they head for the deepest parts anyway which only helps to make the job easier. After 30 rod-bending minutes the fish finally gave up. It was a typical Cassien carp of 45lb 2oz in peak condition – but strangely familiar. It was only later when back home that I looked through my album and found that I'd had the same mirror some eight years earlier in the North Arm, when it had weighed just 20lb 12oz. It was good to see how it had grown since our last encounter.

That fish, which became known as 'Dent Back' signalled the start of a final run of good fish. The next morning saw me land two more fish, a common of 24lb 8oz and another good mirror of 41lb 8oz. It felt as though the action could just go on forever. The thing here was that I wasn't on a group of fish that I was slowly picking off. These were fish that I was catching as they passed through and every time they arrived, they were quite possibly oblivious to what had gone before. The next day was one of those lovely calm, sunny days where you could easily forget which time of year it was. It was certainly warm enough just to be out in a tee shirt and that was one of the other plus points of fishing this particular swim, it was that it was quite a sun trap. The morning had been quiet but I had been sitting there enjoying the sun and just watching what was going on. A few times I noticed that small trails of bubbles had been rising from the weed beds to my right in about 10 to

15 ft. No action had occurred so far but I was sure that this was due to carp moving through the weed and picking up baits and sure enough at 2.15pm, when the sun was just at its highest the rod being fished close to where I'd seen the bubbles just ripped off. This was perhaps the most enjoyable of all the battles, the water had cleared a lot by then after the heavy rains of the previous weeks and I could see the fish twisting and turning way down below the boat – I could see that it was a good fish too – I thought that it could well be another 50 and so I didn't rush things – not that I could anyway. It was some time before the fish was safe in the net and I could go back and find out for sure. At 48lb 10oz it wasn't quite as big as I'd thought, but it's fair to say I wasn't worrying too much about that. It was one of those fish that sticks in the memory longer than most, probably just for the circumstances more than anything else. It wasn't the end of the action that day as the same rod went off again just over three hours later with yet another nice mirror of 40lb 4oz.

I thought it might be a little bigger but at 48lb 10oz I was more than happy.

Time was running out fast now and I figured that it was time to give up with the tiger nuts on one of the rods. They obviously weren't as good as the boilies and although I'd only put them on as a test in the first place, it was clear that I was just wasting a rod. In the end that one rod had been baited with the nuts for 23 days and in that time just one fish had picked them up. The tiger nuts were replaced with a single 24mm MC/Addicted boilie and for a change it was placed on the inside of the weed beds in about 9ft of water. I could see the bait clearly as it rested on the sand close to the weed, it looked a good spot and it was so nice to be able to lower it down by hand and drop all the freebies around just where I wanted them. It looked good and sure enough at 5.30 the next morning I received an

Last fish of the trip and yet another forty.

absolute belter on that rod. It was the final proof (if I needed it) of the difference it can make having the right bait. Really, I could have changed that rod over to the boilie a lot sooner, but I wanted to see what would happen and in less than 12 hours after changing over the rod was back in action. Mind you, it wasn't all that straightforward as the fish had charged through the weed beds and through one of my other lines making it all a bit messy in the half-light of early morning. Eventually, I managed to unravel the whole lot and in amongst a clump of weed was a plump mirror of 42lb 4oz. It meant that out of the last six fish, five of them had been above 40lb, a result that wouldn't be easy to achieve anywhere in the world but on Cassien it was a bit special. It was actually the final fish of the trip as we had to pack up and leave shortly afterwards, but what a trip it had been! We'd fished five different swims in all and had action from all of them. But there was more to it than that, it was the consistency of the action and the quality of the fish that was so pleasing. I hadn't gone more than two days without a fish during the whole session. The final week had finished with a flurry of forties, I'd also topped it off with the 51lb 12oz mirror but of course the most prominent memory was arriving back in the swim that day to see that huge mirror which Joan had just landed, waiting in the net to be photographed! It was a session to remember for so many reasons. I'd done my homework and the decision to spend the whole session in the South Arm turned out to be a very good one. It's not often that everything goes right, but this time it really did and after all of those years spent in the North Arm I could only wonder why I hadn't tried the South earlier?

Carping in a Cooler Climate

Rainbow Lake

Humble Beginnings

Many people probably think that Rainbow Lake has only just recently arrived on the carp scene. In terms of monster carp, that is probably true, as in the last few years it has become the most prolific water we have ever known for big carp. But for the humble beginnings of this most intriguing water, we have to go back much further to the early to mid-1990's. In fact it was John Stent, who was the fishery manager at Boyer Leisure at the time, who we have to thank for starting it all off. John Stent was looking at opening a water in France on a commercial basis and the water he chose to concentrate his efforts on was none other than Lac de Curton, situated near to the town of Hostens, a few miles south of the city of Bordeaux. At the time the carp stock of Lac de Curton was more or less unknown, it may well have already held a few decent fish, but it was mainly fished for bass and pike before that time and it was unlikely that there were enough fish in there to attract anglers from England and Europe all the way down to fish there. In The mid 1990's there weren't many people that were prepared to travel long distances for their fishing and commercial waters certainly weren't as popular and as numerous as they are today.

The lake needed to be stocked and somehow John Stent managed to secure the purchase of more-or-less the entire stock of a lake further north, near to the town of Brive, known as Lac de Causse. This particular lake had been quite popular with travelling anglers for some time, but the local authorities had decided to drain the lake and remove the carp for various reasons; quite possibly because they didn't particularly like the carp anglers which were starting to fish there in greater numbers every year. Needless to say this wasn't too popular with the people that had fished Lac de Causse in the past, but the deal was done and the carp, which had lived in Causse for many years, were now moved to their new home in Lac de Curton.

Rainbow Lake – a different challenge.

With the new start also came a new name of Rainbow Lake. No one was quite sure how the carp would fare in this new venue, it couldn't have been more different to their previous home with its many islands, sandy banks and the pine trees, which surrounded the entire lake. Many thought that the water would just be too acidic to really suit the carp, but time would tell.

There was a fair bit of publicity for the opening of Rainbow, and I remember people such as Ken Townley and Bill Cottam being amongst the early visitors there and a couple of videos were made of the fish being introduced and of the anglers fishing, and catching some of the fish. A little while later there was also a TV programme made by Liam Dale, when he fished out of what is now known as swim 19! But despite the publicity and the attention that it received, Rainbow Lake never really attracted too many people in those first few years. I think it was mainly down to the distances involved. As I said, back then people weren't prepared to travel such long distances for a carp fishing holiday, especially when there were a few more established places much closer to home in the north of France. So for awhile after that, Rainbow Lake went off the radar a little and not much was mentioned or heard about the lake.

The mini bus trip was a totally new experience for me.

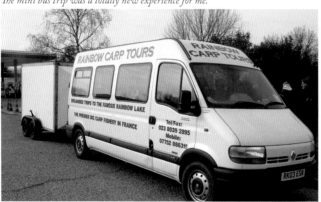

Fast forward to 2003 and I spotted a couple of good fish in Carp Talk, which were described as coming from a venue in the 'south of France'. They were both big fifties if I remember right, but I couldn't recognise the fish or the background in the pictures, I just knew that neither of them were from Cassien. A few weeks later it all became a lot clearer when I received a call from a guy called Paul Hunt. It turned out that Paul was now running trips to Rainbow Lake and wondered if I would be interested in any reports for Carpworld magazine. Of course I had already been writing the 'Worldwide Carp Column' for that magazine for a year or two by then.

It was good to hear about the lake once again and find out what had been happening in the years since I'd last heard about it. It turned out that the lake was now in the charge of Pascal Jousseaume, whose father had owned the lake for many years, and in the meantime there had been a further two or three stockings of carp. It seemed like Rainbow was faring pretty well and the carp had also settled well. One thing that did make my ears prick up was when Paul mentioned that the two carp that I'd seen earlier in Carp Talk were in fact Rainbow carp! During his regular trips to the lake Paul had himself caught some decent fish and over the next few months his reports included himself with fish of 62lb, 67lb and 68lb! These were great big carp by any standards and by September of 2003 one of them had moved on to just over 70lb – the first Rainbow carp to top that weight.

Lac de Curton had become Rainbow Lake.

I was certainly taking an interest in what was going on down there, but up until then I'd never really had any interest in any of the commercial waters, preferring to do my own thing on the large public waters, but it was certainly looking attractive, although I suppose I would have to say that Lake Raduta was itself a commercial water in its own way, but few people ever viewed it as one. The change for me came during another conversation with Paul towards the end of 2003. He had only done trips during the summer months up until then, but they were proving to be popular and he was looking to expand. Up to that time the lake remained more or less empty in the winter and Paul had the idea of going down in February, one reason for that was to take various stuff down in preparation for the new season ahead and also to see how it would fish at that time of year. He asked if I would be interested in coming along and fishing for the week and I couldn't help but say yes. For one thing there was very little else going on for me normally in February, and secondly it would be nice just to see what Rainbow Lake was all about.

From memory I think that there were ten of us in all for the trip, with Paul and Mandy and including Mark 'Gooey' Gooch, his friend James, Mickey Hill and son Christian, all of whom had been there a few times previously with Paul. I have to admit that it felt a bit strange going down that first time in the mini bus. I was so used to just loading the car up and going off with Joan that this was something entirely new to me and it was a little bit out of my comfort zone, but all of the guys on that trip were great, especially Gooey who I've kept in contact with ever since. Mickey Hill was 'mother' for the trip, looking after everyone on the ferry – although that basically meant James, who had rather a liking for vodka if I remember rightly and spent most of the journey down flat out on the floor of the mini bus!

It was quite pleasant when we arrived. The sun was out and it wasn't quite as warm as could be expected at Cassien, but it was certainly better than England that was for sure. I soon met Pascal for the first time, a really nice, genuine man, who welcomed us all in for a cup of coffee. Pascal thanked me for coming down to fish his lake, which I thought was really nice and I thanked him straight back for having me there. He filled us in on what had been happening and a few people had fished the lake over the previous weeks, in fact there had been a 25kg mirror out just the week before. It all sounded very good to me, I looked out across the lake and it looked just like all of the pictures I had seen in the past. The surroundings were still quite green because of all the pine trees which of course keep their colour all-year round and there were just as many islands as I thought there would be – loads of them in all shapes and sizes.

I was due to fish in swim 11 with Paul and Mandy, the Black Beach as it is often called. But first job was to drop everyone else off in their various swims. The whole lake was empty apart from two Dutch guys who were there for the week in swim 19. As we made our way around we came past one empty swim and I remember Mickey Hill leaning over my shoulder and saying

Swim 11 the famous Black Beach.

"That's a good swim that one. You don't catch so many fish in there and it's deep water, but some of the big fish get caught from there."

That was swim 18 and it did look good, but then all of the swims looked good as we passed them and I was more than happy when we got to swim 11, but what Mickey had told me was logged away in the old memory bank.

Swim 11 has more room than most other swims on the lake with quite a chunk of open water out in front, although it still has several bars running through from right to left. Most of the islands are just the parts of the bars which are exposed and although there were still a fair amount in the swim, they were mainly either side of the swim, leaving a fair bit of open water out in front. It all looked pretty much the same to me and I didn't mind which side I fished at all. Paul seemed to prefer the idea of fishing on the left, although there was more room on the right. I was happy enough with that and set about getting the house up and the rods out.

Although it was February it was a nice enough start to the week.

I sat down in the boat and switched the echo sounder on. I was expecting it to be like nothing I'd ever seen before and I wasn't disappointed. I think the best way to describe what was out there is to say that it looked like an upside-down egg box. Literally as soon as it seemed to be dropping off, the bottom would rise sharply up again, sometimes to within inches of the surface, before dropping off again to depths of anything up to eighteen or twenty feet! What surprised me most was the steepness of the slopes. Most of the features seemed to rise very sharply and almost form a point at the very top and then they started to drop away immediately. There weren't quite so many flat areas on the tops of the bars, which I'd expected to come across and there were literally just a mass of features and depths to choose from. I was used to huge depth variations from fishing other waters such as Cassien and Raduta amongst many others, so I wasn't exactly shocked by what I was confronted with, it was just a matter of deciding which of the features to fish. I was in no doubt that the carp would use the bars as roadways for their travels up and down the lake and I had visions in my mind of placing my baits on one side of a steep bar, while several carp would swim along, just on the other side of the bar, oblivious to my baits being there at all. The thing was that people had fished there regularly and fish had been caught regularly, so it was just a matter of making a start and taking it from there. I was sure that it would all become a lot clearer after a day or two, when I'd had more chance to have a look around and maybe even caught a fish or two.

One main channel of water, closest to the bank, runs right through the swim and more or less along that whole side of the lake. There seemed to be two main bars running right through that section and I was sure that they would be good features to fish at some stage, but really to me, it was the area further towards the back of the swim which looked the more likely place to get a bit of action from, so I more or less disregarded the first fifty metres of water in front of me and concentrated on the water beyond that. At the very back of the swim was again another long island. Although there was at least one gap in that island, it did form the boundary of where I could fish to. But left and right of that were other islands at varying ranges and on closer inspection it became obvious that those islands were actually joined up by the various bars. Looking at the islands and more so the channels in between, it was a lot easier to picture where the carp would swim through. From what I had seen so far it appeared that most of the lake consisted of these channels and there was very little plain, open water, even if it appeared that way on the surface.

Baits were placed at varying spots in between various islands and just over bars. The right side of the swim did allow me to go a little further out than on the left and it was the extreme left and right of the swim that looked the ideal places to intercept any fish moving in and out of the swim. On the right there were two or three small channels leading through between the two largest islands and I was sure that fish would pass through there from a big area of open water just the other side. It was a very similar scenario on the left, only the channels were just a little wider, but beyond those the lake opened out into the

I was interested to see how Paul went about things.

main central area of the lake, an area of water controlled by the Island Swim, where Mickey and Christian Hill were setting up.

I knew little really of what the Rainbow fish liked, and so I went with what I was confident in, which were the MC/Addicted baits in 20mm and 24mm sizes. That bait had worked for me everywhere I had taken it and had no reason to think that Rainbow would be any different. I was sure that the big, hungry fish would love a bit of good quality food. I guessed that they had seen their fair share of preserved readymades and particles in the past and so quality bait should make the difference – it always did. I already had my rods out by the time Paul returned to the swim with his gear. He of course had to sort everything out for the other guys; boats, water etc. so it was getting quite late by the time he was ready to get everything sorted, but I was interested to see how he went about doing things as he had a lot of previous experience of many of the swims on the lake.

No big ones for me on that first trip, but they were very pretty.

He knew of one spot on the top of the second bar between our swim and the next swim down, swim 12. There was no one in that swim for the week, in fact there was no one in any of the swims down to our left, so it did make sense to fish down that way a bit. Paul's second rod made me sit up and take notice a little more. Out to the left along the island margin, there was a small gap with an old fallen tree lying across the channel but above the water line. I watched Paul go out and although the line had to go around a slight corner, he actually crouched down in the boat and poked the rod right underneath the fallen tree, so that the bait was presented just the other side of the tree. I can't quite remember where his other two rods went now, but I do remember looking at his baits, which were much smaller than mine, either 14mm boilies or a couple of tigers on the hair and he was baiting up with a mixture of small particles. It was something I'd used many times in the past, but it seemed like all of his presentations revolved around smaller baits compared to my bigger ones. But time would tell and it was only the very start of the week at that point.

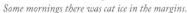

Some mornings there was cat ice in the margins.

As confident as I was, I was still expecting Paul to get the first one for some reason, so I wasn't really surprised when he woke me up at some stage during the night.

"I've had one, do you want to see it?"

To be honest it was cold outside and I was a bit reluctant to get up, but I was pleased I did as on the mat was a really nice-looking common of 35lb.

"That's not bad for the first one!"

I said. It was quite apparent straightaway that Paul is very much into fish care and not too bothered about keeping the fish out of the water too long for pictures, so a couple of quick snaps and the fish was soon back in its watery home.

It was good to see one on the bank, and a nice fish at that. I knew that there were obviously quite a few that were bigger than that swimming about, but it was February and pretty much an unknown quantity, so at that stage any fish was a good 'un. There were no more occurrences through the dark hours and I was looking forward to breakfast. For a change Paul's other half, Mandy, was cooking the meals for everyone on the trip. This was no small task and it was actually all prepared in the trailer that was used to transport all of the gear to the lake. Once all the gear was unloaded, the trailer was then converted into a kitchen, complete with shelves, cookers and lots of food. Meals were obviously organised very much around Paul's appetite and at six feet something and 22 stone, the bloke gets through a bit of grub! So the breakfast that came out and was handed to me wasn't for all three of us – it was just for me. Mind you, I've got to say that on a cold February morning, there was nothing better to see than a pile of steaming bacon, sausages, eggs, beans, mushrooms, toast etc. etc. etc.

Mandy at work in the 'kitchen' with another belly-busting meal about to be served.

While Mandy sorts out all of the food inside of the 'kitchen', it was Paul's job to deliver it to all the guys around the lake, so as he set off in the van to do that, I sat back – or rather collapsed back in my chair and wondered if I needed to undo my trouser button or not? I felt like I was unable to move for awhile, but the next thing I knew I had to get up as one of the tips on the right bounced over and line started to pull from the tight baitrunner. I guessed that there wasn't too much chance of landing the fish from the bank and sure enough the line was already grating and sticking. I had the boat positioned in readiness, so it was just a case of getting in and pushing myself out onto the water. There was a bit of a breeze blowing, but with the aid of my little electric motor, I was able to negotiate my way in between the lines safely enough, which makes a change as I have been known to make the odd cock up here and there where lines are concerned. As soon as I got above the fish it came free and I could tell that it wasn't too big, but it was surging about all over the place like a small common, and that was exactly what it turned out to be, a common of 24lb. As I made my way back to the bank Mandy was just walking across with a cup of tea.

"You've got one then Steve, well done."

Mandy clicked off a few pictures for me before I slipped the fish back. My 24mm bait had done the trick as I'd hoped it would and I was off the mark – now for some of those monsters!

I think I was expecting the action to pick up sharply once we got the baited areas established and the right spots sorted out, probably because it was a 'commercial water' and for some reason I thought that meant that the fishing would be much easier than what I was used to. But of course, that is rarely the case, and waters that appear to be easier from the outside looking in, are very rarely like that when you actually get there. Mind you, I suppose a fish each after just 24 hours on the lake was hardly what you would call struggling and I didn't doubt that there would be more to come. Mickey and Christian hadn't started so well though. They weren't keen on the Island Swim as it meant a fair bit of long-range fishing, which Mickey certainly wasn't that keen on, so they wandered across in the boat and announced that they would be moving across to swim 5, across the other side of the lake from where we were, nearer to the entrance. I remember thinking that it sounded like a good move as that was the swim where the 25kg fish had been caught the previous week. Gooey and James were down in swim 8 to our right and they were doing much better. There were obviously a lot of fish down there in front of them and they'd already landed a few, including one of 45lb for Gooey. He'd caught that one on a double tiger nut hook bait and again I had to wonder about the small baits.

The next action wasn't quite what I wanted, as it was on Paul's rod the next morning while he was off around the lake delivering breakfast. It was a 24lb mirror from the rod furthest down to the left on top of the second bar. I didn't like the idea of catching fish on

We both had runs at the same time –
Paul landed this 44lb mirror – I just made a complete cock-up of it all!

someone else's rod, as to me that seems like a wasted fish, as there was no merit in the capture for me. All I had done was to play the fish in, but that was the agreement and it had to be done. Mind you, Paul returned the compliment later when I went for a shower. I left the rods out as he was staying in the swim and when I got back he had landed a 26lb mirror on one of my rods, so it's all swings and roundabouts.

The weather, far from improving, deteriorated quite quickly. It got colder and flurries of snow were soon falling, and in the mornings cat ice was forming along the margins. Paul had that all covered though, especially for the evenings. He had a large gazebo, complete with sides, with tables, chairs and heater inside. For the evening meals it was lovely to sit in there and thaw out and eat a hot meal in comfort. We also had a film to watch afterwards on the portable DVD player and it was all quite pleasant really. Of course, it was just as we

The weather took a turn for the worse.

were sitting down eating that evening when one of Paul's rods went off. We all rushed out into the cold. It was the rod under the fallen tree, but Paul soon had the fish moving towards us. Just then one of mine went off too and I legged it across the frosty ground. But just as I picked the rod up, everything went slack. I had been cut off about twenty metres in front of the rod tip. I wasn't sure what to do, but first I had to help Paul whose fish was nearly ready for netting. It looked a more powerful fish and was a chunky mirror of 44lb, a great fish to land on a cold winters evening. I knew that whatever had taken my bait still had a lot of line attached to it, so I tied a lead onto the end of the line which had broken and went out in the boat. I figured that it wouldn't be hard to pick up the line, which should be lying across the bars. It took a little while but I managed to find the line and I took the lead off and tied the two ends together. I followed the line and it went right out to the back and through a little gap which I hadn't even looked at before. In the narrow channel where the fish had gone it was difficult to manoeuvre the boat and I felt the engine 'clonk' on something, I picked it up to see one blade of the propeller missing. "Not good" I thought, but I carried on and the line went up the channel and then doubled back around a small branch and I came back almost to the small gap, but everything ground to a halt amongst a mass of roots and tree stumps. I hadn't felt the fish at any time but was determined to at least get all of the line out of the water. I had been out a long time and every now and then Paul and Mandy shouted across to see if I was alright. But I was on a mission and wasn't about to give up. In the boat was Paul's little pike rod, so I lowered the snap tackle down to try and pick up the line the other side of the snag, but only succeeded in losing the snap tackle. I was also losing my patience, it was freezing cold and I wanted to get back to the warmth of the gazebo where I could see the lights glowing in the distance. I started prodding around under the water with the rod and just heard 'snap'. I knew what I'd done and lifted the rod above the surface to see the last ten inches gone. That was it, I'd had enough and just grabbed the line and heaved. Up came a mass of twisted branches, rod tips and snap tackles and beneath that was a common of about 25lb. "So there you are" I said to myself, and with one flick of the tail I was covered in spray and the fish shed the hook and disappeared into the depths. I returned to the bank rather sheepishly to explain what had gone on. Paul had landed a 44lb mirror, while I had broken a rod, broken a propeller, lost his snap tackle and after all of that lost the fish too! I told you I do make the odd cock up here and there – but at least I knew that the fish had got away safely.

It turned out to be a good move for Christian and Mickey.

Before the end of the week I managed to land a couple more fish, both mid – 20's, one common and one mirror. Christian had made the most of his move and had banked a 42lb mirror and Gooey and James also kept catching, with Gooey landing another fish of 45lb towards the end. In fact all of us on the trip had caught at least one fish, which I thought was quite a result. There were the four forties landed and all of those had been caught on

Gooey and James were having a great time further down the lake.

Mark 'Gooey' Gooch with a 45lb mirror from the first trip.

tiger nuts, which I made a mental note of. I had caught one fish every day, except for the final day when I had two, but they were more or less all around the same size and the large, quality baits had not produced the large, quality fish, which I'd hoped they would but I remember feeling fairly happy that I'd at least got amongst some fish. Nowadays that same result would be viewed as a bit of a disaster – not just mine but the group as a whole I suppose, but that shows how much the lake and the carp changed in a relatively short time. But I had made a start and I was keen to have another go at this fascinating lake.

Back for More

The next chance came in the October of 2004. Paul phoned me one evening and said that he had a spare place on a trip and asked if I would be interested. Well I was interested anyway, but even more so when he mentioned that I could have swim 18 if I wanted. By then swim 18 was establishing itself as the 'big fish' swim on the lake and in particular, the biggest known carp in the lake, known as the Big Girl had always been captured from that swim, or at least from very close by. Paul pointed out that it could be tough in there and the week could easily end in a blank, or on the other hand I could catch a few and possibly, if I got lucky, catch one of the big ones. 18 was that sort of swim, it was more of a challenge but it generally produced more big fish and that was something that really got me going.

After the cold, frosty days of February, it was lovely to arrive in the October sun. In the south of France the summer goes on for a bit longer than most of Europe and it looked lovely. I had no idea of how the lake was fishing but I was just pleased to get back and have another go. Rainbow Lake was now starting to become more popular and word was

October arrived and I got my chance to fish swim 18.

spreading that not only was it a great lake to fish, it also held some cracking fish. I had written an article after the first trip and Paul mentioned that his bookings had shot up soon afterwards, so people were now very interested in what Rainbow had to offer. I should say that the owner, Pascal, along with his wife Nadine and sons Paul and Max all make the Rainbow experience a very good one by always making you feel welcome and at home once you arrive, which was always going to help make it more popular. I've fished some great lakes over the years, some where the owners are obviously only interested in the money and the atmosphere isn't always that great, but it is never like that at Rainbow.

What I also liked about swim 18 was that it was more of a one man swim. People do fish it in pairs from time to time, but it is generally regarded as just a one man swim. That suited me more as I liked the idea of fishing alone more and was looking forward to the week ahead. The hustle and bustle of getting everything sorted out was soon replaced by the peacefulness of the lake after being dropped off in the swim. The van and trailer disappeared off up the track and all of a sudden I was alone with a pile of gear to sort out. I stared out to the island margin around 80 or 90 metres away. Large branches appeared from the surface like antlers. This was where the soft bank had given way over the years and whole trees had fallen into the margins to form safe holding areas for the fish to live in when they weren't out looking for food. Those were the hot spots in the swim, that I already knew, and it was obvious to see straightaway. A strong but very warm breeze was blowing

I had two fish on the bank before most people had got their rods out!

in from the south west, into the bank where I was standing. It looked perfect and I just wondered what might be sitting out there in those snags. Maybe the Big Girl was there?

I couldn't wait to get the rods out, everything else could wait, but first things first and I wouldn't be able to relax until I was fishing. Beads of sweat ran down my forehead as I scrambled around looking for all the bits and pieces that I needed. I had thought about my presentation after the previous trip. I still reckoned that the MC/Addicted was the best bait that I could be using, but perhaps the fish weren't so keen on large baits here. I always find that bait size very much depends on the natural food that the carp feed on in the water you're fishing. At Cassien, for instance, the carp are used to feeding on crayfish and mussels and for that reason they are quite happy to accept larger baits. But where they are used to feeding on smaller food items, it stands to reason that they would prefer smaller baits too. To be honest, it wasn't all that clear just what the Rainbow carp did feed on naturally. No one seemed to really know, but it was obvious that there weren't any crayfish or mussels present – or at least very few. So it did make sense to cut the bait size down a little to 18mm's as opposed to 24mm's and perhaps go with a snowman set up. It was always hard to fish Rainbow with the sort of refined, delicate set up that I thought might help to fool the fish, in fact it was impossible just due to the nature of the lake. With all of its islands, bars and snags, it really does demand that you use tough gear and that has to come at some expense where presentation is concerned, but you do what you have to do. Braided lines, strong hooks and heavy leads are all very much the norm for Rainbow anglers and even if that does

It was obvious where the fish would be.

come at the expense of a run or two, it's worth it just in the knowledge that you have more of a chance of landing any fish that you do hook.

I knew all of this from having already been there once, so the rods were already set up ready to go. I just needed to put on some fresh hook baits and get them out there! Even though I hadn't even looked at swim 18 before, dropping the baits out didn't take long at all, which was probably a good thing as it meant less disturbance. Basically, there were three spots along the island margin which looked to be the obvious spots. The water is quite deep along most of that section, in fact between swims 18 and 17 the water is at its deepest, going down to around 35 feet. The deep channel covers most of the water out in front of the swim and only starts to rise sharply just in front of the island. This doesn't leave much room really for positioning the baits, especially with the fallen trees in the margins, so it leaves you with the obvious spots, which are the same spots where everyone else fishes too. So that in itself can cause its own set of problems as you never really know what bait has been left out there by the previous occupants, but it doesn't stop the fish going there to feed; it might even help it as the fish always know that there will be a supply of food waiting for them there.

I should think that I had all of my baits in place before anyone else had even started sorting their gear out. It was around 2pm by the time I was sitting back behind the rods munching my first of many croissants. I'd hardly finished my lunchtime snack when at 3pm the first one rattled off, well I say 'rattled off' that's not really the right description for a take at Rainbow as the method of fishing there involves mainly fishing with either very tight baitrunners or totally locked-up. It was still early days for my Rainbow fishing and I was just fishing the baitrunners tight then, so the rod tip just pulled down sharply and the rod bucked and jumped in the rest. I was surprised, but at the same time I was more than ready for it. I had already gone through the game plan in my head and the way to do it was to walk back with the rod under tension and ease the fish away from the snags. It sounds impossible when you potentially have something huge on the other end, but if you don't allow them to build momentum in the first place then it throws them off balance a bit, giving you the chance to get them moving towards you. I had used the same methods to good effect a couple of years earlier when fishing at Snagmere down in South Africa, so I knew that it would work if I could get it right, and it did work. Slowly the fish headed towards me, and once away from the snags it headed for the deeper water and I could play the fish in relative safety from the bank. I soon had the first fish of the trip on the bank, a 29lb 4oz mirror. I didn't think that it was worth bothering anyone else so I set the tripod up and rattled off a few quick snaps myself, with the aid of the air ball cable, which you just need to kneel on to take the picture.

Sometimes it's nice just to be there.

I hardly moved from the bivvy all week.

It was all done quite quickly and the rod was soon back out on the mark. The whole process couldn't have taken long as the same rod went off again at 4pm. The same process of walking back with the rod under tension did the trick and I had my second fish on the bank, this time a pound bigger at 30lb 4oz. One of the guys fishing in swim 19, 'quiet' Dave Vaughn, had just got in the boat for a look around in the swim and had spotted me landing the fish and came around to see if I needed any help. But the fish was already photographed and returned by then, but it was good of him to offer. He was surprised to hear that I'd already had two and to be honest I was just as surprised myself! I soon found out why they called him 'quiet Dave'. That bloke can talk for England – in fact he can probably do it for the whole of Europe! I couldn't get a word in so I didn't even bother trying, I dread to think what would happen if he got on the phone to Rob Hughes! All joking aside though, he's a really great guy, they both are.

It might have all started quickly, but it soon slowed down. It was almost like there were some fish in the swim feeding and I had just caught them off guard, something which has happened to me many times since, but this was my first experience of it. Two more runs came to the same rod over the next 24 hours but both were lost the same way. They just managed to reach the snags before I could start walking back. It was almost as if they'd learned their lesson after the first two runs and made an extra effort to reach the safety of the branches. It was amazing how quickly they got rid of the hook; it's something that I've noticed many times over the years. I don't know how they do it, but almost as soon as there was a bit of grating on the line it all went solid and although I was out in the boat quickly, by the time I got there the hook was neatly embedded into a branch both times. I wonder sometimes if when we have a fish on the bank which is difficult to unhook, we wouldn't just be better off giving it a bit of wood and saying "There you go, you get it out for me!"

Perfect October conditions.

It was a disappointment for sure, as you never know what you are losing at Rainbow, but in such circumstances it's just not always possible to land them all. The important thing is that if you are going to lose fish, then they get away without having to trail any gear, and especially lead weights. The system I use involves using the Solar lead clips, which do release the lead very quickly and that always helps. However, two lost and two landed wasn't the sort of result I was looking for. I couldn't really get to the rods any quicker as I was already perched behind them in readiness all day long. In fact Paul Hunt did ask if I'd been a heron in a previous life. The only solution was to move the baits away from the snags a little more. I wasn't too keen on doing that, as moving them away also meant them going into slightly deeper water and maybe away from where the fish were feeding.

It was the best of the week, but I'd hoped for more.

I needn't have worried, it proved to be the right thing to do and over the next 24 hours I landed three more fish, two commons and a mirror. Again, they were all around the same size, with two of them weighing 28lb 12oz and one going 29lb 12oz. There was one difference though, and that was all of those three runs came to the rod on the far left, whereas the previous action had all come to the rod on the far right. I figured that it didn't really matter as long as I was landing the fish.

Until then the weather had been good and the action was steady, but the next day dark clouds arrived early and it rained all day – well it was more than just rain, it absolutely chucked it down, and the indicators remained motionless. I did wonder how a change of weather might affect the swim. A change of weather is often just what is needed, especially if it brings wind and rain with it, but it had the opposite effect in 18. It seemed that the fish liked to come up into the snags to get a bit of sun on their backs in the day and obviously have a feed while they were there. Most of the action, apart from one run, had come during the day, whereas other swims around the lake were mainly 'night swims'. Obviously, the rain just kept the fish in their usual haunts and they hadn't ventured into the snags that day.

Thankfully, the rain only lasted for one day and I was awake early the next morning to see the skies had cleared and the sun was rising behind the trees. I sat behind the rods willing one of them to go off. Time was running short and I wanted at least one more before leaving. After watching intently for a couple of hours, I literally just turned my back to put the kettle on when the alarm sounded. It's amazing how many times that happens isn't it? This time it was the middle rod of the three and the first sign of action on that rod all week. I hoped and prayed that it would be a good 'un, but although everything went to plan and I landed the fish without too many problems, it weighed 36lb 8oz. Hardly a Rainbow monster, but still the best fish of the trip. The sizes might actually surprise some people as these days we always tend to hear about much bigger fish, but the best result on the trip fell to one of the guys fishing in swim 14, who had a fish known as 'Ten Scales' at just over 50lb for the first time. That fish is now one of the known big 'uns having reached a top weight so far of 75lb, so you can see that many of the fish were still just growing then, and I often wonder how big some of those fish are now. It might not have been the sort of result I was looking for, but I really enjoyed fishing in swim 18 and I was determined to have a few more goes in there as soon as the chance came along.

Freezing February

The February trips to Rainbow were to become a regular fixture for Paul Hunt and his Rainbow Carp Tours and with another trip planned for the early part of 2005, I was more than happy when Paul rang up and said that there would be space for me once again in swim 18. I had only been away once since the last trip in October and that was for our normal Christmas trip to Cassien. Those Cassien trips are generally the longest trips of the year for me and also my favourite, it has to be said. Once again it didn't disappoint, and although it was tough as always, I did come away with some decent fish up to 52lb 12oz and I just thoroughly enjoyed the whole thing. But as soon as I'd returned from Cassien my thoughts were once again directed towards Rainbow. Normally I would be resting the rods during the first two or three months of the year, or I would turn my attentions to barbel fishing, which is always exciting, as well as being something different to keep my enthusiasm up. But an early Rainbow trip was something to fill the gap and thoughts of fishing there were starting to fill my mind more and more. There was something else to consider too, and that was the events which took place at Lake Raduta in 2004. The fish kill which happened that year had wiped out much of the existing Raduta stock and so I

February 2005 arrived and it was freezing cold.

knew that the fishing had, at least for the near future, come to an end on that water. So Rainbow Lake had very much come to the rescue in terms of having a venue to fish that could replace the void left by Raduta. It was a big void to fill as Lake Raduta had been a large part of my angling life for the last six years, but it looked like I had found somewhere just at the right time.

February hardly seemed like the best time to be on the banks of Rainbow, but any chance to fish there was worth taking and I counted the days away until I was finally boarding the mini bus again. For the first time I was seeing familiar faces as it was mostly the same guys that were on the bus one year earlier – Gooey, James and 'Mum' for the week, Mickey. This time we did all get a bit involved with the vodka, but Mickey made sure that we all got to our cabins okay and were present and correct in the morning – what a top man!

The lake was once again bathed in sunshine when we arrived, almost like it was giving us a nice welcome – or was it lulling us into a false sense of security? The long range weather forecast said that it was going to be getting very cold in the week, so we had no illusions that we would be in shorts and tee shirts or anything like that, all we hoped was that we could end up with a fish or two.

It was almost like Groundhog Day to start with. Okay it was a bit colder than it had been in October, but the sun was shining and there was a slight south westerly breeze blowing, which I had come to realize were just about perfect conditions for swim 18. Out went the rods on the spots which were now familiar to me – and just as before, I was literally into the first fish before any of the others had got any of their rods out! I was expecting it, to be honest, but it wasn't quite the result I was hoping for as a 15lb common came wriggling into the net. "Well at least I haven't blanked" I thought to myself as I unhooked the little blighter and returned him to the chilly margins. Another run came to the same rod at 4pm, but that didn't go to plan when the fish slipped the hook after a few seconds. I didn't even have the chance to feel what it might have been, but at least it looked like it was going to be a good week again – how wrong I was.

As promised, the weather took a turn for the worse and it got cold, really cold! I remember that one night I got into my two sleeping bags, still in my one-piece suit, with the door of the bivvy zipped up, and I was still cold. Swim 18 is a little bit more exposed

It was tough-going but it was hardly surprising.

than most swims and I knew all about it. It didn't do the fishing any good either and it quietened down quickly after that first afternoon. It was the same for everyone and very little happened during the next couple of days.

The next occurrence for me came on the Tuesday afternoon and after feeling relief that something had happened, it soon turned to disappointment when the fish again fell off. I figured that they weren't feeding all that strongly, and that perhaps was the reason for not hooking the two fish well enough. I was still sticking with the MC/ Addicted baits, as they had caught all the fish so far for me at Rainbow and for that matter, on all the other

waters I had been fishing. But something that Paul Hunt said to me that evening when he brought dinner round got me thinking. He said that he didn't think that the Rainbow carp liked Monster Crab all that much. I found it hard to believe as they always seemed to like it, wherever it was used, but with Paul's experience of the lake, it was something I had to think about.

I wanted to stick with the Monster Crab, but the seeds of doubt had been sown.

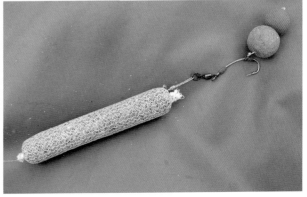

By Thursday afternoon it was obvious that it just wasn't happening. No more action had come my way and most other people were in the same boat, although I think that Dave Vaughn had caught a 46lb mirror from around in swim 5. It was make or break time and I either had to sit there and just hope that something would happen, or I had to change things around and see if that made any difference. I was still fairly sure that fish were visiting the swim, but what Paul had told me was niggling away in the back of my mind. I reeled in all of the rods, not only in an attempt to rest the swim, but also to clear my mind and think of something different to do. I went for a ride around the lake on the push bike, which everyone was supplied with and stopped off at the shower, which always seems to liven me up a bit. It was probably around two hours later when I got back to the swim. I rooted through what I had with me and came across a tin of Dynamite tiger nuts that I'd had for some time. I also had some Bait and Feed Company, Particle 42 groundbait and

I had a dig around in my bags and came up with an old tin of tigers.

With time running out I decided to change a few things.

some Solar pineapple pop ups. I went through it all in my mind and figured that a double tiger nut hook bait, topped with a pineapple pop up, along with a small bag of the groundbait, might be different enough to entice a fish into feeding before the end of the week, which was now fast approaching.

I remembered back to the first trip twelve months earlier when the four biggest fish had all come to tiger nuts, so it was certainly worth a go and I tied up new rigs and changed all the rods over with the same presentation on each. By 4pm I had them all back in position. I obviously didn't go too heavy with the bait as I guessed that there would still be uneaten bait lying on the bottom, so I only sprinkled about ten tiger nuts around each hook bait, which may not seem like much, but the spots I was fishing to were small and I knew that if any fish arrived in the area, they wouldn't have too much trouble in finding the baits.

But I awoke in the morning to see everything just as I had positioned it the evening before. It was the last full day of fishing and I would be all packed up and ready to go by the same time the next day. The weather had changed slightly, it was still very cold but the wind had turned slightly and was now blowing straight in from the south. I knew that Paul would be around any minute with breakfast and just then the middle rod pulled over sharply. I was on it in a flash, there was no way I was going to mess this one up. Paul pulled up behind me just as I had the fish circling in front of me. We could both see that it wasn't massive and Paul said

"You wouldn't normally play a fish of that size that carefully would you?"

I could hardly even answer, I was so determined just to get it in. Thankfully, I netted the fish, my first one since the previous Saturday. The weight didn't really matter but it was a very welcome mirror of 28lb 4oz.

"I'll just drop the breakfast's off to everyone and I'll be back for a chat," Paul said before heading off up the track. It must have taken him about fifteen or twenty minutes for him to do that before he was back behind the swim. Just as he wound down his window the right-hand rod signalled a drop-back. I looked for a second before springing into action. As I bent into the fish, it rose up in the water and swirled close to the trailing branches. Just then, out of the blue, the left-hand rod stuttered into life. Paul looked at me and I

The relief was overwhelming.

looked at him in amazement. Thankfully, Paul was thinking quick and jumped straight out and grabbed the other rod. We were now both playing a fish each.

"Which rod do you want?" He asked.

"This one feels okay so I'll stick with this one" I replied.

After sitting there all week more or less just twiddling my thumbs it was mad to now have two fish on at once, especially with the other rod still leant up against the bivvy! The fish came slowly towards me, on the surface for much of the time and I could tell that it was at least better than most of the others. It didn't do so much, but it had that bit more weight to it and with a sigh of relief I lifted the mesh around it. I made sure everything was okay before going over to help Paul, who now had the other fish ready for netting. I had certainly done the right move as I could see that this fish wasn't as big as the one I'd landed just seconds earlier. In fact it was a grey, leathery type of fish, weighing 33lb 4oz. We took a couple of pics of the fish just for reference, it wasn't a fish that either of us could count but between us we had banked it, which had to count for something though and with that one safely back we then returned to my fish, which was a cracking looking mirror of 46lb 4oz, a totally different looking fish to the other one, and not only the best fish of the week, but my best fish from the lake at that point and one that I was well pleased with.

The biggest of three fish in 45 minutes and I could leave with a smile on my face.

The whole episode had taken just 45 minutes from start to finish. Three fish in 45 minutes after almost a week without action was weird to say the least, but it does show that sometimes it does pay to change things around, as the change of baits had obviously worked. But it also shows that it's always worth sticking it out until the end no matter how bad it looks. Some of the other guys were getting despondent by then, one had even packed up early. Three of the guys came around soon after, not knowing what had just happened, and said that they had reeled in for the morning and were looking forward to going home.

"I've just had three in 45 minutes" I said.

At first I'm sure they thought I was joking, but a quick glance down at the mat and landing net showed that I was telling the truth. I could hardly believe it myself as it had all happened so quickly, but then that's just how it goes sometimes and it felt like just reward for staying positive and grafting it out until the end. It can all seem so easy sometimes and other times it can feel like everything is against you, but it's often how you deal with the situations that makes all the difference. It still wasn't exactly a fantastic result, but I went home the next day with a smile on my face.

Payback Time

I felt like I was making slow progress at Rainbow. I either seem to get lucky straight away with a big fish, or I have to work really hard for them. There still weren't the big fish there in the numbers that they are today, but I wanted one of them more than ever. Throughout the trips I'd been on so far, the fish had got bigger and bigger. The first trip my best was a mere 26lb, while the second trip I had them to 36lb and the third trip to 46lb. So the fourth trip would surely produce a Rainbow 50 for me, which was really what I was aiming at around that time. Of course two of the three trips which I'd been on had taken place in February, hardly the best month for carp fishing, let alone for the big fish, so I felt like I'd yet to really get it right time-wise.

It was Paul Hunt who again helped me out for the next trip. I just happened to phone him one day when he was down at the lake and he said that he was just off to the club house and would see if there were any free swims for a drive-and-survive trip if I wanted. It was very kind of him to do

By April it had warmed up and it looked good!

that and the great news was that swim 18 was vacant for a week in the early part of April. I know how difficult it is to book swims for other people – heaven knows, enough people have asked me and it is almost impossible to do, but I just happened to call at the right time and I was very grateful for Paul's help. It would be the first time that I would be making my own way down to Rainbow, so I was looking forward to that. It meant that Joan could come along for the first time and I could also take all the extra bits and pieces which normally had to be left behind. Another very important factor was that I felt April could be one of the better times of the year to be at the lake with the water temperature rising and the fish more willing to feed in the build-up to the spawning period, so all in all it was another eagerly-awaited trip!

With the temperature rising, everything became more active.

The drive down was a bit of a cock-up really. We drove all through the Friday night, arriving at the lake late Saturday morning. It was the right time to arrive, but I was absolutely knackered by the time we got there. What we should have done was arrive on the Friday evening and then stop over somewhere for the night and be fresh for the start, but it was how it was and we were there, that was the main thing. Swim 18 had been vacated by Terry Stock, who was still down for another week, but had moved along to swim 19 for the remainder of his time. We chatted for awhile and he said that he had really wanted to stay in 18 and was going to ask if we fancied swapping with him? It seems funny now but 18 really was the place I wanted to be in more than anywhere else so I don't think that I would have swapped, although most people would have I'm sure. In any case, Terry was already set up with the rods out by then. Besides being a decent bloke, Terry was as keen as anyone I'd seen on Rainbow and a good angler too as the following days would show.

By now I knew the spots well.

The bottom only shelved up just in front of the snags.

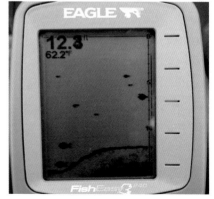

Following someone like Terry into a swim is never a real confidence booster as you know for sure that the fish won't have had much of a rest. As it happened, he had taken about ten fish to just over 40lb, so there might have been a few left for me. Also down for his first trip was Rob Hales with a few friends including Des Taylor. I hadn't seen them since the early Cassien days, so we had a bit of catching up to do. Rob was booked into fish swim 21, but didn't like the look of all the islands and snags and had swapped with a French pair on the Island swim.

"Let me know if you get a big one" said Rob "I just want to see what one of them looks like".

"Believe me mate I'll be calling everyone if that happens!" I replied. I only hoped that the chance would come at some stage.

First job, as ever, was to get the rods out. There was always that early chance of a fish and I didn't want to miss out on what seemed to be almost a certainty. I put the sounder on, although there was no need to as the spots were already decided upon, but it was interesting to see that the water temperature was up around 16 degrees. I figured that anything above 15 degrees would be pretty good for that time as it was still warming up. I went straight in with the bait that had brought me success towards the end of the previous trip in February. Each rod had two tiger nuts and a small Solar pineapple pop up attached. The only difference this time was that I'd gone a bit more technical on the rig front and opted for the 360 rig, incorporating a size 6 Long Shank Nailer tied to around ten inches of 25lb Armaled Kik-Bak hook length. The 360 rig was really designed for use with pop ups, but for some reason it seemed to work well with snowman-type set ups too and considering that the Rainbow carp were well used to seeing all sorts of presentations by now, I figured that it might give me a little bit of an advantage in tricking

For a change I had to wait a little for the first one.

one or two of those big, wily old fish.

Whatever I thought those tactics might do, they didn't work – well not immediately anyway. For a change the first afternoon passed by without a bleep. I wasn't expecting that and although it didn't worry me too much at the start of the trip, I did feel that an opportunity had somehow been missed.

Maybe it was going to be tougher than I thought. I was sure that it would be more productive than the February trip, but back then I'd received two runs in the first couple of hours before it went very quiet for many days, so I wondered just what was in store this time around.

Everything remained quiet until dawn was just breaking the following morning, when the middle rod just exploded into life! Fishing swim 18 is always a bit stressful and as much as you try to relax, you always have to be aware that should something occur, you need to spring into action as quickly as possible. The hook baits are always close to the island snags and a few seconds either way can make all the difference. Thankfully, even though I was in a deep sleep when the run came, I managed to do everything on auto-pilot and soon had the fish away from danger. It was obvious from the fight that it wasn't one of the monsters I was after, but at 32lb it was a decent enough start to the week. The first fish of a trip is always a good one to get – it means you haven't blanked, for a start! But it sort of settles the nerves a bit, it had taken a little longer to come than I'd hoped, but it was only the start of the first full days fishing and there were sure to be more chances.

It looked good out there but the indicators remained motionless, not only for the remainder of that day, but for all of the following day too! Had I got the tactics right? Were the fish visiting the swim and not feeding on my baits? I couldn't be sure but I could see Terry in swim 19 going in and out in his boat several times during the day, so perhaps he was stopping the fish from getting through to me. All of those things were going through my head. I felt like I should be catching more, but I wasn't. Eventually, at 11am

Des had only just left the swim when I landed this near forty.

on the Tuesday another pick up resulted in an 18lb mirror. I was pleased to get the action, but I was hardly overjoyed with the result. I was almost halfway through the week already and I only had two mediocre fish to show for my efforts. Always in the back of my mind though, was the February trip when the best of the action came in one brief spell near the end, so I knew that anything was possible at any time and all I needed was a bit of luck to be on my side.

Wednesday morning started much better, a strong westerly wind blew up early on and as the waves came into the bank from either side of the island in front of me, it left a calm area in the lee of the wind right where the baits were positioned. With the sun shining down and a slight scum forming on the surface it looked spot on and something just had to happen. At 8.30am the left hand rod was away. Des Taylor had been around for a chat and had only just left when it went off. The great thing with Swim 18 is that as soon as the fish are away from the initial danger, you can enjoy the fight from the bank without having to panic or jump in the boat as is the case with some of the other swims. The fish was soon lying in the bottom of the net, a nicely-scaled mirror of 39lb 4oz. For the first time it was really looking good out there and during the day I landed another three fish, all around the mid-twenty mark. Four fish in the day was a bit more like it and it felt like I was getting somewhere at last.

All of the action was coming during the day so I wasn't too bothered when it all tailed off towards darkness. The weather had changed and the fish had responded, so another day like that would be just what the doctor ordered! Only the following morning couldn't have been more different. The wind had dropped and the clear skies had been replaced by grey clouds with light rain already falling. It might have been different but it still looked good and I was confident enough, but as the hours passed by everything was quiet again.

We sat huddled under the umbrella looking out and just waiting for something to happen. At 11.50am a single bleep alerted me to the right-hand rod. It was only a liner but it was the first indication of any sort on that rod all week, and all of a sudden all of my attention was focussed on to that rod. I was sure that a fish was down there feeding and had bumped into the line by mistake. I was waiting for something to happen any second – and at bang on midday the right-hand rod was almost ripped from the rests! I leapt from my chair and picked up the rod all in one movement and tried to walk back, but the fish was having none of it and I could feel the powerful thrusts

The right side of the swim had been quiet all week, but all of a sudden my attention was focused there.

of the tail hitting the line some distance away. I could also feel a bit of grating from the branches on the line. They were very tense moments and I just prayed that I could gain enough line. Inch by inch I edged the fish back, but a powerful surge almost pulled me off of my feet and I had no option other than to give line. Miraculously, the fish stayed just clear of the branches and again I just inched it back towards the deep channel. I saw the line cutting down in the water which signalled that the fish was going deep and away from the danger areas. For the first time I took a deep breath and I felt my whole body relax just a little bit. The fight was far from over but I was in more control now. The fish kited from left to right and back again in the deep channel and gaining line was a very slow process. I wasn't going to rush things and just got a few more turns on the reel whenever I could. Eventually, the fish was nearing the slope on my side of the channel and it was all going fine until, to my horror, everything ground to a halt. The fish had found a snag down there somewhere and I couldn't even feel it on the end. Surely it wasn't all going to go wrong now? I took the only option I could and jumped straight in the boat, it was only a few yards out to where the fish was, but the different angle made a big difference and I felt the line beginning to give. Slowly, the line grated around the unseen object, until all of a sudden I was back in direct contact with the fish. Realising what had happened, the fish tried to put some distance between us again and I heard one of my other alarms sound as the lines crossed. There was little I could do other than just hold onto the fish, by then I just wanted

I had no option but to take to the boat.

to get it into the net no matter what. Slowly, I was able to ease the fish nearer and nearer to the surface. It was starting to tire for sure, but then so was I!

All of a sudden it was on the surface coughing water at me. I reached out with the net and as the fish was over the cord I lifted but the fish just slid backwards into the lake. It was the first time I realised just how long the fish was, I thought I had it in the net but most of it was still hanging over. But the fish knew that it was beaten and on the next attempt I made sure that it was well over the cord before I lifted. As it sunk into the bottom of the net I just laid the rod down and took a few seconds to get my breath back before punching the air. I knew that this was the fish that I had craved so much. I didn't recognise it, but it was big, that was all that mattered. I knew that it had to be a personal best, a fish that would beat the Cassien mirror that I'd landed some 18 years earlier. Trying to lift the fish out from the margins only confirmed what I thought. The sling was zeroed and as we struggled to lift the fish, the needle settled on 68lb 4oz! It was hard to describe my emotions, to wait that long to beat my PB was enough, but to beat it with such a stunning fish was just incredible. As promised, I called Rob and Des and they both came to lend a hand with the pictures. It was incredibly hard lifting a fish of that size up but I managed somehow, but pictures never seem to do a fish justice really, although I did get some great pics. I fully expected Paul Hunt or Pascal to recognise the fish straight away, but neither of them knew it, in fact no one knew the fish at all, which I find staggering. Surely it must have been caught before at lower weights, but somehow it had obviously avoided capture for some time before it had picked up my bait down in those murky depths. It only made the whole experience even more special.

At last the one I wanted – 68lb 4oz and a new personal best.

I was blown away by the fish and couldn't really get my head around fishing properly after that. It wasn't the end of the trip of course and the following day the same rod was away again, but I let Joan have that one and she duly netted her first Rainbow carp, a common of 40lb 12oz, which was actually the biggest Rainbow common I'd seen at that point. And around in swim 19 Terry was still going at it. I saw him come back in the boat punching the air so I went around just in time to see him with a magnificent mirror of 64lb, which became known after that as the 'Terry Stock' fish. It was a great period to be fishing Rainbow Lake, it was the time when it was just taking off as a really big fish water. Of course, it had already been running as a carp fishery since 1994 and it was now 2005, but really little seemed to have happened in those years compared to what we were now seeing.

It was Terry Stock's turn the following day with the fish which was named after him.

Of course, it was just the start of it all down there and what has happened even in the short time since I caught that fish is nothing short of amazing and no doubt it will continue to amaze us for many years yet. But as time goes on and we look back, it is often the early years which we remember with most fondness, and that is the way it is for me at Rainbow. I would go on to catch bigger fish and more of them, but those early trips were full of excitement and of the unknown. We really had no idea what the lake might hold, sure we knew some of the big fish, but to be able to capture a fish of that size and have no one recognise it, is nothing short of remarkable and for that reason (along with the size of it, of course) it will remain one of my most memorable captures. There have been many wonderful big fish waters that have come to light over the last twenty years or so, Cassien was of course the original one, but since then others such as the Orient and Raduta, have given us many heart-pounding moments and excitement far beyond what we could dream of. I've been lucky enough to fish all of those waters quite early on in their history. They are all great waters and will always remain so, but the baton has been passed on now to Rainbow Lake, a water where the carp are larger and more numerous than ever previously thought possible. You have to fish there to understand what the place is all about. Looking in from the outside, not everyone can see why it is in such demand these days, but once you have been on the banks for a few days it all becomes much clearer and you soon get bitten by the Rainbow 'bug'. It is simply an incredible carp water. I've fished many of the best and it is undoubtedly right up there with them and I don't doubt that the best years are still to come, but it would take something really extraordinary to top the capture of that first big fish – that was special!

It was just an amazing carp – even more so as no one recognised it!

2006 – A Vintage Winter at Cassien

The Cassien winter session of 2005 had been a real head banger of a trip with low water levels, too many anglers and very little action to show for my efforts. Every now and then it just goes like that and it's all part of the fishing there, you just never know how it's going to turn out until you are there. But after what had probably been my toughest session ever, I felt like a really good trip was well overdue and little did I know, but the winter of 2006 was about to make up for it in style.

About every four or five years Cassien seems to come up trumps and produce a really good session for me. Several different factors come into play, perhaps the main one being the water level. Generally, the lake doesn't fish so well if the water level is on the low side and in the years leading up to 2006 it was nearly always well down, particularly in 2005 when the level had been lower than I'd ever known it before in the winter months. This was mainly down to prolonged periods of warm, dry weather through the summer, but also down to the local electricity companies who use the lake water for generating electricity which can have an adverse effect on our fishing. The story doing the rounds was that the local power companies were now selling electricity off to Italy and the demand on the Cassien water had become greater than ever. This all resulted in the water levels during the summer of 2006 being at an all time low much to the frustration of the anglers, who were finding it tough going.

I only hoped that it would be better than the previous year.

But heading towards December the news was beginning to look a lot more promising. I bumped into Stephane, a local French angler, while I was at the Braunfels show in Germany during November and he told me the news that I wanted to hear – that after several heavy storms the lake was now virtually full up again! That was music to my ears and all of a sudden I couldn't wait for my next trip, which by then was only a matter of days away. However, it wasn't particularly straightforward this time around. Venture had been building momentum through the year and we were due to be at the Carp Expo show in Austria for the 3rd and 4th of December, which gave me the problem of when to actually leave for Cassien. I wanted to be there before those dates really to get settled in for our stay, but it would be more practical to go afterwards. It was a tricky one and in the end we couldn't help ourselves and decided to go down earlier rather than later and would just have to fly up from Nice to Vienna for the show which would be easy enough, but it left another problem of what to do with our gear while we were gone? We would have to cross that bridge when we came to it, the main thing was just to get down there and get the rods out!

We loaded ourselves onto the Channel Tunnel train just after midday and Joan and I drove down in one hit, only stopping for fuel and a quick coffee on the way, arriving at Pierre's restaurant at around 2.30am the following morning. Normally, by the time we arrive at the lake I'm just about shattered and ready for a few hours kip but for some reason I felt wide awake. It was quite mild outside and the first thing I had to do was to walk to the waterside to see how it looked in the moonlight. It's always a special feeling to step outside the car for the first time after arriving, just to take in some of that lovely fresh air and soak up the incredible atmosphere which Cassien always has. I stood looking out where the margins should have been but the water wasn't there, in fact it had dropped by around four metres during the week leading up to our arrival – not good. The level dropping so quickly is something that's always likely to happen these days, whereas it just never happened in years gone by. But knowing that it was always likely to happen I'd sort of prepared myself for it so rather than being put off, I figured that I had plenty of time in front of me and a lot could happen between now and the end of the trip - which was of course some weeks away.

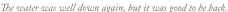

The water was well down again, but it was good to be back.

After a few hours sleep, daylight approached and I could see a few anglers about on the bank and in boats, but not all that many. Just as I was surveying the lake a Dutch guy pulled up in his boat at the base of Pierre's, heading for some supplies from his car. He had been on the lake for about a week and said that the North arm had started to fish well after some heavy rain but the water level hadn't risen at all. That was good and bad news. The fish had obviously responded to the rain but the fact that the level hadn't risen after the storms meant that they were still draining water off. The North Arm sounded a good bet, but it was the South Arm that I was more interested in. At least the one swim that I fancied most was still free, so I took no time at all to load some gear into the boat and secure it before anyone else could sneak in. I've learned the hard way in the past that any delays in getting sorted out can end in disappointment as swims can be taken before you know it and then be out of the equation for a couple of weeks or more. Just because I had plenty of time at my disposal didn't mean that I could be complacent.

Even at four metres down the lake looked far better than it had done the previous year and although not perfect it was just nice to be back, there's nothing like that feeling of just arriving for a long session, knowing that there's plenty of fishing time ahead. It was certainly warm enough in the winter sunshine, beads of sweat were running down my forehead after climbing up the steep bank with all the gear. We weren't planning to move around too much this time if possible and with that in mind we had brought the big stuff with us. The Cassien 2-Man bivvy is all about space and comfort and as a session tent it's easily the biggest and most comfortable I've used – it's strong too, so whatever the weather had in stall for us I knew we wouldn't have to worry.

In the afternoon sun it was the perfect opportunity to get out in the boat and have a good look around. The various weed beds around Cassien often play an important role, but they do tend to change a bit from time to time, depending on conditions. During the summer with the very low water levels most of the weed beds had literally been on dry land so I wasn't sure just what would be out there. It was soon apparent that there wasn't much weed around at all and it was probably only just starting to grow again after being decimated by the harsh conditions. I dragged a rig along the lake bed in certain areas and sure enough I retrieved short lengths of bright green, fresh Milfoil. Even though it wasn't much to go on I was sure that it would still be enough to hold much of the carps natural food such as crayfish and would be the ideal starting place. The weed was mainly in around 13 feet to 15 feet, which was a reasonable depth for the time of year anyway. I doubted that it would be growing any thicker in other parts of the lake so even though there wasn't much out there, it was better than nothing.

Bait for this trip would be a combination of baits from Solar. I hadn't used the BYT before but had a supply of 22mm's already air-dried. Although it was a new bait for me I already had great faith in it after seeing at first-hand Simon Crow's results on a previous trip to Austria, where he landed several good fish, in particular some nice mirrors. Just in case, I also had some of the Club Mix in 18mm, again all well air-dried to keep them fresh for the duration of the trip.

The feeling of sitting back with the first cup of tea once the rods are out is just wonderful. The nice thing was knowing that there was plenty of time in front of us and not really having to do anything other than enjoy it and try and catch a few fish along the way. The first few days were actually quite slow and they passed by quickly without a bite. It wasn't totally unexpected. The low water levels were certainly partly to blame but it often takes a little while to get in tune with things and for the fish to find the food. It certainly didn't bother me unduly and I wasn't thinking about moving. I'd made that mistake the year before, when after a few days without a bite I moved out of the swim and it cost me dearly. A mate moved in there after me and started catching straightaway and ended up having a right result – a lesson learned, as they say.

One morning whilst sitting out by the rods a car whizzed along the South Arm road tooting its horn, which signalled the arrival of our good friend Gary Hillson. Gary is fantastic company and we've shared a few winter sessions together enjoying good meals, even better wines and catching a few along the way, so it was great to see him drive past knowing that he would soon be joining us. The great thing about fishing with Gary is that although we tended to meet up most days for a social, we had different ideas on how to fish the lake and we rarely seemed to fish the same areas, which is something that helped us both as we could always swap ideas and info and try different things.

Around mid afternoon we saw the boat laden down with gear skipping across the surface towards us and so the kettle went on for the usual cuppa. We hadn't seen each other since the previous winter so there was a bit of catching up to do before the conversation of course turned to the days ahead. He said that he fancied the more mobile approach this time and planned to fish several different swims if he couldn't find consistent action. It would be interesting to see how the two methods panned out as we were intending to stay put for as long as the fish would allow – if and when they turned up. The other great thing was that he liked the idea of fishing our swim for a few days while we were in Austria, so that solved the problem of what to do with our gear – perfect! In fact Austria was on us before we knew it and with the water level slowly dropping and no fish as yet for us, perhaps it wasn't a bad time for a little break anyway.

Joan was presented with a rather special Birthday cake on our return from Austria.

It was a bit weird to be leaving the lake so early into a trip, but it had to be done. It was the first time that I'd ever used Nice airport. I know that it's always been popular with many people travelling to the lake as it cuts the journey time down so much, but I've always driven and probably always will but I have to say that Nice airport is just lovely – especially the view you get of the bay as you take off. It's easy to see why the people with money want to spend so much time down in that part of the world, it is a bit special.

The carp show was a really good one. The people of Austria are so welcoming and always make us feel at home, in particular our friend Kurt Grabmayer, who was the main organiser, and his mate Jay Jay. The shows are always hard work but they never feel like it at the time as there is so much going on and so many people to talk to that the time just flies by. Of course, all the time I was there I had Cassien on my mind and I was keen to know how things were going back at the lake. I couldn't believe it when Gary sent a text saying that another big storm had been through the region just after we had left and the water had risen by one metre – but more than that he'd caught a mirror of 35lb!! What! I couldn't believe it at first and thought that he must be having me on, it seemed all too much to happen in the space of a day or two but it was all true and the show just couldn't go quick enough after that. It was obviously starting to happen and I didn't want to miss anything. We flew back in on the Monday, a little late after missing a connecting flight, but back into the warm French sunshine all the same. I was itching to get the rods back out, but that had to be put on hold just for a little while. It happened to be Joan's birthday that day and we had a meal arranged at Gerard's in the afternoon, care of Gary along with Martin and Rachel Russell. It was a great day with lovely food and a selection of Gary's favourite American red wines and even a special birthday cake surprise as well for Joan. As usual, once the wine was flowing the celebrations went on longer than expected and it all meant that fishing was out the window for me that night but it didn't stop Gary helping himself to another Cassien carp of 26lb while I slept soundly just a few feet away.

It was really good to wake up in the bivvy again the following morning, even though the old head was still a bit fuzzy. The lake now looked totally different to just a few days earlier, the water was still rising and it was more coloured than before. All of a sudden there was a totally different feel to the session and I couldn't wait to get fishing again. Gary was more than happy to have a couple of fish under his

It was always going to happen! Joan with our first carp of the trip at 43lb 8oz.

belt and moved further down the South Arm near to the Pylon and it was obviously the right move as by the next morning he had scored with another mirror of just over 30lb. I went down armed with my camera and as he held up the fish I realised it was one that I'd caught about 18 months earlier at 17lb, so the fish from the previous stockings were still growing at a very healthy rate. Gary had only just returned the fish when a text message came through on my phone. We both joked that it would be Joan with a fish as it's become a running joke now that she catches one every time I leave the rods – and guess what – it was from Joan!!

"Can you come back I've got one in the net!"

I looked at Gary and we both just laughed, I don't know how those fish know that I've left the swim but I'm sure they know somehow! I raced back in the boat, sad that I'd missed out but pleased that our first fish was on the bank all the same. Lying in the net was a chunky common of 43lb 8oz that had given Joan a real run-around, but she'd landed it alone from the bank without any real problems. It was great to see another good fish on the bank, but I still had to get off the mark myself after nearly a week on the bank! Two days later it would be my birthday and another meal and celebration, I just hoped to have a fish to celebrate by then. It was looking more likely to happen all the time and thankfully at 3.30am on the very day of my birthday, my alarm burst into life and it was as if they'd never been away. After a good tussle out in the boat I slipped the net under a pretty mirror of 35lb and that was it, I was off the mark at last!

Got one at last! A Birthday mirror to get me off the mark.

The wine tasted even sweeter that day. This time it was a selection of Italian reds – and boy were they nice! The meal of roast lamb followed by crème broullet was just fab and sitting inside, nice and warm and dry by the fire I failed to notice what was going on outside. It was absolutely chucking it down out there! It was a great day to be 'off' the lake as otherwise it would have been a day of being confined to the bivvy, but I knew it would only improve our chances of more fish over the coming days. Making our way back to the swim in awful conditions and feeling a bit the worse for wear it was tempting to head straight for the sack and not to get the rods out, but I knew that the chances were too good so I made the effort all the same. The first run came before I'd even closed my eyes. A 28lb mirror was determined to drag me up the South Arm but I won the day – or night in this case. By morning I'd had another three runs, all of which I had to play from the bank as the wind had got up so much that it just wasn't safe enough to go out in the boat. One fish was lost when it found a snag. There was little I could do about that but I did land another fish of 26lb and one of around mid-doubles. The rain had stopped and the skies had cleared but the southerly wind was blowing gale force down the arm and it looked so different to the first week but it looked so much more carpy.

The water came up and it blew a 'hooly' but the fish liked it.

Gary had also scored with a couple more fish from his swim up to mid-30's but a couple of quiet days afterwards made him move down to opposite us. It seemed a good idea, it was as if the wind had moved the fish more towards us and judging by the previous couple of days they were on the lookout for food too. There were very few other people about by then, which only made the situation better for us. Less lines in the water definitely makes the fish less wary and they are quite nomadic if they are allowed to be and will cover a great deal of water, but at the same time they will also come back to the same areas where they know food can be found.

We were due to meet up in our swim for breakfast the next morning but Gary had another fish to photograph so instead I made my way across to him. Not a big one this time, a low-twenty mirror, so I was soon back at base just in time for the right-hand rod to roar off at just gone midday. The long, slow fight told me that it was a better fish but it was difficult to see it in the murky water. Eventually, I saw this big flank covered in large scales rise up from the depths and I bundled it into the net first time. It was a real cracker of 48lb 8oz and I knew that Gary would want to see that one as it was a real beauty and one that I hadn't seen before so I called him across. It's always better to share a moment like that with close friends and it was all turning out quite well after the slow start. No sooner had we photographed and returned that fish than my left-hander was away and I was out in the boat again. It was less than an hour after the first run but I could tell it was another good 'un. The fight was even harder if anything but it ended the same way and I was soon holding up another beauty of 49lb 8oz for the cameras. What a cracking brace of carp to catch in the space of an hour! We wined and dined on the bank that afternoon and talked about our prospects for more fish. We all agreed that it was 'big fish' time right now and conditions were just right for it – few people around, mild weather and rising water level – the perfect combination!

They don't come much better than this South Arm beauty!

A near fifty to complete a fantastic brace both caught in less than an hour.

I felt very confident that night but nothing happened and there were no messages from Gary on my phone when I switched it on. I looked out early in the morning as the mist was rising. Joan put the coffee pot on and then I noticed Gary rowing across the lake towards us. "He's either seen the coffee go on, or he's had a good fish and his phone's not working." I remarked to Joan. Gary arrived with a serious look on his face.

"My phone's packed up but I just had to come across and tell you – I've had a 64lb mirror – and I see you've got the coffee on!"

Wow! What could I say, I shook his hand and we sat down over coffee and he recounted the story of how he'd had a slow take at 4am and gone out only to find that his engine wouldn't work properly. He played what was obviously a very good fish very gingerly but was still amazed when he saw the size of the head that was coming up to the net. His engine had packed up and so had his phone but he'd got himself a new personal best which was all that mattered.

I left Joan in charge of the rods, which of course was tempting fate but pictures had to be taken and Gary's swim was only about two hundred yards away. As he put the fish on the mat we just gasped. It looked huge – it was huge! I didn't recognise the fish at all and Gary didn't at first but it proved to be a fish that he'd caught some years earlier at 47lb, a rarely-caught fish and one of the real prizes that Cassien gives up every now and then. He proudly struggled with the beast while I clicked away before returning it to the depths where it had recently been dragged from.

It was a special moment – Gary with his new personal best.

This was starting to be one of those very special sessions. From a slow start it was now building up very well and in the space of a couple of days we'd landed our three biggest fish of the trip so far. I wasn't expecting to top Gary's superb mirror, but I was sure that there was plenty more to come. We still had time on our hands and it was just looking better and better. We were in a very fortunate position. It isn't very often that Cassien is quiet these days. It is one of the worlds most popular carp fishing destinations and is busy for much of the time. But just for now it was different. For some reason the people weren't arriving, perhaps put off by the low water levels of recent times or tough previous sessions. Either way it was brilliant to look out every morning and not see any bivvies or boats anywhere else. This of course was also having a very positive effect on the fishing and we'd experienced some consistent action from a good stamp of fish after a fairly slow start. That is the thing with Cassien, it can all change so quickly. Less than two weeks earlier the water had been low and clear, it hadn't been really busy but enough anglers were about and the fishing had been really slow. Now the fish were really responding to the conditions and lack of pressure, and it's not something that you can predict or plan for, you just have to make the most of those rare times when they occur.

22mm BYT's and size 4 Solar Stronghold hooks – the winning combination.

What was becoming apparent about my fish was that they were nearly all coming during the day, whereas Gary's were virtually all coming in the hours of darkness. That suited me as I'd rather have a good sleep and then catch fish during the day when I can see what I'm doing. It was a little strange why we should catch fish at different times, though, as even the two fish that Gary had caught from my swim earlier in the trip had both come at night, but as long as they kept coming I wasn't going to worry too much about it.

Over the next couple of days I landed three fish, all around 31lb. These came between midday and early evening. The pleasing thing was that I'd only lost one fish since the start, in a snag which I could do nothing about. Otherwise, every fish had been landed okay. It was good because I'd been trying out the new Stronghold long shank hooks from Solar

The action was just getting better and better.

and they were proving to be every bit as good as I'd hoped. As soon as I saw them I knew they had good potential, being needle sharp but also strong, but you never quite know how things will work in practice until you try them, but they had proved themselves to me and have become one of my favourites.

One quiet day followed for me, although Gary caught another one if I remember rightly. The next morning a group of canoeists arrived with their tutors using motor boats. They raced up and down the lake causing a bit of disturbance in the swim, but as the ripples lapped the shore one of my alarms bleeped a couple of times and the tip just bent over a little and stayed there. Gary thought that the boats were to blame but I knew it was another fish and immediately took to the boat. The fish hadn't gone anywhere but it felt really heavy. A long battle followed and I was really getting excited but eventually when it surfaced it wasn't as big as I thought it would be, mind you at 43lb I could hardly complain, but they do play tricks on you at times. I didn't know it at the time but that was to be the start of a really consistent spell of action that would see me catch fish every day over quite a long period, something that isn't easy to do in the winter on Cassien. During the previous years session, at the same time, I had fished for almost five weeks and caught just four carp in that time and Joan had just one. This time around it was like fishing a different water completely.

The boats had just gone by when the tip pulled over.

It gets light in the winter at around 7.45am but with the high surrounding hills the sun doesn't actually appear until about 9.15am. If the nights are really cold, which they can be, then the frost doesn't melt until the sun is up. Fortunately, we were experiencing a really mild spell – so mild that some nights I had to sleep out of my sleeping bag in just a tee shirt! That isn't normal in the winter, I can assure you, but it was very pleasant all the same. It was nice just to get up at around 8am and watch the day unfold while Joan put the coffee pot on and sorted breakfast out. Normally by the time we'd finished breakfast the sun was just appearing. However, this time breakfast was interrupted at 8.30am by a screaming run. I've got to say that it's my favourite time to get a run even though, on this occasion, my coffee was left to get cold. With the mist rising from the calm water it was really atmospheric stuff being dragged around by an angry carp. I've always liked rods that were meant for playing carp as opposed to casting 'broom handles' and the Venture VXR-1's are without a doubt the best rods that I've ever used in that respect, especially when the fish is down deep underneath the boat and I can watch the tip bend over until it disappears beneath the surface. What was even more pleasing was when I saw the fish go into the landing net. I knew it was another good 'un. Joan was standing at the edge waiting and, as ever, she'd already got the mat and the sling ready for the fish. The fish was hoisted on the scales and the needle swung around and stopped on 52lb 4oz – a nicely-scaled, dark brown mirror and a really good start to the day - another cracking Cassien carp. It was a nice social day with Gary cooking one of his special pasta dishes (Pasta Hillsoni) along with a couple of bottles of Chardonnay. He loves cooking on the bank and comes up with some real corkers, one day he presented us with breaded scallops for starters followed by Nile Perch – nice one Gaz - no baked beans and fried sausages for us! The day was made complete when at 6.15pm one of the closer rods spluttered into life. That particular rod had

The coffee got cold but it was worth it for this lovely 52lb 4oz mirror.

been quiet for awhile but it was one area that had produced fish for me in the past so I felt happy to persevere with it and while it had taken a bit of time to go off, with a 42lb 4oz mirror on the end it was worth the wait.

It looked like being a good afternoon!

Things were good for us and besides eating well we had one more wine afternoon to fit in, with a selection of Australian reds from the D'Arenberg producers. These are my real favourites and I'd looked forward to that day. If you like full-flavoured red wines then look out for one called 'Dead Arm', that's my personal favourite, although 'Dead-Head' would be a better description once you've drunk a bottle or two of it!

The following two days produced a common of 27lb and a mirror of 36lb 8oz for me, but the runs were drying up for Gary. He'd obviously done well from the swim after catching a superb 64lb mirror previously, but after a few smaller fish in subsequent days little else had happened and with time running out for him, he was looking for one last

It was turning out to be a very special trip.

throw of the dice and a move to another area. The water had continued to rise and the lake was now not far off from full level. With that in mind he quite fancied the idea of the West Arm as often the fish will head for there when the water rises well. We were definitely staying put as my action showed no signs of stopping but it would be interesting to see how he got on for his remaining few days. He packed his boat and came over for a cup of tea before heading off to his new area.

Sometime during the evening a text message came through saying that he had found loads of fish and they were jumping constantly, even in the daylight, and he was really confident of something happening. Even though it was only a text message I could sense Gary's excitement and I was sure too that he was going to score quickly and was keen to put the phone on the following morning to see what he'd caught. In fact he'd caught two fish by breakfast time, a 35lb mirror and a fabulous common of 51lb. We always make the effort to go and photograph each others fish, but the West Arm was some distance away. I figured it best to walk around the tracks rather than go by boat, but just as I had set off Gary sent a text saying he was coming to us first for a coffee. I was pleased he did as no sooner had I sat back down in the swim than another fast run resulted in a good-looking common of 42lb 4oz for me.

I'd just sat down when the rod went off with this cracker on the end.

Gary was very excited about his new swim but time was running out for him and he only had one night left. After coffee I walked back to his swim with him – although it was more of a trek than a walk, taking almost an hour. Back at his swim I could see fish jumping immediately but already someone else had moved in close to him and while we were looking over, the guy had a run and landed a small fish from very close to where Gary had been fishing. This didn't please Gary too much but we set about photographing the fish anyway. The 51lb common was a real beauty and turned out to be the fish that I'd caught during the making of the Cassien DVD at 44lb so it was good to see that fish again and at a much higher weight. It just shows how those fish get about. I'd always thought that it was very much a North Arm fish as most previous captures that I knew of that fish had come from there but here it was in the West Arm and feeding in an area that had been dry land a few weeks earlier! The Cassien carp never cease to amaze me with how much they will travel and where they will travel too.

I left Gary to get his rods out while I started the long walk back. Inevitably, the call came through from Joan when I was about halfway there that she'd caught a fish but this time it was a smaller specimen of 24lb. It's got to the stage now where I just expect it to happen and it's more of a surprise when it doesn't – not that I mind her catching, of course, it just makes me wonder why it happens so often? I'm sure that the big guy up there is just looking down and playing games with us sometimes.

Gary arrived the next day all packed and ready to go. He'd only had one more fish and that was a small one so he'd done the pics himself. It was a real shame that he had to go but all good things do come to an end and as I always say you cannot stop time from marching on, all you can do is make the most of it while you are there. We had shared so many good days together that it did leave us with a slightly empty feeling when we saw him heading off for the last time.

A move to the West Arm paid off for Gary with this 51lb beauty.

All the time, the lake was just getting quieter and for the first time Joan and I found ourselves to be the only people in the whole of the South Arm, which reminded us very much of the early days when it was about the only other time you could experience the lake like that. It was a very special feeling I can tell you and one I'll remember for a long time. For some reason I didn't get a daytime run that day but two in the night instead. Don't ask me why, but I had changed my rigs and put different hooks on for some reason and when I went out to play the first fish the hook just popped out as soon as I was above it. Why I had changed hooks I don't know but I immediately went back to the Solar long shanks and when the next rod went off a couple of hours later I had no worries and safely landed a 37lb mirror.

The bait and baiting strategies were obviously working very well. A lot also depends on the conditions on the lake, as I've already mentioned, but the baiting has to be right all the same. I was using a combination of the BYT and Club Mix from Solar. I only used a single 22mm BYT as a hookbait throughout the trip though. I was confident enough in both baits to bait up with a mixture of the two. The important thing was to use the right amount in the right areas. At the start of the session I was catching fish between 14 feet and 17 feet. It was the same areas that I was still catching from but of course the water level had risen a lot since the start and the depths on those same spots were now between 21 feet and 26 feet. It's possible that the fish would have fed on other spots but all the time they were working I couldn't see any point in changing them and the water was warmer due to the conditions so that would probably explain why they were happy to feed that little bit deeper. I don't tend to use a lot of bait in the winter – perhaps half a dozen baits right on top of the hook bait and then another 15 to 20 freebies around the general area. I only normally replace the hook baits every two days but I still bait up every day with a few freebies as I

What a great time to be out there playing a carp.

know that quite often fish can move through and clear you out without giving you any indication, so even if no fish have been through the swim, the small amounts that I put out wouldn't harm my chances in any way.

It was certainly doing the job anyway, as it has done for several years and I landed another two fish up to 27lb 12oz the next day to make it four carp inside of 12 hours. If everything could have stayed the same then I'm sure that I could have just kept on catching at the same rate, but it was bound to change sooner or later. The following day it was back to normal with the daytime run at 2pm producing a 36lb 8oz mirror. That made it a 2pm run two days on the trot, so the following day, which just happened to be Christmas Eve, at 2pm I was sitting behind the rods ready for it to go and sure enough bang on time off it went. It was difficult to tell the size of the fish other than it felt pretty good. The fight must have gone on for around 20 to 25 minutes before a big creamy flank broke the surface. I had just been enjoying the battle in the afternoon sun, it is normally the time on most waters when you least expect to get action and for me it was the perfect time to get a bend in the rod and this was looking like a serious carp! Indeed, at 52lb 2oz it was a serious carp and only a couple of ounces short of my best fish of the trip. It was a typical deep-bodied Cassien mirror but one that I didn't recognise at all, no doubt one of the many young fish that have grown on so well. It was a great early Christmas present – and of course the next

I was ready for the 2pm bite and I wasn't disappointed.

afternoon I was there waiting again, expecting to get my Christmas Day carp at 2pm, I sat behind the rods with the video camera all ready and guess what – it didn't happen! It was the first day for quite some time that nothing happened, but I suppose that if they're going to have a days rest then it might as well be on Christmas Day.

The thing with Cassien is that you know sooner or later that the crowds are going to arrive and the next day that is exactly what happened. Out of the blue, boat loads of people started arriving from all directions and before long all of the points that had remained empty for so long now became filled with anglers. On top of that the water started to drop again – and quite rapidly. At one point earlier we thought we would have to move the bivvy back, but now we had plenty of open bank space in front of us. As I said earlier it's amazing how much can change at Cassien in such a short time. A few weeks before it had changed for the better and now everything was starting to head the other way. It was still Cassien but it totally changed the atmosphere of the trip and I knew that it would change the habits of the fish too. I wasn't unduly worried as we now only had a few days left anyway and in a way it felt as if it was coming to a natural end. If the lake had only just started to fish well then I wouldn't have wanted to leave, but I felt as though I'd been more than lucky with the way things had gone so I couldn't complain.

'Merry Christmas'!

The following morning I had a very nicely-scaled mirror of 34lb but for the first time the action was starting to spread out a little, I couldn't see anyone else catching but the fish just appeared to know what was happening and were slowing down a little. During the couple of remaining days I had one more fish, which turned out to be the smallest of the trip at 13lb and although it is always a wrench to leave Cassien we knew that we'd had the best of it. You never know what you'll get at this amazing lake but this time most people stayed away while the fish came out to play. The following year could be completely the other way around. In a way that's what makes Cassien so exciting and all the more rewarding when it does go right. It was certainly a lot better than the year before – in fact it was one of the best.

The Triple Crown

Long sessions are something that I've grown into over the years but in the summer of 2007 I did something that was quite new for me. I would be away for three weeks but that would combine consecutive visits to three totally different lakes – Cassien, Serreire and Rainbow – my own mini version of the Tour de France! The aim, of course, being to catch decent fish from all three venues; I knew what the lakes held and I had previous experience of all of them, but they are all very different waters in their own right.

It all came about by chance really. We had been to Bob Davis' beautiful Lac Serreire over the last few years in August to celebrate birthdays and wedding anniversary's besides doing a bit of fishing. So that was like a permanent fixture on the calendar and a very pleasant place to visit during what is generally the hottest month of the year. But then Cassien cropped up again. We'd only returned from there a couple of weeks earlier but Venture partners, Rob Hughes and Rene Hawkins were due to be down there around the same time and so it would be good to meet up and share a bit of time on the banks of that most famous of waters. There was also talk of doing a bit of filming for either 'Extreme Carp' or a DVD of some sort. I've done a fair bit of filming in the past with Rob and Jon Jones (Shoes) and have normally enjoyed it a great deal so I was always up for a bit more of that. It would be better to fit that time in before going on to Serreire I thought, as it would be a little more hectic than normal, especially with the lake still closed for night fishing. Then a call came through from Jason Colenso who is Rob's partner at Angling International, he said that he'd booked swim's 18 and 12 down at Rainbow and one of those would be free if I fancied it. Well the dates for the week at Rainbow would be following straight on from Serreire and my first reaction was that it would be too much after fishing the other two lakes – but then I thought "What the hell, why not?"

I'd only been home from Cassien a week or two.

Rainbow is only a three-hour drive down country from Serreire and it would be nice to fish there again, so I rang Jason back and said that I'd be more than happy to take him up on his offer. So that was the plan – three separate week sessions, but all bunched into one trip! But the starting point was, of course, Cassien.

The July trip had been another good one with a few good fish.

People often say to me that they wonder how I can keep doing all those long journeys year after year. To be honest I like driving abroad, whilst the motorways in England are normally nothing more than long car parks, the roads of Europe – and especially France – are an absolute pleasure to drive on with plenty of open space and nice scenery, the worst part is inevitably getting out of the country - and then back in!

An hour-and-a-half drive down to the Channel Tunnel shouldn't have been too much grief, but as we got to within a few miles of our escape from England everything ground to a halt, which then became a very slow crawl. After some time we discovered that the M20 had been shut and we were told to follow the diversion signs which, although we looked hard, just didn't exist. However, after driving round in circles we did find the queue for the tunnel, which was also at a stand still. There was obviously something serious going on, but no one seemed any the wiser as to what it was until a guy next to us in the queue heard that there had been a power cut in the tunnel and that everything was a bit chaotic. We all gradually inched forward until we got to the ticket desk where the news was that there would be at least a five hour delay for us getting onto the train. There was nothing we could do other than sit and wait, but gradually the back log began to clear until eventually it was our turn to board.

By the time we got to Calais I was already tired so we only made it to Reims before I needed a few hours of 'shuteye'. That was probably the worst thing I could have done as when I awoke in daylight it seemed to be quite busy. A quick wash and brush up at the services and we started what I thought would be the remaining six to eight hours drive – Wrong! Just after starting out we saw a sign that said 'Bouchon' I'd not come across it before but soon found out that it meant traffic jam! In fact we came across a great deal of 'Bouchon's' all the way down, so to all of you out there - just remember what it means. The journey which would normally take fourteen hours from leaving home to arriving at the lake took us an incredible twenty-eight hours! There were times when I thought we just weren't going to get there at all, but arrive we did and what a relief it was to see Philippe at Pierre's restaurant, especially when he walked over with a couple of very welcome hot coffee's.

All of a sudden we were at Cassien again and all the troubles of the journey down were forgotten. Philippe had some good news, apparently a few decent fish had been caught recently, but whilst opening up in the morning he had also seen plenty of good fish showing around the base of the restaurant where the boats and pedalos are kept. He suggested that we stayed not far away and had a go there in the morning. It seemed a good idea, it was already getting late and tiredness was once again creeping in. Russian angler, Yuri Begalov, was also staying there that night after fishing for the day. He'd caught a couple of fish around low 30's over the previous days so it was good to get some first-hand news on what had been going on since we'd been away.

A couple of bottles of Rose later and I was ready for bed. I had seen some fish showing in the area so it would certainly be worth a go whenever I woke up, but I must admit that I wasn't all that keen on an early start. As it turned out, any thoughts of a lie-in disappeared before the sun was up. I forgot that it was now Sunday and the busiest day of the week for the restaurants and people were arriving early for their various activities. Through blurry eyes I assembled a couple of rods but it didn't look the same as the previous evening, the fish weren't showing any more and it was looking far too busy for my liking.

We stuck it out for a couple of hours but with swimmers, boats, pedalos and wind surfers all getting dangerously close to the lines I thought it best to look for somewhere quieter in the North Arm where we could at least rest a little easier. There were quite a lot of anglers on the lake this time around. You never know from one week to the next how many will be there, as people from so many different countries visit Cassien but as always I hope to find it as empty as possible, but it was not to be this time around. No matter how busy it is, there are always some places which are out of the way and we headed for one of the small bays which rarely get fished by carp anglers.

With three different lakes to fish over three weeks I had worked out in my own mind the way I wanted to approach each one. Each water would require totally different tactics, bait sizes etc. Actually, it's a point that people tend to overlook. I often get asked what is my approach for fishing in France and it's an impossible question to answer, as I fish all waters differently – but I will go through what I used on each water as I come to them, but to think that all French waters are the same would be a big mistake. The size of the baits

I use really depends on what the carp like to eat as natural food, if they eat large items such as crayfish and swan mussels as the Cassien carp do, then they are far more likely to accept larger hook baits. On waters where the carp feed on smaller items like blood worm or zebra mussels then they will generally go for smaller baits too. Thankfully, the Cassien carps liking for large baits has often been a blessing in disguise with the number of nuisance species about. I had plenty of 24mm Club Mix and BYT boilies with me but was also aware that I might have to use plastic hook baits if things got too bad. I decided to play it both ways. I would use boilies on two rods and plastic baits on the other two and just see where I went from there. Boilies would normally be my first choice but making sure that you have a hook bait on is the main priority.

In the confines of the bay there wasn't too much water to play with. In front of me it dropped slowly off to about fifteen feet where it then dropped sharply down to around twenty five feet where it then levelled off. The edge of the drop-off looked the obvious spot and I placed three of the baits along the ledge but tried the remaining rod in the deeper water. I baited fairly lightly as it was already getting to mid afternoon and it would only be around six hours fishing time before having to pack up for the night. I must admit that it was tempting to put more freebies out just to be safe, but I must have done it right as around an hour later one of the rods with the plastic bait rattled off and the fish tore off so fast that it almost beached itself on the far bank! Luckily, in the restricted area it couldn't go far and I soon had it in the net. The long, scaly mirror weighed just over 25lb and made a decent enough start.

Less than an hour later, the same rod was away again with a hungry-looking 28lb common. Two fish in quick succession gave me the impression that the lake was fishing well, but in reality it was more like I had just stumbled on a few fish which were keeping out of the way. That was it for the day and the following day I persevered in the same swim but it produced nothing. Those small out-of-the-way areas do get a bit claustrophobic – especially if you're not catching, so a move to the main area of the lake was in order. Even

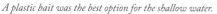
A plastic bait was the best option for the shallow water.

with more anglers around, it was easy enough to find a swim that hadn't been fished for at least a few days, maybe longer. Although I've had years of experience at Cassien I still have to trust to luck a little with a new area as the fish tend to move around so much and you never really know if they will be there or not.

It wasn't long before a couple of fish gave away their presence and although it looked good, no action was forthcoming for the rest of that day. For a change I decided to stick more bait out in an attempt to get their heads down. A few kilos of boilies plus some mixed particles and pellets all went out in the hope that it would get them going over the next day or two as I would definitely give it another day or two there in the hope that fish would move in. There was a lovely plateau just out in front of the swim, where it dropped down to around 30 feet before rising up again to a peak of 16 feet. I baited all around that spot and another margin spot just out to my right before calling it a day.

The weather was different the following day. The usual blue, sunny skies had been replaced with cloud and a little drizzle, but it looked good for a fish or two. I placed a couple of baits on the plateau, one in the close margins and one in the deeper water in around 55 feet just to have all options covered. It was the deep rod that went first around mid-morning but the excitement soon faded as I realised the culprit was a catfish of around 40lb. I was still moaning about that one when one of the plateau rods signalled a drop back. I stood there looking as the indicator rose again and I was soon out in the boat following whatever was on the end. It was soon clear that it was a carp but it wasn't fighting particularly hard and I thought it might be small until in the gloom I saw what looked like a good fish slide into the net.

"Please be as big as you looked" I said to myself and indeed it was! At 53lb 8oz it's one of my better Cassien fish and one very reminiscent of the old original fish that once graced the lake – a real corker! That one fish made the whole trip more than worthwhile.

It was one of the most impressive Cassien mirrors I'd seen.

Really there's not much to say about the trip after that. I fished another day in the same area and then moved to the South Arm briefly but no more action came my way. Three fish may not seem much but I only fished for five and a half days in the end, so really it was an okay result, especially with the big one. Rob Hughes did film the fish but his trip turned into more of a family holiday, which didn't bother me at all. I'd enjoyed it immensely. We celebrated with pizza's at Pierre's and then a few bottles back at the Hughes residence and then my thoughts were turned to the next destination on the tour – Lac Serreire.

If I thought the drive down was bad then we were in for some more of the same on the drive up to Limoges. We were due there in the afternoon but it was almost dark by the time we rolled down the small lane leading up to the lakes. Lloyd and Precious (the dogs) were first as ever to greet us, closely followed by the rest of the Davis clan. It was great to see them again and catch up on what had happened since we last spoke to each other. The small lake, which we were due to fish hadn't been doing great things but August always was hit-and-miss there.

"Give 'em some food to get 'em going" Bob said. He knew the lake and I would certainly take his advice on board, but it was late and there was a bivvy already set up for us so any thoughts of fishing could be put off until the next morning.

Now I had to switch off from Cassien and get into 'Serreire mode'. I knew how I wanted to fish. The small lake, or Badgers Holt as it is commonly known, is home to some stunning fish but they are under pressure every week during the season, so I didn't want to crowd the place with too many lines. Also, I wanted to pin the lines down as much as possible, so I would use putty on the end of the tubing, then have a flying back lead on the line and after that also use a normal backlead at the rod end of the line. One thing I certainly found

Definitely the best way to start the day.

was that light backleads were better than heavier ones and the Solar Absailer back lead clips were the best to use as when reeling in or playing fish. I've often found in the past that other backleads will fall off, whereas the Solar ones don't.

I had quite a variety of bait to use. Firstly I had around 20kg of Solar BYT in 10mm and 12mm sizes with matching pop ups. I also had around the same weight in pellets of various sizes. On the particle front, I had plenty of hemp and the Combi-Seed Mix from The Bait and Feed Company, which I could make up as I needed and to top it all off I had 16kg of Frolic dog food, which I hadn't used much before but I felt that it would help and finish off a nice mixture of good bait.

A fantastic Serreire mirror that nearly pulled my arms off!

It takes a bit of confidence to bait up quite heavily when the fish haven't been particularly active, but sometimes you have to take the bull by the horns, as it were. I had no doubt in my own mind that I would catch fish at some stage – how many and how big I had no idea, but after the first 24 hours passed without a fish I could see Bob getting a little edgy. I know how much he wants his visitors to catch well and of course he wanted his advice to pay off. When I did get a run I went and lost it like an idiot after being taken by surprise, but before the day was out I did land two lovely mirrors both of which weighed 33lb 8oz. Apart from weighing the same they couldn't have looked more different, the first being a dark brown 'wood carving' whilst the other was a deeper-bodied grey fish. Sighs of relief all round!

Although the lake is only small, the way I went about fishing it required a fair bit of hard work. Most of the spots I wanted to fish were in the margins but required precise placement, which couldn't be done just by casting alone. For the two rods on the left I had to cast the leads over onto the adjacent bank, I then had to go around and attach the rigs while Joan held the rods. I then walked one bait right down into the far corner where I then had to wade out under some overhanging trees in about four feet of water, where I could then feel around for a firmer spot to place the lead. The other rod was a little easier as I only had to walk it around to the pontoon midway down the same bank and then lower it into position. The two rods on the right were in similar positions at the other end of the lake. I had found a firm spot amongst soft silt on the far margin, but the adjacent trees meant that I would have to cast to that one, but with a pole marker in place the job was made easier. The last rod was to go way down the near margin to the right, next to the well-known white tree. This just meant walking back down the bank, dropping the bait and then passing the rod around the trees as I made my way back. All in all, quite a performance to get four baits into place on a small water, but I was determined to fish well and although it did take quite a time to do them all, I did feel confident with all of them. As Bob pointed out, with a bait boat it would have been a hell of a lot easier, but I didn't have one and didn't really want one. I've nothing against them but it's more satisfying doing it the old fashioned way – and a bit of hard work never hurt anyone!

Everything had to be pinned down on the bottom. *BYT snowman on a short rig.*

The two right hand rods both produced in quick succession, the first fish being a mirror with half a tail that I'd caught a couple of years back at 28lb but now it had moved on to 37lb 4oz! Testament to how well Bob has run his waters. The second fish was an absolute 'stonker' of 38lb, one which hadn't been out for some time and was absolutely gorgeous.

The fish were now getting their heads down and the heavier baiting was paying off. I was also keeping the bait going in at least a couple of times a day as well as topping up when a run occurred. The next morning produced two more stunning mirrors of 34lb and 40lb 12oz plus the old warrior common which I got at 40lb at last (40lb 12oz to be exact) It was my third capture of the fish and I'd just missed out on getting it at 40 before, so I suppose it was third time lucky! Later that afternoon I had a nicely-scaled 28lb mirror that Bob recognised as one of his stockies that had put on silly amounts of weight since being introduced – it was actually the only fish that I would land under the 30lb mark.

One of two forties that morning.

The carp were constantly showing over the baits.

Little BYT snowman's were doing the biz amongst all the food I was putting out. It's amazing how sometimes fish only need some food to get them going. I suppose you can never be sure if it's the right thing or not, but then that's why it's always good to listen to the people who do know the places well. Action was certainly coming at regular intervals and with good fish too, mainly around mid to upper 30's. But later that night I had a real surprise when the rod on the far-right margin went off and after a lengthy battle I was looking down at a nice big mirror of 48lb 8oz that I didn't recognise, in fact Bob had only seen it once before himself a year or so ago so it was a special one for sure. But it certainly wasn't the best surprise. That was saved for early the next morning when the bait in the far left corner was picked up by a slow, plodding fish. It felt good from the start but didn't do anything drastic. The width of the fish as it went in the net was incredible and I had no idea how much it would weigh. Once on the bank, though, I recognised it as one Joan had caught previously at 46lb, but this time it pulled the needle round to 54lb 4oz. It was a fish that I'd wanted to catch since I'd seen Joan with it but the weight was a real bonus! One more mirror of 34lb 10oz graced the net before the end of the week, but what a week it had been! 13 fish landed and 4 lost was a very pleasing result but the 54 meant that I'd now had 50's from both of the first two waters and now it was time to move onto Rainbow – could I possibly make it 50's from all three waters? Well there was only one way to find out, so Saturday morning the gear was all packed away once more and after a quick stop at the shops for fresh supplies, we were on our way again, this time heading south towards Bordeaux.

This rarely-caught mirror of 48lb 8oz came as a nice surprise.

A proper 'chunk' of a fish at 54lb.

The chance to fish Rainbow Lake this time around came out of the blue during a conversation with Angling International director Jason Colenso. Unbeknown to me, he already had a couple of swims booked for the week following on from when we would be packing up from Serreire.

"I've got swims 18 and 12 booked and you can have 12 if you like – or at a push you could have 18" said Jason.

I called Jason back and said that I would take him up on his offer and would happily take swim 12. I think he was a bit surprised that I didn't try to haggle for swim 18 as I've fished there a lot in the past and done pretty well from there on the whole. But just putting big fish on the bank isn't the whole story for me and although I felt confident that I could do well in 18, I fancied the challenge of a swim that hadn't been particularly kind to me previously. Of all the swims that I have fished on Rainbow so far, swim 12 has been the most difficult to come to terms with. In all I'd been in there three times before, once when I'd caught plenty of fish but 'only' up to 45lb and the other two sessions had produced just three or four fish with the best going just over the 40lb mark. Don't get me wrong, I still look upon fish of those sizes as very good but when you know what's possible at Rainbow and see some of those huge fish on the mat, it gives you a different perspective to what you have on most other waters. I figured that I was due a good session in 12 and the challenge was drawing me into it.

Most people arrive during the Saturday morning for the change over in plenty of time to find out what's been happening and to have a chat with the previous occupants of whatever swim they are due to fish. Well, we were only leaving Serreire on the Saturday morning and with a bit of shopping to do it was inevitable that we would arrive a bit late. Personally I don't mind that, I prefer to arrive to an empty swim that's at least had a couple of hours rest and I'm sure the other anglers appreciate being left in peace to pack up. I know it's one of the things that does grate on me a bit when I'm trying to get everything sorted and packed away and then the next people arrive early and stay there talking while I'm trying to enjoy the last moments of the trip. I know not everyone's the same but I like to give people the space anyway.

The start of 'stage three' of the Triple Crown down at Rainbow Lake.

I suppose it was around 4pm when we rolled up to the gates. The club house was empty so we went straight around to the swim. We passed 18 on the way, Jason had yet to arrive and it did look good in there as always. It did cross my mind that I've normally managed a fish really quickly from there and it was hard to drive away knowing that, but who knows what 12 had in store? As ever the swim was spotless and had been brushed clean. Pascal and family take great pride in what they do and making everything look tidy for their next guests is a really nice touch. Although you always know that people have not long gone it's nice not to see the evidence all around.

A simple set up for Rainbow consisting of a single tiger nut and a BYT pop up.

I knew in my head what I wanted to do, although I think that the travelling was starting to catch up and it was hard work just putting the rods together. Thankfully, I had been planning for what I would need during the previous week and had several rigs and leaders already tied up. As I've stated on many occasions, the hardest part of my fishing is having to change everything virtually every time I load the car. Every lake is different and requires different gear and a different approach. Long gone are the days when I used to target just one water for the year – but then I love what I'm doing now too!

It didn't take long to get off the mark.

For the first night I just wanted to keep everything as low profile as possible. Even a couple of hours with no lines in the water can have an effect on the fish and sure enough some fish were showing along the bars in front of the swim. Normally as soon as the rods go out the fish realise it and can go quiet, so all I was going to do was fish the near margin and maybe catch one or two fish off guard and give the main part of the swim a rest. I knew that some good fish had been caught from the margins before and I could always start spreading out the next day.

Down to the left of the swim is a small bush, which looks insignificant but produces a fair bit of action at the right times, even though the water is only just over a metre deep there. One bait went there and the rest were just spread around the drop off in front which generally seemed to be at about 20 metres range. There it dropped sharply from about 2 metres to 4 or 5metres and it looked a good interception point for any fish moving through the swim.

As with the tactics, the bait needed to be 'tweaked' to suit the situation. The Rainbow carp see a vast array of baits and I'm sure that they eat most of them to some degree, but they can also be moody fish at times. I've tried all sorts with varying degrees of success. Both the Club Mix and BYT from Solar have performed very well, but then so have particles and ground bait mixes. Sometimes a mixture of all of those gives a bit of an edge. Certainly a tiger nut and boilie combination has worked for me when things have been a little tough so I went with that on all rods, just one or two tigers and a BYT pop up. I would fish that over a mixture of Particle 42 groundbait, a small particle mixture and a few handfuls of small BYT boilies and a sprinkling of tigers. As ever when using tigers I find that not using too many seems to be more productive than filling the place in with them, whereas with boilies it can be the other way around when things are going well. The water out in front looked well coloured which was a good sign that there were fish in the area and that they had been feeding. I remember turning up one time and being able to see the bottom all over but not seeing a sign of any fish and that session was indeed a struggle – it looked much better this time.

It seemed to take an eternity to get fishing but all rods were in place by dark and stage 3 of the Triple Crown was underway. It was about 2am when I was jolted from my sleep by the first run. It was the bait down the left margin by the bush that did the trick, one of the old favourite spots. Swim 12 is literally full of bars and snags and certainly on the left side it's often best to take to the boat to play and land the fish. But down the left margin isn't too bad if all goes well and after a few heart flutters I had the first fish boiling under the tip. Joan did the honours with the net and a 40lb 8oz common was soon being held up for a few piccies.

Apart from that one fish, the first night passed quietly. Of all the rods, the one that went was the one I thought most likely to go. The other margin rods remained quiet and although the plan to catch them off guard hadn't entirely worked, there were still fish showing out in front so they were at least fairly relaxed, but it was time to start looking for some better spots.

The swim really is like an upside down egg box, with all sorts of features spread right through. There are two main bars that run parallel to the bank, which come very close to the surface in parts, but there are all sorts of other bits and pieces out there. Most of the nastier stuff is on the left of the swim. Most of the features are strewn with old tree stumps, which become more exposed all the time as fish feed there and dig away at the silt. That's the reason I always use a good lead release system. Heavy leads such as 8oz or 10oz Korda Grippers help to give a really good hook hold on the take, but then it's important to get rid of the lead in order to have more chance of landing them, it seems to work well most of the time, anyway.

With so many features it's hard to know exactly where to start but at least there are a lot more options than in swim 18 which is more or less down to three or four areas. Along the far island margin is a small gap which leads through to the main part of the lake. It's one of those spots that needs you to be on the ball but it is a good spot and sure enough, as soon as I looked out there I could see several patches of bubbles rising to the surface, which I was sure were from feeding fish. One bait was dropped there and two more were placed on the nearer bars in about 11 feet. I stuck with the left margin rod as it had already produced one fish.

The gap rod looked sure to go off before long and it was only there for about ten minutes before the tip lurched over. The first moments of the battle are always tense but after that it's not quite so bad on the right of the swim where the bars and the snags are less severe. The resulting fish was another common of 41lb. The weather looked bang on for it, after a few hot weeks some stormy weather had blown in from the Bay of Biscay and it was forecast to last for most of the week. The gap still looked the best chance of a run and over the next couple of hours I had two good mirrors of 44lb 2oz and 42lb 4oz before losing one to a hook pull all on the same rod. But the best was yet to come when again the same rod went off. The fish actually came away from the danger area much easier than the others which made me think that it might be smaller but as the huge-framed fish rolled in the edge I knew it was much bigger! It looked at least mid 50's – maybe 60 but the scales gave a reading of 58lb 8oz. A special fish in more than one way, it completed the hat-trick of 50's from the three different waters that had been the aim from the start and however unrealistic it had seemed, I had somehow pulled it off!

It was a great run of action which hadn't gone unnoticed. I had still yet to see any other anglers but on the Monday morning had a visit from the people either side of our swim. The guys on the left in swim 14 had still yet to catch, apart from a few tench, while on the right they had already been down for two weeks catching plenty of good fish, although it had slowed up a little for them. All were decent blokes and it was good to have a chat with them. The two anglers in 14 had been fishing in the bottom of the gulleys between the bars

It looked massive as it came to the net and I knew that the Triple Crown was complete!

and I suggested that they might be better off fishing on the tops of the bars as it had proved to be better for me in the past. It certainly worked for them as they started catching from the next morning onwards.

Late summer and early autumn seem to be among the best times to fish around the area of the lake I was in. Like any water the fish move around and are not always there, but they do seem to arrive in larger numbers after the really hot weather starts to fade for one reason or another. I was

It was hard to believe that it was August.

confident that there were more fish to come and kept faith in the same areas. I was also going to keep my eye on other areas that could produce but I wanted to leave certain parts of the swim alone if I could so that the fish weren't pressured out of the area. Anyway, all the time those same spots were coming up with the goods I was prepared to stick with them. And produce they did! The next day seven fish were landed up to high 30's, not quite living up to what had occurred the first day but still very good all the same.

Then the action started to slow up a bit. It could have been for a number of reasons. The stormy weather had turned into a day of persistent rain which was quite heavy at times and they never seem to be the best feeding conditions. It could also have been that after the initial burst of action the fish were a bit more wary. Either way just two fish of 18lb and 34lb followed but it was still action all the same. It is a common occurrence at Rainbow for the action to slow midway through the session; Paul Hunt, who is obviously there more than most with his organised trips calls it the 'midweek crisis'.

As ever I needn't have worried and it was just a case of being patient, as better conditions the following day brought the fish on the feed again. There were still periods of heavy rain but mixed with clear spells and a decent breeze. It's funny how the groups of fish stick together as it seemed to be one common after another up to 38lb, although during one of the heavier downpours I did manage one very long mirror of 45lb 12oz.

The bottle rig came into play later on in the week.

Most of the fish had been coming to the gap rod which had been consistent all the way through, even on the odd quiet day. The other spots had produced the occasional fish and it's easy to let things go by when you are catching from one area. But with only a couple of days left it was now the time to have a look at other possible spots. One area that I had ignored on purpose up until then was the far island margin over to the left. I had caught from there on previous trips but it does mean fishing right across all the bars and taking to the boat every time a fish is hooked. But it did look a good area with a small bay leading off the island and it had been free of lines for awhile.

Fishing to that spot meant changing things a little and using a bottle rig. Just leaving the line to run across the bars is asking for trouble; sure the fish can still be landed but the line does tend to get caught around all manner of things. The bottle is nothing more than a small drinks bottle of whatever size you feel happy using. I opted for one that would stay on the surface even under tension. The neck of the bottle is attached to a Solar Absailer backlead clip via a short length of elastic which helps to eliminate false movements in windy conditions. Once the rig is dropped the bottle is then clipped onto the line, it is then stopped at just over depth with the aid of a Powergum stop knot. It might seem a bit strange to have the line coming directly down from the bottle to the rig but it doesn't seem to put the fish off and it's a tactic that many anglers have used at the venue with success.

The bottle has done its job and another good fish is on its way to the net.

It wasn't long before the bottle rig did the trick with a mirror of 33lb. But instead of the usual screaming run it was just a drop back followed by the line tightening up. Perhaps the fish was confused by the different angle of the line. It definitely looked to be a good move when the next run again came to that rod. But despite using the bottle, the fish was still around a snag by the time I got above it. I had no idea what was on the end but poked around with the tip under water and thankfully everything came free. As I heaved, the shape of a big common rose to the surface. It was all over quite quickly really but in the net was one of the nicest big commons that I've ever laid eyes on – a classic-shaped fish of 51lb 4oz. That just sums up why it's good to leave areas alone sometimes for later in the session. It's always tempting to try and cover all the best-looking areas straightaway, but leaving something as a backup and also a safe area for the fish can pay dividends. I had done the same on Serreire with good results a week earlier and now the same tactic had worked again.

It was one of the nicest big commons I'd ever seen.

If anything, the bottle rig rod became the top rod towards the end but, as ever, time was fast running out. On Friday the rain came back with a vengeance after a brief sunny spell. The heavens opened and it was one of those situations where I couldn't see the islands 100 metres out in front. I remarked to Joan that I had been in similar situations when I had fished in swim 14 some time earlier and every time the rain was at its heaviest I would get a run. I had no sooner got the words out of my mouth when the gap rod burst into life. I had no choice other than to run out and get drenched. It was all good fun really and another nice common of upper 30's was on the end.

Thankfully, on the Saturday morning the skies cleared and it was possible to get most things dry. One of the early jobs is to go and retrieve all the markers from around the swim. Of course with the bottle on the line, I had forgotten how much it raises the line and went through it with the electric motor. It meant taking the propeller off and unravelling the line, which I've done many times before, but I could see that the bait had been dragged into the deepest part of the swim of around 25 feet. I should have reeled it straight in but with only an hour or so left I thought I'd just leave it. Whilst packing the Cassien bivvy away I heard a few bleeps and looked around to see the line tightening up and the bottle moving across the surface like one of the barrels in the Jaws movie! I just laughed. All the times we try and get everything as precise as possible and then a bait that's just been dragged along the bottom and into a deep channel gets picked up in less than an hour! It wasn't a monster, at 33lb 4oz, but it certainly had my name on it.

So that was the end of the three-week journey across France. I've done longer sessions for sure but moving around the venues made it seem like a longer trip and it felt like we'd been away from England for ages. To expect all of the waters to fish well and come up with the goods had been a lot to ask for, especially in August, but that is exactly what happened. All three waters had produced fish over 50lb, in fact the final tally was four 50's and eight 40's and I was pleased, to say the least, and it had been such an enjoyable journey – one of our favourite trips for sure. But it hadn't come easy, every lake had to be treated as a different session with different tactics and baiting strategies but it had all worked out okay. I was ready for a few nights at home in my own bed but was also looking forward to the next trip. This one had been different but I would love to do it all again sometime.

Dawn breaks on the final day of the trip.

Until the Next Time

Well what can I say? Over 140,000 words and I hardly seemed to have scratched the surface of all the fishing I've done over the last twenty years or so – never mind the rest which came before that! I always knew that it would be a struggle to fit it all in and in the end I didn't even come close. I suppose it reflects just how much fishing I've done through my life and how many incredible and unique places I've been fortunate enough to visit in my quest to catch more carp.

Enjoyment has very much been the main reason for everything I've done and everywhere that I've been, and I've always been of the same opinion – if I'm not enjoying it, then I'll do something else, but fishing is just in me, it's in my blood and I cannot imagine what life would be like without it. When I was younger I used to notice other people and how they had their lives set out. Work Monday to Friday, take the kids out on Saturday, wash the car on Sunday etc. etc. There's nothing wrong with any of that, but I just knew that it wasn't for me, I wanted to be out fishing somewhere and everything else sort of fitted in around that. Thankfully I found someone in Joan who wanted to share that life with me, as it would have been very difficult otherwise – just the thirteen Christmases spent down at Cassien alone speak for themselves. I'd done all the parties and sitting in front of the TV watching the Wizard of Oz and again don't get me wrong that's all great but there's nothing quite like waking up on Cassien on Christmas morning – especially if there's a fish to be photographed!

What could be better than spending Christmas day on Cassien?

But along the way there have, of course, been times when it hasn't all gone right and that's all part of a carp anglers life. It doesn't always go right and we cannot catch them all the time. It's how you deal with it which makes all the difference. I'm not keen on crowds and not too keen on the politics of carp fishing, which are hard to avoid sometimes. When I started fishing abroad I found an escape from both of them, at least for awhile and that is why I have fished away so much. The space and freedom, not to mention the solitude, was something that struck a chord with me straightaway and I loved it. But I still love my fishing in England too and I still try to fit in as much as I can. It doesn't always end up being too much as so many other things are always going on in my life. The important thing is I still love it and even after a long trip away, when I'm pleased to see my own bed again, give it a couple of days and I'm already thinking of where to go next!

At that moment it was the greatest bit of fishing in the world!

If there are times when it's getting me down or I'm not enjoying it as I should, then I just move on to somewhere else after a different target in different surroundings and that has always done the trick. It hasn't always been carp either. At one time I really got into barbel fishing and for the first year it really took over everything that I did. It was so refreshing and new that I couldn't get enough of it and if I remember right, I only caught one carp in England that year plus whatever I caught whilst I was away. Did it matter? Not one little bit, I loved every minute of it and caught loads of lovely barbel and chub and by the following year the hunger for carp came back with a vengeance. I still fish for barbel and chub every year, as well as other species such as perch and pike. I remember one time when I was fishing up the River Kennet when it was in flood, it was tough going on the main river just to hold bottom in the strong flow. I looked over the back of where I was to a small stream which had now swelled and coloured up. It looked perfect for trotting a float down with the old centre pin. So that was what I did and it just so happened that the perch had also gone to that side stream to escape the fierce current. I didn't catch loads, but it was incredibly exciting and I caught a few stripy 'sergeants' up to 3lb 4oz. At that moment it was the greatest bit of fishing in the world and you couldn't have dragged me away from it.

I've had some great times barbel fishing, this is my best so far of 14lb 7oz.

Of course how ever good any of that is, there is nothing which compares with the buzz that carp fishing gives you. There is something about those big scaly mirrors and commons that sets them apart from the rest. Their individuality, their character, their history – not to mention their size and fighting qualities, all go towards making them the most popular fish around today. I started in a time when carp were only just becoming mainstream and many people still looked at you a bit strangely when you told them what you were trying to catch. It's changed a lot since then and now for many people a carp might well be the first fish they catch. I was brought up in very much the old traditional style where I started off catching minnows and worked on to roach and perch, before finding how awesome pike were, even if most of them were about 6lb! Carp, however, sat right at the top of the fish pyramid and when I did eventually move on to fishing for them my life changed forever.

At the time of writing this, it's now thirty four years since I caught my first carp and little did I know when I bundled that 16lb mirror into my landing net down at Brooklands Lakes in 1974, that all those years later it would lead to this! The fact is that the fire still burns inside me as much as it ever has and my desire for new challenges and to go out in pursuit of certain fish has not diminished at all - I'm very pleased to say. People often ask me how I can be so enthusiastic about fishing after all this time and it's easy because I don't have to build my excitement up for fishing, it is just always there. Perhaps the fact that I fish so many different places helps with that. Variety is the spice of life as they say and for me it's very much the case as there is always something to look forward to. I couldn't have spent a whole year fishing Lake Raduta, but a couple of trips through the year were

always eagerly anticipated and in the meantime there was always a big old English mirror hiding away somewhere that I would be chasing after, and in the winter time when many anglers start to get a bit disillusioned with things, I would have a month or so at Cassien to look forward to, there is always something good just around the corner.

A trip to Austria saw me bag this surprise personal best common.

As I said earlier, I've done so much fishing that a great deal had to be left out of this book, so inevitably there will be a follow up, or at least that's the aim as it's taken me long enough to get this one finished, I can only hope that I can get moving a bit quicker next

A big, wild common from my favourite river – the mighty St. Lawrence.

time. I've done a lot more fishing on Cassien than I've been able to write about in these pages and I've had to settle for picking out the most memorable and perhaps some of the more successful trips too. I've had tough trips there and I'll hope you'll forgive me for missing some of them out, I had to miss so much out but even the tough trips at Cassien were still great. I also had to leave out many successful trips to that great water. In 2000 I shared a session there with Tim Paisley when, in one morning alone, we had fish of 20lb, 30lb, 40lb, 50lb and 60lb but Tim has already covered that trip better than I ever could in his books 'Carp' and 'Memories of Carp' so I didn't want to go over it all again. Then there was my longest session there when I started off with mirrors of 47lb 12oz and 50lb 6oz, or the 1996 winter trip when I caught my first Christmas Day carp, amongst many others – all very special memories, but there just wasn't the room for them all to go in. But besides Cassien I have been to some fantastic waters in far away places and had some cracking results. Austria was one place which was never on my list of places to visit until we got invited over and what a trip it turned out to be! All of us caught some lovely fish and I ended up with a personal best common. That was a special trip for sure, but then so were the times I travelled over to fish the St. Lawrence River in the USA and Canada. I've fished twice on the American side of the river, somehow winning another World Carp Cup with Tim Paisley along the way and it was a place I just fell in love with. The people were so friendly and the fishing was out of this world. Okay the monsters aren't there, or at least they're very hard to find, but the whole package was one that I really enjoyed. Over on the Canadian side I caught even more fish and ended up with probably the best result that I've ever had in a single week of fishing. The action was just incredible and that was all from totally wild river carp, many of which might not have ever seen a hook before. That's all still to come as well as much more – Morocco for instance. I was lucky enough to be the first English angler to catch a carp from the Bin El Quidane reservoir, in the end Simon Crow and I caught loads of fish, and stunning fish they were too. Simon caught a 43lb mirror which was right out of the top draw and I don't doubt that it's one of his favourite carp ever.

Crowy was rightly over the moon with this Moroccan mirror.

Then of course there's Rainbow Lake. I cannot say much about this place that hasn't already been said, but it is simply the most extraordinary and phenomenal carp water that has ever been discovered and the amount of big carp that continue to grow even bigger every year is just mind-blowing! My chapter on Rainbow Lake in this book is all about the first few trips for me and those early trips to any water are always special and very memorable for me. But what has happened since for me is almost make-believe stuff. While writing the book this year alone I've had another three personal bests; two mirrors of 68lb 8oz and 70lb 8oz and a common of 67lb 12oz which at the time of writing was the last carp that I've caught. I'd always wanted a 70lb carp and hoped that Cassien might provide it at some stage, I'd also hoped for a common over 60lb one day, expecting that Lake Raduta might be the place to do it. Well, both of those ambitions have been achieved from Rainbow Lake in the space of a few months. It just shows how incredible it is there and they are all stories which will have to wait until next time.

Looking outside the window now it's cold and wet, and I don't think they'll be having it today. As soon as it warms up a little I'll probably be off just around the corner. There's a nice mirror that lives not too far away and it's on the wanted list! It's not meant to be too difficult to catch but I haven't managed it yet and I don't think I can give up until I've had her, sometimes it just takes longer and I can be patient. Then when spring comes it'll be back down the other lake just a few miles further away where one very special old carp hides away, that one is right at the top of the list and is undoubtedly proving to be the biggest challenge of all – but I like it like that. In between all of that there will of course be a few other trips away and looking through the diary my next year is already starting to look quite full again.

I hope you've enjoyed reading through these pages. I can't say that it's all been easy, as to be honest, writing a book is one hell of a job when it comes down to it and I still can't believe that I've almost finished it now. Catching fish and sitting behind the rods is certainly a lot easier than putting it all down on paper – at least for me it is, but I do have to say that I've really enjoyed putting it all together and reminiscing about all those great times, because they are all great times for me. Carp fishing has given me a life that might be a little different to most peoples but it has been diverse and interesting to say the least. For a start I've now visited fifteen different countries outside of England just to go and fish for carp. It's hard to imagine what else I could have done which would have allowed me to see that much of the world. But there's a lot more to do yet and there are places I still want to go to and fish that I want to catch. Who knows, I might get there this year but if not it doesn't matter I'll just keep doing it for as long as I'm able. So, if there's a message to leave you with, then it's *just get out there and enjoy your fishing.* The more you enjoy it, the easier the hard times are to deal with. I try to take a positive lead out of most things and if a trip hasn't gone well then it only spurs me on to do better next time. Catching carp, especially big ones is a challenge and we all like it that way otherwise we wouldn't be doing it, would we? All I know is that if you enjoy your carp fishing half as much as I do then you've got many great times ahead of you. The next trip can't come around soon enough for me and whether it's just around the corner or a thousand miles away, I just know it'll be good. Carp fishing has

I love the camaraderie of the trips away. Great times spent with great people – long may it last!

reached many countries around the world now but it is still very much enclosed in its own small world. Unlike most other sports and pastimes, many people outside of carp fishing have no real idea or concept of what we do and yet to us it is one of the most important things in our lives. It's ruled the best part of my life and will continue to do so, I'm sure. Whether it's the hunters instinct in us or the need to be out in the great outdoors I'm not sure but what I do know is, like most of you reading this, it's something I've just got to do! I love fishing for carp and everything that comes with it, the travelling, the scenery, the people, the challenge, the solitude and the camaraderie and most of all the carp themselves. I don't know how many carp I've caught in my life – but I do know that it's not enough! There are places to go, fish to catch and challenges to take up and all I know is I can't wait to get out there again for more of the same – bring it on!

One for next time – after a long wait I finally got my 70lb carp.

The last carp I caught whilst putting the finishing touches to this book – and it turned out to be my biggest common ever!